Dare to Be Great

Previously published as:
Every Saint Has a Past, Every Sinner a Future

Seven Steps to

the Spiritual and Material

Riches of Life

Terry Cole-Whittaker

Jeremy P. Tarcher/Penguin

a member of Penguin Group (USA) Inc., New York

Most Tarcher/Penguin books are available at special quantity discounts for bulk purchase
for sales promotions, premiums, fund-raising, and educational needs. Special books or book
excerpts also can be created to fit specific needs. For details, write Penguin Group (USA)
Inc. Special Markets, 375 Hudson Street, New York, NY 10014.

Jeremy P. Tarcher/Penguin
a member of
Penguin Group (USA) Inc.
375 Hudson Street
New York, NY 10014
www.penguin.com

New Thought Library Series Publisher: Joel Fotinos

All scriptural quotations are taken from the King James
Version of the Bible.

First trade paperback edition 2003

The Library of Congress catalogued the hardcover edition as follows:
Cole-Whittaker, Terry, date.
    Every saint has a past, every sinner a future / Terry Cole-Whittaker.
        p.   cm.
    ISBN 1-58542-095-6
    1. Spiritual life.   2. Hope—Religious aspects.   I. Title.
    BL624 .C642   2001   00-054376
    291.4'4—dc21

ISBN 1-58542-271-1 (paperback edition)
Printed in the United States of America

10   9   8   7   6   5   4   3   2   1

Book design by Chris Welch
Title page photo © Maura Rosenthal/Mspace

I dedicate this book to my husband, Sergy,
and to my honorable teachers.

Acknowledgments

No one does anything alone, as it is always a team effort that takes a project from start to finish. This team was heaven-sent, beginning with my longtime literary agent and friend, Elizabeth Backman. Beth has stuck with me through the years, and this is our fourth book together. She is the glue that has kept me on course, as this book was a long time in gestation before it was birthed. Beth is also the midwife, so a big "Thank You, Beth." My husband, Sergy, was my cheerleader and coach all through the writing. Every team needs a coach, and I had mine. I literally could not have done it without him by my side. Who was going to be my publisher? As Spirit would have it, I was introduced to Joel Fotinos through a mutual friend, Reverend Paul Tenalglia of New York. Joel and I met for lunch while I was on a speaking tour in New York City and we became friends. He believed in me and I believed in him, so we made a deal. Joel is the publisher of Jeremy P. Tarcher, a division of Penguin Group (USA) Inc., and there you see how everything works out. God found the perfect right publisher for me and it was Joel. One last person was needed and that was an editor. Joel selected Sara Carder, who is on staff at Jeremy P. Tarcher. It was Sara's magic touch that gave the finishing touches where needed. She was a pleasure to work with, and I am very grateful to her, for it was her talent that tied up any loose ends. I would also like to thank copyeditor Barbara Grenquist for her excellent work. There are others on the team who have helped along the way, and I am grateful to each of you as well as to those whose names I do not know. Thank you for the contribution each of you has made to this book. Most of all I am grateful to God for the opportunity to write this book and for bringing us all together in this project of love.

Contents

Dear Reader,

As I have included many valuable exercises in the book, I suggest that you use a notebook for your answers. A notebook will give you more space to record your thoughts and ideas, and besides, if you would like to loan this book to a friend, your answers will be kept private. The word *sacred* actually means secret and some things are for your eyes only. I also look forward to hearing from you about the wonderful results you are receiving from following the Seven Step Sacred Treasure Map to the Spiritual and Material Riches of Life. You can reach me on my Website, terrycolewhittaker.com. I have a wonderful gift waiting for you when you contact me on my Website. Warm regards,

Terry

Website
terrycolewhittaker.com

Introduction

Did you know that every great person was first an ordinary person just like everyone else? It's true, but instead of following the crowd, they followed the seven amazing steps that are contained in this book. Your question may be: "How could it be that every person who has attained wealth, enormous success, lasting happiness, enlightenment, and fame took these seven steps?" My answer is: "They had to, because these are the steps that every person who achieves anything of value must take."

Although there are various streets that a person can travel to reach their destination, there are certain specific things that every person must do regardless of the route they take. For example, we need to know where we are going before we get in the car, unless we want to end up who knows where. Highly successful people, besides being certain about their destination, think and do things that the average person never thinks or dreams of doing.

Compare those whom you consider to be the most outstanding people who have ever lived with those who aren't. Each has a set of creative tools, including the ability to think, feel, desire, speak, hear, imagine, and act; therefore, everyone has this much in common. The difference has to do with what people do with their creative tools. Some use these tools to suffer one regrettable situation after another while others win victory after victory. Same tools, different results.

Perhaps you are thinking that some cannot help themselves because they have handicaps, but many famous people were handicapped and attained greatness in spite of it. Beethoven went deaf but continued to compose exquisite music that is still appreciated today. Franklin Roosevelt, former president of the United States, was paralyzed and could not walk. Many who have achieved prominence were plagued with every sort of disadvantage you can imagine, but their passionate desire and strong will made them rise above their circumstances and attain prominence and fortune.

If you desire to fully express your talents; build your dreams into reality; associate with successful, high-minded people; travel to the most beautiful places in the world; have inner peace; be spiritually enlightened; have wealth; own a lovely home; be happy in your relationships; do wonderful works that make a difference and help others; or receive community and global recognition for your talents and contribution to society, then you will have to *dare to be great*.

Courage Is the Price of Greatness

Courage is the price one must pay for greatness. Pressure to remain average and to settle for that which is common is applied to us from every direction. Once a person raises their head a little above the others, envious people are quick to criticize. Many schools teach the young to be less than who they are as they encourage them to conform and lose themselves in the mass of humanity rather than cultivate and express their creativity, uniqueness, and talents and rise to the top.

As a young woman, I knew that I didn't want to be just another number; instead I wanted my life to count, to matter, and to be everything that it could possibly be. Looking around at the way others lived, I saw some achieving a grand life, but most were "living lives of quiet desperation," to quote the American philosopher Ralph Waldo Emerson. I wasn't going to be one of those people who missed out on my chances, so I vowed that I would seek to make the most of what I had. Full of hope and the expectancy of my possibilities, I set out on a mission to have the best of everything.

Diligently, I searched the archives of ancient wisdom; read about the lives of famous people; took classes on success motivation; associated with the most successful, intelligent, and famous people I could find; and applied what I was learning. With this remarkable knowledge, I am happy to say, everything I have ever wanted has come to me—but not without daring, boldness, and enterprise on my part. It takes a sort of bravery, as we must rise above the opinions and criticisms of others, leave our mistakes and failures behind, push past our own fears and doubts, and face each of these challenges as a necessity and truly a blessing in disguise. With each victory we become stronger, and in time we become fearless and positive and can face any challenge with confidence.

What Does It Mean to Be Great?

Your next question could be: "What does it mean to be great, and isn't it a bit egotistical to even desire it?" My answer is: "We're supposed to desire and endeavor to be the most fully actualized people we can possibly be and do whatever we can to uplift and improve society with our talents, products, services, and projects." It would be foolish to think that God has put us on earth to hide our talents and live out our days in a miserable and wretched condition. Intelligence is meant to be used intelligently to raise ourselves to the highest point possible and to help others do the same.

Designed for Greatness

I believe that every person is destined for greatness as a rose is meant to blossom into a fragrant thing of exquisite beauty. What can be said of the rose that refuses to blossom other than "How sad"? What can be said of the person who is unwilling to bring forth the greatness that is within them other than "What a pity"?

Greatness means to be who you are, not perhaps who you think you are but who you truly are—a spark of the Divine. Since God, by definition, is the reservoir of absolute and limitless beauty, intelligence, love, bliss, opulence, strength, genius, and power, we, being made from God, since God is all there is, must possess these same qualities within us. As an apple seed possesses the potential to produce an entire tree—thousands and thousands of flowers and apples plus who knows how many more seeds—in the same way, every person, as part of God, possesses enormous possibilities. We have it all; what we do with what we have determines the quality of our existence.

Human beings are designed for greatness and are supposed to reach for the stars rather than settle for mediocrity. A piano that is a masterpiece is meant to be played expertly rather than sit unused in a corner gathering dust. What finer masterpiece than you—a human being? This book is written for you, dear friend. Like me, you have a burning desire to live life to the fullest. *Dare to be great* and great you shall be.

Dare to Be Great

Chapter One

Life Is a Treasure Hunt

> "For where your treasure is, there will your
> heart be also."—*Matthew 6:21*

You Can Attain Love, Happiness, and Prosperity

Here is the greatest news! You will always get another chance to attain the happiness, love, and prosperity you desire, and you will find out why and how right here in this book. Human life is troubled with incessant problems of varying degrees, but these have a root cause and therefore a solution. We can all achieve a permanent end to dejection, and find the solutions we are seeking when we are given the proper knowledge. Those who desire can also attain ultimate bliss in the here and now.

Never give up! You can be certain that all you hope for in your heart of hearts exists and is available in abundant supply. You just need to know how to find it and what to do to get and keep it. Such is human nature that most do not seek to end their worries and find true love and bliss until they reach the depth of despair. Although it is not necessary to wait until we hit bottom before we rise to the top, we can start now. Now is the perfect time to start on a treasure hunt. Everything you have experienced in the past has prepared you for the blessings you will now receive.

Most well-known saints and philosophers underwent a crisis at some point in their lives, as have other extraordinary people throughout time. Instead of giving up and succumbing to permanent discouragement, bitterness, and dejection, they sought to find the solution. In fact, this is the higher purpose of tribulation.

Use Unhappiness to Bring You Happiness

Distress can awaken us from our slumber of ignorance and impel us toward the ultimate goal of life: supreme unending bliss free of misery. I know it sounds strange that God would set it up that in order for us to be blissful we must first experience misery. But we are only miserable to the degree that we are trying to get what we want without the proper map and directions.

Life is designed in a certain way for a specific purpose with a perfect system for us to follow that we may obtain and enjoy supreme happiness, love, peace of mind, and prosperity. Regardless of our past or present situation, age, sex, religion, race, health, education, or finances it is possible for us to reach the pinnacle of life's treasures and riches.

We shouldn't despise our suffering or poverty nor should we seek to continue to suffer or be poor. Unhappy and difficult times are a wake-up call for us to seek and find a better way. Some become accustomed to their suffering or they take their medications to be able to cope, but they are missing the point and they will ultimately fail to achieve a permanent solution to their problems.

Dejection is common to almost all of us during times of imagined or real loss, abandonment, rejection, humiliation, and defeat. Instead of falling into the pit of despair and grief, the most intelligent people not only rise up to fight once again, they also seek to find out how life works so they can finally get it right.

We can only get it right when we know what right is. Do you want to hit a home run? Find out how to hit a home run and then get up to the plate and swing at the ball with all your might and intention. If you fail, go back to the instruction book, make your corrections, and go at it again until you achieve your home runs. But don't give up your dream. Give up what doesn't work and do what does.

Forget Three Strikes and You're Out

Three strikes and you're out is only a rule in baseball and in the criminal law books of some countries. According to the Supreme Law of the universe, chances are without limit because life and you are an ongoing *forever* adventure.

The first time I realized that I was eternal and would never die, I felt great distress. Yes, it was a relief to know I would never die, but I wanted my misery to end. My mind was torturing me on a regular daily basis for as yet I did not know how my mind worked or what to do to make my mind my best friend rather than my worst enemy. I thought, "If I have to endure this mental anguish, then why would I want to live forever?"

At that low point, I decided that it was time for me to control my mind and learn how to be happy. Eternity is a long time to be miserable or poor, especially when the Creator desires for us to be prosperous and happy.

Hope Is Eternal

I had to write this book for the number-one reason that people are not living as they would love to live because they don't know the spiritual and material rules of successful, happy, and abundant living. Using my life in search of this profound knowledge, and having finally attained it, I felt compelled to teach and share it with the greatest number of people possible.

This is not a book about regret, but a book of hope, hope for what is possible for any and every person to attain. This is a book about what works. It's about what anyone can do to recover from a loss, build an empire, gain true love, be happy, peaceful, and prosperous, know more about God, succeed in their endeavors, and make spiritual and material advancement. Will it take long and will it be difficult to get? No, it only takes an instant once we let go of our attachment to misery and struggle.

Detaching Yourself from the Useless

You and I know that there is an enormous emotional pull that keeps us attached to the events, mistakes, and even successes of yesterday. People around us can make it even more difficult for us to release the past and live in the present. Old friends and family tend to view us as we were and not as we are.

Family and friends may feel the need to continually remind us of what we did that wasn't okay or of what we failed to do. Sometimes they don't say anything; they don't need to. Resentment, anger, and judgment pervade the very air that we are breathing in their presence. A moment-to-moment release of the stale air must take place for us to take in the fresh.

Relationships are vital and nourishing when they are forever fresh and new in each instant.

A relentless stream of thoughts and conversations about a dead past forces us to perceive and believe that hope is gone when the truth is, hope is eternal. There is a greater opportunity, and that is to learn how to live fully in the eternal here and now.

The past is valuable to the degree that we can take the love, lessons, and successes and apply this knowledge to our present situation. Nothing we can do will change yesterday, bring back what was, or allow us to regain the lost moment. But changing our perception and understanding will give us the ability to use crisis as a stepping-stone to success. Eventually with greater understanding we can end crisis once and for all.

Today Is the First Day of the Rest of Your Eternal Life!

In order to proceed toward a brighter day and toward the greater rewards available to you in this moment and in all your moments to come, you will first need to believe that every moment is the start of something wonderful. **Today really is the first day of the rest of your eternal life.**

The potential for you to experience anything that is or has been available to any person is available to *you* in this moment. Who and what you are now and who and what you desire to become are what is important, not who and what you were yesterday.

We can all have a truckload of regrets if we choose to perceive events in this way, and most likely we have all done something for which we are not especially proud. But we must go forward, armed with the proper knowledge, and try and try again until we reach our ultimate goals.

Every Saint Has a Past, Every Sinner a Future

What would Mary Magdalene's future have been if, instead of accepting forgiveness from Jesus, she had continued to worry about how others saw her or what they were saying or thinking about her? Her neighbors would never see her as changed for they would always see her as a prostitute no matter how reformed and pure she became. She confessed her mistakes and asked for forgiveness and it was given. There was no need for her to immerse herself in shame and guilt for more than a minute, for she had seen the error of her ways and chosen a new life.

Mary would always be guilty in the eyes of the townspeople, but she was always pure in the eyes of Jesus. If Mary had not been degraded, her example of surrender would not have been so strong. Her past was the very fuel for her transformation and 180-degree turnaround toward spiritual freedom.

Saint Francis comes to mind, as another example of a sinner turned saint. A cheating merchant and thieving soldier of fortune, after being wounded in battle, he was lying in a coma in his room when he had a profound change of heart. Awakened by the sweet sound of a bird, he somehow saw clearly the purpose of life. After his transformation he left his old life, never to return.

Here a cruel person had become a saint, not by lamenting his past and beating himself every day for his mistakes but by seeing another way to live and living it. All he did was change his direction and walk forward into a life of freedom.

One more sinner comes to mind: Saul. What would have happened to Christianity if Saul, the tax collector and persecutor of Christians, who later became Saint Paul, had not had a change of heart? As Saul he violently murdered Christians by throwing them to the lions to be eaten alive. Did he wallow in guilt after his awakening? No, he left his old life behind in a flash when he was given revelation and a higher taste, a taste of the supreme bliss of the love of God.

Did he think, "My life is over because I have made so many horrible mistakes"? No, he left it all behind and walked forward into the light of a new day with the knowledge of a new way to be.

Shame and Guilt Are Destructive and Useless Emotions

Sally had tried for years to stop drinking. After each drinking session she would feel guilty about drinking and about what she did while under the influence of alcohol. Her shame and guilt grew, and her drinking continued. Trying something new, she surrendered her problem to God. Praying with all her sincerity she asked to have this curse of alcohol and her addictive behavior taken from her. Instead of feeling shame and guilt when she drank, she would make it all right. She refused to feel guilt and shame the next day. Sally observed the motivation behind drinking. Noticing how she felt during and after drinking, she came to dislike the uncomfortable feelings, her inappropriate behavior, the taste in her mouth, and the stench from her body. One day, she lost the taste, thanks to God. Now she is living guilt-, shame- and alcohol-free. She feels good, thinks clearly, smells good, and is a successful human being.

Everyone Has Failures and Everyone Suffers, Until . . .

No one can become great without failures. But we can also give up failing when we have the right knowledge and instruction as to what to do that works. With knowledge we can pick ourselves up, dust ourselves off, and start all over again, as the song goes. Each moment can be a turnaround point, as it was for our aforementioned sinners who became saints.

A sinner can be transformed into a saint in a flash. A morose person can become happy in the twinkling of an eye. A failure in business can become a success and reap great rewards. An old person can become young at heart. Sickness can leave and health can be restored through the power of prayer. A loser in a relationship can become a winner when she learns how to love. A fool can become a genius and even a respected scholar, if he is determined and does the work required.

There Is Hope for Everyone, Without Exception

There is hope for everyone to satisfy the longings of his or her heart and soul, if he or she is willing to seek out and apply the knowledge of how to make his or her dreams come true. Very few ever take the time to discover what they are truly seeking in their heart of hearts. Besides knowing what you desire, it's equally important to gain the knowledge by which you can attain your goals. Knowledge comes in two parts: what to do and what not to do. Both are equally important.

Maps Point Out the Dangers to Avoid

For example, you may be on the right road but you are not aware of the detour, cliff, or swamp ahead and it is dark. Darkness means ignorance and the light means knowledge. The solution is knowledge in the form of what

I call a treasure map. A good map, besides giving you an overview, points out the best route to take that will get you to where you want to go in the shortest amount of time and also guarantees you the most pleasurable and safest journey possible.

Everyone, without exception, is traveling the road of life in search of happiness, love, and prosperity. Traveling on horseback, camel, elephant, in a jet or car, walking, running, and crawling in hopes of obtaining the objects of their desires, people have endured every kind of hardship and challenge to reach and find the treasures of their minds and hearts.

Most fail in their attempts to attain lasting happiness and prosperity, falling victim to unforeseen dangers, losses, and obstacles. Some, instead of being beaten by these same challenges, have risen above, gone around or though, and continued until they reached their desired destinations.

Everyone Needs a Map

A map is the answer. With a map, we know what is around the corner and exactly how to reach our destination and find the treasures. Trial and error is actually the most inferior method for getting what you want. One could search lifetimes by the trial-and-error method and still never find the treasures. Someone who uses a tried and proven map can reach the treasures quickly, almost effortlessly.

Maps are not always on a flat piece of yellowed paper worn thin from age. Maps can take the form of a book, information delivered in the classroom, or words of wisdom and direction whispered in someone's ear by a sage, expert, or wise teacher.

Seven Steps

The miracle of this **Seven-Step Sacred Treasure Map** is that it works. It will take you where you want to go, as it has others. These seven steps took me from my starting position as an insecure and frightened child to the attainment of every one of my important goals and the fulfillment of my cherished dreams. By following these steps and with God's help and the assistance of many wonderful people, I was able to become the author of many best-selling books, a globally recognized and award-winning motivational and inspirational speaker, a counselor to the "stars," a business consultant, the minister of an international television ministry speaking to millions each week, and someone who had become fearless.

A warning: This map won't work if you desire to live in your dead past and suffer, or if you enjoy self-pity, strife, worry, and resentment. You can be happy or feel regret, but not both.

Agree to Get the Most from Your Eternal Life

Before you begin this new and wonderful adventure, I invite you to get ready. Getting ready means you agree to go forward taking with you only those memories and things you can use today to achieve your present goals and dreams.

Carrying luggage full of useless stuff is a heavy burden that will only make your journey difficult and tiring. Besides, with empty bags you are free to collect and take with you the most valuable and precious treasures you find along the way.

Preparing for Your Journey

> ### Agreements
> #### (Place your name on the lines)
>
> I, _____, agree to say good-bye to any regrets, resentments, or heartaches.
>
> I, _____, agree to take the lessons, gems, and pearls of wisdom from my past and leave the rest behind.
>
> I, _____, agree to set new goals and use the Seven-Step Treasure Map to achieve them.
>
> I, _____, agree that today is the first day of the rest of my eternal life.

You are ready to begin your journey. On this journey, be sure to take the best of yesterday with you because the gems and pearls of wisdom you have gathered along the way are valuable assets. Unless we look back and take the wisdom and valued experiences we have gained on our path, we may believe our lives—and thus we—are worthless. In truth we are very, very rich. This wealth is part of our cosmic bank account, and it's always ours to draw from to help us meet our every present need.

How I Came upon These Miraculous Seven Steps

It wasn't until I had achieved most of my life's goals and dreams that I was able to look back and understand exactly what I had done that got me to the treasure house of the spiritual and material riches I had desired. Hindsight is important, for when applied it gives us foresight. I didn't start out with the map; it was given to me step by step over a period of time.

My First Taste of the Mystical

My hunt for the spiritual and material riches of life started when I was about six years old. *Treasure Island, Sinbad the Sailor, Aladdin and His Wonderful Lamp, Lost Horizon, The Secret Garden* and *The Jungle Book*, my favorite stories when I was a child, gave me my first taste of the mystical, magical, and marvelous. Adventure, hidden treasures, secret passwords, miracles, and special mystic powers became my secret desires.

Old trunks hiding in forgotten corners of my great-grandmother's friends' attics fascinated me, and when she visited her friends they would let me climb the stairs and play to my heart's content. Again and again I would look through those same old trunks hoping to find a lost treasure map or some priceless jewels and gold coins. Costume jewelry, dusty love letters, worn clothes, and mementos of a life lived long ago were the only treasures I would find, so I would put on the clothes and jewelry and read the letters once again.

Treasure hunting was my secret mission, and I reveled in tales of lost gold mines and hidden treasure, and stories of the poor girl who becomes rich, happy, and famous.

Escaping to the movies, reading, and hearing fairy tales and stories of adventure and opulence stimulated my imagination. I didn't know at the time that people are the architects of their own lives, but even then I was building my foundation and designing my life by what I chose to hear, read, and see.

People Can Change, If They Desire to Change

Psychologists tell us that by the time a child is five years old she is over 80 percent programmed for the rest of her life and on a set course, unless she actually at some point makes a concerted effort to change her direction. Decisions we make as children when we are dependent upon others for our survival continue with us, as adults, long after those childhood days and dependencies are no more. People can change their conditioning, but it takes great desire and work.

We get attached to people and this can mean trouble, as we tend to take on the qualities of those with whom we associate. I watched as my family members suffered through their interactions, and it was strange to me that they would keep coming back for more as if they enjoyed all the suffering. It didn't mean that they needed to get rid of each other, but just not to be so attached or so serious about it all. No one, except my great-grandmother, seemed to take responsibility for his or her mental, emotional, or financial condition, always blaming it on someone else.

As the family was busily engaged in their emotional dramas, I was busy seeking out ways to get what I wanted. I had desires and needs in those early years that led me to seek the practical knowledge of how to earn money, despite the fact that I was too young to get a job. My younger sisters and I had no allowance because Mom worked long hours as a waitress just to stay abreast of the house payments and keep us in groceries, so if we wanted something extra or special we had to be ingenious and creative. Necessity is the mother of invention, even for a kid.

One of my ways of getting money was selling stuff to the neighbors, and the second-best gold mine was the sand under the outdoor monkey bars at the grammar school. Kids would play on the monkey bars and lose their money, and after school I would go out with an old window screen, sift the sand and find at least a dollar in nickels and dimes every time. No, I didn't work to make them lose their money. I just went hunting for whatever had been lost.

There was a blessing in having to be creative in finding ways to get money, as it made me into an entrepreneur. I was about five years old, and already I knew that my parents were not the source of my good. Whatever was to be was somehow up to me.

GEM

This lesson would stay with me and develop into the realization that God is my source and others are my avenues. Others are never the origin of our supply, and if one avenue dries up there is always another.

This was just about the time when I noticed that I could wish for something and it would happen. Each evening, right at twilight, I would stand outside and make my wishes on the very first star that appeared in the sky. With all my faith and belief I would say, "Star light, star bright, first star I see tonight, I wish I may, I wish I might have this wish I wish tonight." Following this statement, I'd ask for whatever I wanted. Not knowing much about God except the little I had learned during my infrequent trips to Sunday school, wishing on a star, as did Pinocchio's father, seemed like a grand idea. The movie *Pinocchio* had made an enormous impression on me, for it gave me the notion of the power of a higher presence that could make my wishes come true.

The Good Lord was already fulfilling my innermost desires, even before I knew how to pray, only I believed it was the power of the first star. Faith is a powerful force; I really believed in the manifesting power of this first star, but it had to be the first star. Sometimes I just talked with the star as I would with a loving, nonjudgmental, caring friend.

I had felt as if I didn't belong with my parents, and right around this time of my nightly "star ritual" and by some stroke of good fortune my mother sent me to live with my great-grandmother, Nanny, and great-grandfather, Grandpa George. Overnight I was lifted out of one life and placed in another that was more in keeping with my hopes and dreams, even at such an early age.

The Power of Belief

I had wished for a better life, and it was given to me. Already I had recognized the cause-and-effect relationship between my wishes and what was happening, but I did not know the science behind it all. Of course I never told anyone about this newly found treasure of wishing upon a star. Who would have believed me, anyway, as I was just a little girl? If you want to hear of wonderful things, ask children to tell you their secrets and just listen.

> Take a few moments to write about your very first spiritual experience. Remember that first unusual and mystical experience when you knew there was something happening beyond the normal course of events or what others believed.
>
> $\bullet\ \bullet\ \bullet\ \bullet\ \bullet$
>
> Describe your first mystical experience in the space below.
>
> What happened?

A New Life Overnight

Instead of being just a little girl in a crowd, I had become a little princess, who was showered with constant love and attention, plus a good measure of caring discipline. Prosperity, excellence, and opulence were all around me in God's majestic creation of the Sierra Nevada Mountains of California.

Pristine snow-covered mountains encircled our home in the tiny valley below the most southerly glacier in North America. Huge pine trees whistled in the cooling summer breezes, and the sounds of the roaring creek sang me to sleep each night. I ran with the deer, picked fragrant wildflowers, rode horses bareback, and drank from pure streams of crystal-clear cold water fed by the ancient glacier.

Away from my parents' distress, I was sheltered and protected from harm and free to run and play to my heart's content. I didn't know much about God, except from Nanny, and I didn't know anything about the laws and principles of success, but here I was with *my* people in the most beautiful place I had ever seen. Later I would learn that nothing happens by accident and there is a cause behind every effect and result.

How did all this happen? Was it because it was my fate and coming to me as the result of my prior endeavors and desires in some past life? Was it happening because God had heard me crying for help and knew this was best for me, or was it both or something else? Anyway, life was good and I was secure.

Years later I learned the science of creativity and how the Divine works for us, as it works through us. Nothing happens by accident. There is an impersonal law of creativity working in everyone's life. Everyone is using this law either consciously or unconsciously. Most use this creative law of the universe unconsciously and have no idea why things are happening as they are.

The Creative Law of Life

We co-create our lives as an artist paints a picture. Wishes, thoughts, beliefs, desires, and actions are our artist's tools. Our desires are made manifest to the degree that we ask, as I had asked the first star. Since the star has no power of its own and all power comes from God, I was actually praying to God only I didn't know it. I had faith in the star, and it was my asking and faith that made an impression upon the Universal Creative Mind.

My desires, beliefs, and mental concepts created a form into which the creative substance, known as God's energy, was poured. This is much like pouring water into an ice cube tray. When the water is frozen, out comes the cube in the exact form of the mold into which the water has been poured. The water has no choice other than to take the form of the mold or container into which it is poured. Creative substance has no choice but to take on the form of our mental concepts, beliefs, and desires. This is why it is very important that we consciously choose what we hear, think, say, and do, as these are mighty implements of creativity.

Good thoughts and deeds bring good fortune. Jesus taught us this science when he said, "It is done unto you as you believe." You might say that each person has a wish-fulfilling tree called the mind and whatever we wish for with sincerity and intensity will tend to take form in the outer world. If people only knew the power of the mind, they would be careful about what they think, believe, and wish for.

A Gift from Beyond

One day something very special happened that would point out the direction of my future life's path by giving me a taste of something beyond this world. Running between the birch and pine trees, through the sweet wildflowers and over a small stream by a rusting vintage Model A Ford car, I arrived at my secret hideout. Quietly sitting down in the tall grasses, as was my practice to wait for my friends the deer and chipmunks to show up and play, I felt a familiar presence.

My beloved Grandpa George had recently passed away, which for me was my only deep sorrow, as he had been my best friend, and I had been his shadow and sidekick. Grandpa George took care of the resort he and Nanny owned and we called home, Glacier Lodge. When he painted cabins, so did I, and when he worked on the water pipes, so did I. Losing Grandpa George was tragic for me, and all I could do was think of him and remember the perfect love that I felt from him and for him. If only he hadn't died . . .

Feeling someone behind me, I turned around to see who was there, and it was Grandpa George. It was he, I was sure, but his body looked not exactly as I remembered him. Then he talked to me, and I knew it was my beloved pal and protector.

Tears of love were streaming down my checks, for I missed him so. "But he is still alive and right here with me, as if he had never been gone, even for a moment" was my thought. I listened intently to every word he spoke, but more than the words I felt his love and concern for me.

"Terry Nan, my precious, I have been given permission to come back to tell you something you need to know. You will help many people because this is your desire and your work. You too have challenges to overcome and when you do, you will help others to also be victorious over their challenges.

Don't worry, for you are being guided and protected, so you will pass through each and every test and challenge, as you do the right thing. Above all else, seek to know, love, and serve God. Try to do the good in each situation, and all will be well.

Terry Nan, know that I am alive, and when you think of me I will be right there with you for a little while longer. Now I know there is no end to life, and I want you to know this truth and not be afraid."

Just as he had appeared, he disappeared. I sat there for a few moments not quite knowing what to do, but I trusted that Nanny would know, so I ran home and excitedly told her every detail. Nanny and I could talk of such things, and experiences, as they were not strange to her. She considered them to be a gift from God, and not to be questioned, only cherished.

At such an early age I was beginning to understand that there are two worlds, the one in which we are living and another. But where was this other? I had so many questions, but really no one to ask, for Nanny understood, but she too was just learning about spiritual matters and the power of positive thinking. Oftentimes I served as her counselor and cheerleader, and other times she was mine.

Besides the questions I had about dying, which was my greatest fear, I also wanted to know why some people were happy, wealthy, loved, healthy, and successful and others were not. What could I do to guarantee myself the best possible happy and wonderful life? Another fear I had was winding up like so many of my parents' friends, who, in my opinion, were living depressing, mundane, dead-end lives.

To me life seemed to offer a feast of adventure, opportunities, and possibilities to explore and experience. This is what I wanted for myself. How would I get it? How and where would I find a treasure chest full of jewels and gold coins, a magic carpet, and the mystical powers to create what I wanted right out of thin air? Years passed and my questions were not answered, but when I was seventeen, something very special happened that would lead me to the answers I was seeking.

> Write some of your earliest questions and
> realizations about life.
>
> Some of my earliest questions about life were:
> 1.
> 2.
> 3.
> Some of my earliest realizations about life were:
> 1.
> 2.
> 3.

How My Treasure Hunt for God, Happiness, and Prosperity Began

"The journey of a thousand miles begins with a single step." —*Chinese proverb*

t was a simple event that transpired one evening right before I went to sleep. How was I to know that my heartfelt request, as a teenager, would open doors to worlds upon worlds of spiritual and material riches? But it did.

Does God Exist?

Before this particular evening, I had been seriously seeking God by attending the Sunday morning services of the different churches of "organized religion." The truth was I didn't understand what the ministers were saying and oftentimes I would fall asleep out of boredom. There was nothing wrong with church; I just hadn't found the right one for me, as yet.

Each religion proclaimed, "Ours is the only right way." This could clearly *not* be true if each was saying it! One day my question would be answered when ancient, sacred knowledge was given to me that stated, "God is unlimited and every person is unique. Therefore God offers a special path for every person to learn about Him and engage in the relationship that best suits his or her particular personality, understanding, and interests." For now I was on a quest that made me seek my answers, not within the walls of any particular church, but within me.

Lying in my bed one very special night, I prayed. Saying the Lord's

Prayer, as I did every night, thinking it was a good idea, even though no one had told me to do so, I then spoke my heart openly and sincerely, not even knowing if there was a God who was listening.

Begging some unseen and unknown God, in my uneducated, teenager way, I pleaded, "Dear God, I have been looking for you, and I have not found you. Are you there? If you exist, you will have to find me. Please make yourself known to me." Because I was without any formal religious training, the words were unimportant. Neither did it matter whether I knew scripture or had a regular church. What mattered was the sincerity, for this was to become the most important relationship of my life—and somehow I knew it.

Right after this Turning-Point Prayer, wonderful events and circumstances started happening, and I was led in the right direction for me to eventually find this unseen God. Because I was not ready as yet to understand it all, I had to be prepared in consciousness.

Setting Foot on a Positive Path

Exactly two months after my prayer, this unseen God answered me in a big way. I had prayed in earnest, and now it was time for my spiritual education to begin. When the student is ready, the teacher appears. Timing is everything, as there is that moment in time when the right people come together at the right place by divine appointment.

My great-grandmother Nanny's kitchen table was the exact location for the start in earnest of my spiritual journey and my hunt for spiritual and material riches. There had been a big dance at the American Legion Hall, right after which I came home and found the two of them waiting up for me. Nanny and her friend Violet were having a late-night cup of coffee with hot milk, as was their custom, when they decided that we should pray together for the healing of a very sick neighbor.

Seventeen at the time and just out of high school, I cherished these summer months with Nanny. Because my parents had moved to Newport Beach, California, when I was eight years old, I no longer lived with Nanny. Now, our only time together was made possible through school vacations, some weekends, and the summers, when I didn't have a full-time job.

Driving my maroon 1941 Chevy late at night through the Mojave Desert and then up the Owens Valley to Nanny's house, I was filled with the excitement of the prospect of seeing her again. As I approached Nanny's house in Big Pine, it gave me a special thrill to see through the window that her kitchen light was on. She welcomed me with open arms, and I was safe and sound with my spiritual buddy.

PEARL

Change for the better happens rapidly when there are both inner and outer changes in alignment with one's dreams and wishes.

Old Ed, one of Nanny's renters, was in intensive care and was expected to die at any moment. Out of compassion and a heartfelt desire for him to heal, we wanted to help. Violet volunteered to teach us a little something about spiritual mind healing and then lead us in prayer.

Spiritual Healing

First Violet explained how spiritual mind healing worked. She said, "There is only one mind and this Mind is God's mind. Our individual minds are part of God's infinite and unlimited mind because everything and everyone is within this All-pervading Presence and Power. Because there is no distance in consciousness, when something is known in one place, it is known in all places at the same time. When we know and accept the wholeness and health of the person for whom we are praying, this corresponds to the already existing pattern of a perfect person and body in the mind of God. Agreeing in mind with the prototype of God's creation of the ideal physical form calls on the law of correspondents, and a healing will take place," she continued.

"Listen!" Violet decreed. "Instead of believing in the appearances of the person or situation, which is the form of the person's former beliefs and activities, we see, speak, and accept the ideal of what is now desired. This sets a new idea or cause in motion that must take form. Consciousness takes form in the outer world of effects. That which we think, believe, envision, and act upon works as a seed that must grow and take form in the outer world around us when planted in the good soil of a receptive and faithful mind."

She concluded: "The only person or mind we need to convince is our own. At the moment when, with absolute faith in God, we are certain of the supernatural power of God to do anything and we accept the wholeness of the person for whom we are praying, the healing occurs naturally. When two or more are gathered in the name of the Lord, as taught in the scriptures, the healing power of Divine Love and Intelligence takes over and the healing or desired manifestation is instantaneous. In order to be effective as a spiritual mind healer we must have the basic realization that the Divine Spirit is always present, is always permanently available, and all the Power of the universe is at any and every point ready to flow in the direction of our desire."

I didn't understand much of this but it sounded right, so I went along. Later on, before we went to bed, she wrote down all she had said to remind me of the lesson. This is how I remember word for word her teachings as I have kept them throughout the years.

"Remember," she added, "no task is impossible for God, even if it appears impossible to us. God never sees our problems, beholding us as his faultless children. We cause our problems with wrong thinking and conduct. To be spiritual mind healers we need to be of the same mind as Christ Jesus. We need to see others as God sees them, perfect parts of His Perfect energy." Violet then instructed us to uncross our arms and legs, close our eyes, and relax.

"I will now speak the words of healing in prayer. Your task is to accept Ed's healing through faith. Believe absolutely in the power of God to heal Ed's body. Clear your mind of any idea of sickness and see Ed as a whole, complete, and perfect child of God. Know for certain that when your words are spoken, the prayer is answered. How and when that healing takes is up to a higher power."

"Let us pray" were her final instructions. Then she spoke the prayer with authority. Her prayer went something like this: "There is only One Power, One God, and One Truth. That Presence and Power is right here with us now and always. We know, Lord, that Ed is your perfect child whose eternal nature is spiritual. We know that with You, Beloved Father, all things are possible. We ask that whatever lessons he needs to learn from this experience he knows now. Lift up your child to victory and infuse him with your presence. We affirm that Ed is strong, healthy, and able now. And so it is. Amen."

GEM

Ideas, thoughts, and feelings take form in matter. Therefore, if you want something to take place in the outer tangible world, you must first have the mental counterpart, as the blueprint for the desired finished product.

During the prayer I felt something I had never felt previously: a transcendental movement out of the confines of my body to a place of euphoria, peace, and well-being. For those few minutes, all my problems, anxieties, and fears disappeared. A wave of bliss passed through me, and my body seemed to disappear. All that was left was my awareness and consciousness. Something phenomenal had happened.

You can imagine how happy we were when we called the hospital the next morning and were told that Ed was coming home the next day. The doctors said his recovery was unexplainable; they had thought he would die sometime during the night. We, on the other hand, knew it was a definite affirmation of the power of prayer. Old Ed recovered, came home, and

Write your first positive experiences of the power of prayer and your relationship with a Higher Power:

How old were you?

Where were you?

What happened?

What was the outcome?

How has this affected you since that time?

What can you do to apply this gem and pearl to your present situation and reap the rewards?

lived a few more years. But he wasn't the same miserly, cranky old man, as he had had a change of heart. We could sense a remarkable difference in him. Old Ed never talked of it, as if something sacred and secret beyond this world had occurred for him at the level of his soul and not just his body.

Ed was not the only one to have had a healing; so had I. Whatever it was that happened to me that warm summer evening was finer than any experience I had had to date, and I wanted more. Something extraordinary and miraculous had occurred, and somehow I had had something to do with it.

An Unseen Power

Once before this I had fallen backward off a high fence. Instead of crashing to the pavement and breaking any bones, something or someone set me down delicately like a feather. I do not know how this happened or what was responsible, only that I should have cracked my skull on the cement sidewalk. Instead I was protected by an unseen power.

I never said anything to my parents, but the event stayed with me and caused me to wonder how something like this could happen. Gravity was somehow stopped. I thought, "How can a law of nature quit for a moment in time?" But, it did.

Children have these experiences, but most never say anything about them and put them aside as if nothing had happened. As I have come to understand it, events such as this one are windows into the spiritual world and show us the possibilities of mind over matter. They are designed to give us a glimpse of something beyond appearances and to spark our curiosity. The purpose of curiosity is to entice us to seek further in order to find the topmost treasures and solve the "mysteries of life."

List any events that sparked your curiosity and caused you to look further into the "mysteries of life."

1.

2.

3.

4.

In the years to come I would find the solutions to the mysteries even though many persons along the way had told me, "There are no answers and no solutions." These people, as I look back, were unhappy and cynical because their teachers had told them, "Life is an unsolved mystery" and they believed it.

Getting Answers

As the summer wore on, Nanny, Violet, and I would spend each night absorbed in our conversation about spiritual matters and supernatural experiences. Most of the time was spent in my asking questions and Violet answering. For three months, I had Violet as a tutor who fed me the spiritual and practical food I craved. I had my Nanny and now Violet to talk to about God, and the principles of prosperity and successful living. Violet was in her late sixties, her body was slender but not thin, and her hair was mostly white with some light brown in the back. I thought she was very pretty, especially because she always wore a smile on her face. Her violet-flavored perfume preceded her into the room and remained long after she was gone.

"Everything wonderful will come to you if you ask, have the right attitude, believe that it will happen, and you take the appropriate action," said Violet. These words were music to my ears, for they were giving me hope—and more than blind hope or faith in something mysterious but real knowledge and instructions that I could follow to gain control over my destiny. Instead of being confused and fearful about my future, as I had been, I was excited about my possibilities. Life is not a gamble or a game of chance. There are rules anyone can follow and reach his or her goals and have his or her dreams come true. Order exists in the universe and there are principles and laws that govern everything, including us. If we want to succeed, we need to know and abide by the rules of life.

Summarizing Violet's Lessons

"Violet, would you please share with me some of the rules and principles that govern our lives and also an overview of everything you have taught to me in these three summer months?" I pleaded. "Yes," exclaimed Violet, "and I will also write it out so you can keep a copy to read whenever you need to remember our lessons."

"There is One Power and Presence for good, that has no equal or opposite. We are both one with this One God and different, as each of us is a unique and distinct person with godlike qualities. This gives the Supreme Being the greatest opportunity to enjoy the pleasures of infinite variety.

This Supreme Creative Force of Pure Love and Bless is All-powerful, All-knowing, and Everywhere present. Within each of us is the same Loving, All-giving, Perfect Intelligence we call God, the creator and maintainer of the Universe. We live, move, and have our being in this Presence and Power, which works for us as it works through us. "Fear not, little flock. It is the Father's good pleasure to give you His Kingdom," said Jesus. Our work is to give up fear and accept the gifts that God is pouring into, around, and through us now and forever. Anyone who chooses to can live in this Heavenly Kingdom now, and forever.

Whatever this Loving Presence we call God is, we are also, only in a minute quantity. "Verily, verily, I say unto you, The Son can do nothing of himself, but what he seeth the Father do; for what things soever he doeth, these also doeth the Son likewise" (John 5: 19).

All that exits is within God, and God is all there is. Every person is god-like in nature and imbued with divine qualities. Each of us has the power of free will as to what we will do with our power, creative abilities, talents, and intelligence. Someone can misuse her power of free will and bring harm to others and subsequently to herself. This is called evil or error.

The universe is orderly, working according to laws created by a supreme and superior intelligence. When we work with this Superior Intelligence and use the laws of life intelligently, we are able to design our lives as an architect designs a magnificent structure. People are designing and creating their lives right this minute anyway, only most have no idea of what they are doing or why things are happening as they are. People are suffering because of ignorance. Ignorance of the creative law of life is no excuse, for it is working anyway.

Everyone possesses tools of creativity, which include the abilities to desire, wish, believe, think, imagine, hear, see, speak, feel, and act. All these creative abilities are either part of or controlled through the mind. The mind is a mirror meant to reflect the spiritual world; but if left to its own devices without controls, the mind will reflect negativity, fear, poverty, and sorrow. The person must know what he wants to be, do, and have, and then control his mind and use it as a person would drive a vehicle to take him where he would like to go, safely, quickly, and with the greatest amount of enjoyment.

The self, the true person, is essentially asleep. With the driver asleep, an out-of-control mind sabotages and throws the person into danger at every turn. Sacred Knowledge awakens the person much as Sleeping Beauty is awakened by the kiss of the sweet prince. From this point of awakening, conscious people take charge of their lives by controlling their minds and their actions to bring them what they truly desire. With this knowledge, a person is able to live by design rather than by default.

The Outer World Is Created from the Inner

Because the universal law of life called Cause and Effect, Karma, Reciprocity, and "As you sow, so shall you reap" is constantly working, we are creating in every moment. Exactly what we will create is up to God and us, as a co-creative partnership. This partnership is called God and Company, and we are the company. We create with our desires, mind, and imagination using the undifferentiated and formless universal creative energy. This formless energy is flowing in, around, and through us to produce and give form to our ideas and desires.

Each person is essentially an artist. The canvas is life and upon this canvas the person paints what she sees, senses, and feels within. Whoever desires to change the outer must know what he wants to paint and then see it first within the imagination. The goals, images, and desired results are set in mind, which signals and activates the divine creative process to engage and manifest and produce.

The Spiritually Intelligent person is able to tap into the unlimited creative flow of Universal Intelligence and harness it to manifest her heartfelt goals and precious dreams into reality. Those who know of this limitless and creative power and have found out how to access it are called Geniuses.

The world around us is an outward manifestation of our inner world of mental concepts, images, and deep-seated beliefs. What we believe appears in our outer world much as images are projected on a movie screen. The light within the projector shines through the film, thus producing a limitless variety of pictures and movies for the audience to enjoy. Depending upon what is being shown in the movie the people respond accordingly, but it is still a movie. Our movie will change when the images on the film change.

Our concepts, beliefs, dreams, and desires act as the images and sounds on the film and accompanying sound track. The light of Universal consciousness shines through these images that we may experience our desires being made manifest. A person has the power to choose a horror movie or a beautiful movie full of love and every good and wonderful experience.

Jesus taught us this when he said, "It is done unto you as you believe." Thoughts become things when we believe and act on them. Truly, words precede form. Sound is the basic building block of the universe. "And God *said*, 'Let there be light: and there was light'" (Genesis 1:3). "In the beginning was the Word, and the Word was with God, and the Word was God" (John 1:1).

Heavenly Thoughts Produce Heavenly Experiences; Hellish Thoughts Produce Hellish Experiences

The invisible spiritual world is the model for this material world. "As above so below" is the principle called the Hermetic Axiom. This means that whatever is true and workable here has its perfect counterpart and origin in the world of pure spirit, God. Each person is a perfect, whole, and beautiful child of God, made in the image and likeness of the Supreme Being and therefore capable of accomplishing magnificent works by allowing this Power, Person, and Intelligence to express through us. As Jesus said, "It is not me but the Father Within who doeth the work."

Everything here is a reflection of that which is transpiring at the level of pure spirit without any trace of material energy. This is likened to a reflection of a tree in a calm lake. The tree as seen in the reflection is flat and not the real tree, but it is a real reflection. The reflection has beauty, function, and qualities of its own. Money is a reflection of the Goddess of Fortune, but money is not the power as it is a symbol.

The power is God's energy behind the money. Money changes form to suit the time, place, and circumstance, but the power remains the same and continues to flow and empower and enrich those who have a prosperity consciousness. Seashells at one time were money and still are for those who value seashells and barter. Generally speaking, storeowners will not take seashells in trade unless they love seashells. They will take, however, whatever is the agreed-upon means of exchange. Money follows consciousness. One who has a prosperity consciousness has money in whatever form is valued at the time, but money never has her. Prosperity-minded people are clear that they appreciate money, and they are also clear that money is not the purpose of life. Love is the purpose of life.

Pure love exists at the level of pure spirit, and to the degree that the person is allowing pure love to flow through his consciousness and actions pure love will manifest, abundantly. Pure opulence, wealth, and prosperity without the trace of poverty exists at the level of pure spirit and can be made manifest here when the person has no trace of poverty, fear, greed, or miserliness in the mind. Whatever we desire to experience and manifest is already existing in pure spirit as a perfect idea complete in all ways, and our work is to know this and allow this perfect idea to express through us into our outer world of affairs.

We can express the beauty, opulence, peace, and bliss of this heavenly spiritual world to the degree that we accept it and align our beliefs, thoughts, words, and deeds with it. A person can think degraded thoughts of poverty, fear, anger, envy, and sickness or she can elevate her mind to the level of what is called TRUTH. This is what it means to know the TRUTH and operate from Principle.

By aligning our mind and intelligence with God's perfect creation and order, we allow all good to flow to us unobstructed. Our work is to know exactly what we want to be, do, and have, and then to clear our subconscious mind of all limiting beliefs as we allow TRUTH to flow from the Source, God, Supreme Intelligence to us, by flowing unobstructed through us. GOD CAN ONLY DO FOR US WHAT HE CAN DO THROUGH US. If we desire to be happy, prosperous, loved, peaceful, and secure, we must maintain those corresponding beliefs and thoughts and act accordingly. This is the principle of correspondents or, as some call them, mental equivalents.

A person who desires to have a happy marriage must have the consciousness, skills, and knowledge of someone who is happily married. Because we can learn, anyone can learn to develop the right consciousness to obtain anything he desires by building the mental equivalent in consciousness, much as the architect uses blueprints and from these beginning blueprints the structure takes on form.

Thoughts Are Things

The basis of success and failure is in our beliefs and thoughts. Thoughts cause us to act and action produces results. Beliefs, which are concepts we accept as true and absolute, externalize as experiences: poverty thoughts produce poverty actions, which produce poverty results, while the belief in an infinite supply will tend to produce abundance in the life of the believer.

Thought is the food of consciousness, and we live on thought. Low thoughts and thoughts of fear, doubt, and poverty are heavy and they drain and rob us of our Divine birthright. High thoughts, God-filled thoughts, inspire, energize, motivate, and will take us to the top of the mountain and give us the treasures of the spiritual and material riches of life. The higher the thoughts the more elevated, positive, peaceful, and successful is the person. At the innermost and most elevated point possible in the consciousness of any person is pure, transcendental, eternal, and Supreme Bliss. This occurs when the mind is perfectly peaceful and centered completely on the ABSOLUTE TRUTH, without any obstruction or opposition to pure love.

It is challenging to change our ideas about ourselves, but as we persistently remind ourselves of our intrinsic nature as spiritual beings we can change our thoughts to fit the new conception. We can expand our awareness of who we are and our potential by daily dwelling upon the vastness of the universe, the idea of infinity, and the recognition of our unity with the boundless Whole.

God is within the heart of every person and is closer than our breath. God is ready and willing to help the individual in every way possible, but the person must first ask and seek this guidance and ever-ready love and assistance. Prayer is communion with God. The Almighty also knows what is in the heart of every living entity and is the Supreme Master in working everything out perfectly in divine right order and time.

Prayer reaches its highest potential when we raise our consciousness above the limitations of any existing circumstance, accept our ideal, and affirm it. Believing in the unseen Power and Presence of God is the very essence of faith. God is not weak, unhappy, poor, sick, or limited by any situation, person, place, or thing and neither are we at the level of our true selves.

By using Success Mantras, affirmations, and positive prayer we are able to reprogram our subconscious mind and set a new cause in motion that will produce the desired result. What is known in one mind is known in all minds, for we are part of the whole and no one is separate.

Higher thought and all ideas, inventions, art, music, and possibilities are already present in Universal Mind. We can access this realm of higher thought and limitless knowledge, guidance, and help anytime and anywhere, by rising above the limited world of appearances and opening our minds, intelligence, and hearts to this frequency and flow. This operates much like a radio or wireless technology. If we want to bring in a certain station, we must tune our radio receiver to that station. We do this through meditation, imagery, and prayer.

Success Mantras

Repetition of Success Mantras and positive statements of the TRUTH will dissolve old programming, as the higher beliefs and thoughts take over. Once the person accepts this new reality, his or her outer world will change to reflect the new inner one. Spirit is senior to matter, for matter must serve spirit and take on the form spirit commands. This is the impersonal and mechanical law of substance. Substance is inert matter, even though it is still God's energy and holy and divine. This substance is like the clay of the artist, and we are the artists. We are only limited by our own consciousness and imagination and our unwillingness to accept responsibility for our lives and for what has happened to us and will happen to us. Personal responsibility is the key that unlocks the door and allows the person to express and manifest his or her potential and receive the kingdom of God.

All this knowledge is to bring us to the point of perfect understanding of who we are that we may "have life and have it more abundantly," as is stated in the book of John in the New Testament of the Holy Bible.

Good Luck Is an Attitude

"Nothing ever happens by luck or by accident," Violet continued to explain. "There is a cause behind every effect. Even that which appears as a natural disaster has a cause, usually something mankind has done to disturb the balance of nature. Whatever comes to us today has its seed in an event of yesterday or the moment before. What we think and do today are the seeds that will grow into tomorrow's harvest. What we give out or do to others will come back to us that we may choose to do the right and good thing in each moment, if we want to live prosperous, happy, and wonderful lives.

"All good fortune is the result of one using this Universal Law properly. Anyone desiring to be fortunate needs to start with a positive mental attitude followed by the behavior that supports his or her desired results. Building and maintaining a positive mental attitude is absolutely essential."

Two Boys

Violet told us the story of a woman who had two boys. One thought himself to be lucky, and the other thought himself to be unlucky. There is a principle operating here called the "self-fulfilling prophecy." What you believe, think, and say about yourself has the tendency to manifest as a reality by the creative law of mind. The woman felt sorrow about the depressing, negative attitude of her unlucky boy and she sought to change his attitude. Placing a quarter on the carpet in the hallway, she coaxed the unlucky son to walk down the hall thinking he would find the quarter and believe his luck had changed. All of a sudden the lucky boy ran in front of his brother and, seeing the quarter, he quickly picked it up with joy, affirming how lucky he was.

"What to do?" thought the mother. Picking a time when the lucky son was not at home, she placed a quarter in the driveway of the garage and asked her so-called unlucky son to come to her. Because the quarter was in such an obvious place he had to see it and he did, but he wouldn't pick it up. "You put this quarter here, didn't you?" he exclaimed.

Because of his negative attitude, he couldn't let himself get into the spirit of good fortune and bend down and pick up the quarter. Did it really matter how the quarter had gotten there? Of course it didn't matter. What matters is that the quarter was there. The only thing the boy needed to do was to bend down, pick it up, and put it in his pocket with a smile on his face, and his luck would have changed. Good fortune is the direct result of our seeing possibilities, options, and opportunities all around us.

Someone with a negative attitude is cynical and cannot see his good fortune even when it is right in front of him. The boy's mother putting the quarter in the driveway was an act of love inspired by God to help change the unlucky boy's attitude and give him a chance to look on the bright side and thus change his life for the better. Those who expect good do good works and good is returned to them, as this is the Law of the Universe.

Violet completed her lessons by teaching us about the two basic Universal principles: Love and the Law. **"Love determines the goal, and the law makes the achievement possible."** Love of a person, place, thing, belief, or circumstance causes us to desire and act in a way that attracts to us the object of our love. By the same law of attraction, that which we do not accept or desire turns and runs the other way. The law is impersonal, but we are persons. The law obeys, follows, and receives, but it never gives direction or decides what it shall do or create, but we do. The law must fulfill and return to us that which we have impressed upon it by our thoughts, beliefs, and actions. Once something is conceived in the individual mind an impression is made upon the Universal Subjective Mind, and the right people, places, things, and events come together at the right time and in the right way for the desire to be fulfilled."

Time to Apply This Knowledge

What a summer! I had been using this power all along, but I didn't know it. Now I could understand why so many people were suffering. God was not making them suffer; it was their misuse of the law of life.

I knew that it was up to me to use the laws and principles of life intelligently, not to manipulate God, for no one can do that, but to make myself a worthy vessel through which the Higher Power could express freely and abundantly. Everyone has the freedom of choice as to whether or not to be all he or she can be and to express his or her full God-given talents and potential or not. My choice was to use these principles and find out what it was possible for me to attain. Why not find out? What are the other alternatives?

Principles of Success

Sitting at the Feet of Someone Who Knows

No one forced Nanny or me to listen to Violet. There we had sat anxious to receive the next, delicious morsel of what we called "truth." Violet made a huge impact on my entire life, and I wish I could have told her what a difference those three months under her tutelage had made in my life, but she passed away a few years later and I never saw her again after that summer.

PEARL
We may never know the contribution we make to another.
Whatever we contribute in love, besides blessing the
receiver, blesses us even more.

Violet taught me the basics that became the philosophical foundation of my life. This summer was God's gift to me as the answer to my prayer. There was no way I could have planned to find a teacher because, first, I didn't know I needed one and, second, I would not have known where to look or what to look for. Some call this coincidence, but after a lifetime of so-called coincidences I know for certain coincidences do not exist.

Violet had handed me a treasure chest of priceless jewels and wealth in the form of her instructions. I was a young woman of seventeen, bubbling over with passion, desire, and enthusiasm. God had brought the answer to prayer right into my Nanny's kitchen in the form of an elderly woman of knowledge. What a delivery service!

Not that I had found God yet, but if I had been told then what I know now I wouldn't have believed it or been in the slightest way ready. I had a lot of preparation to do, lessons to learn, experiences to go through, and knowledge to gain before I would be given the most sacred of all treasures. We all have to start where we are, and where you are right now is the perfect place for you to be to realize the lessons you need to learn in order to receive your treasures. Each gem you find and pearl of wisdom you pick up and put in your cosmic safe-deposit box will give you the resources, strength, and inspiration you need to help you to reach your destination.

GEM
Any life is worthwhile if the person collects the valuable lessons,
gifts, and treasures along the way.

Look to the past and retrieve the gems, pearls of wisdom, and treasures you can cash in today and build the wonderful life you desire.

Write about the single most important spiritual event that occurred before you were an adult, which changed the course of your life.

· · · · ·

The event happened when . . .

The event happened like this . . .

Write about what happened as a result of this event, what you learned, and how this continues to contribute to you to this day.

· · · · ·

As a result of this event, I . . .

How can you use what you learned from this event to prosper today?
I can . . .

Who was your first spiritual teacher?

My first spiritual teacher was _____.
What were the three most important teachings you received from him or her?
1.
2.
3.

Testing My New Philosophy

Preparing to enter college, I was so grateful and relieved to have something I could use to help me to know what to do to achieve my goals and guarantee that I would have a wonderful life. I remembered and wrote down the Four Basic Principles for Attaining Goals, which I had been given by Violet right before I climbed in my Chevy and drove away to start my college career. That was the last I ever saw or heard from her again, but she is still with me today through all that she taught me.

Violet's Four Basic Principles for Attaining Goals

1. Set your goals as to what you desire to be, do, and have.
2. Believe you can achieve your goals and keep a positive mental attitude.
3. Pray and ask God to help you to achieve your goals.
4. Work to attain your goals as if it all depends on you, and also trust that all depends on God.

My first big test of Violet's principles was presented to me on the first day of college as the registrar handed me the college brochure containing information about all the big events and activities of the 1957–58 school year.

Applying My Newly Acquired Principles

Immediately my eyes fell on the Homecoming football game and the crowning of the homecoming queen, freshman class president, and the school musicals and theatrical productions. These were all for me. Every one of these activities was beyond what I had ever hoped to attain before, but now I had spiritual knowledge and the Four Basic Principles to help me.

My first big obstacle was that the homecoming queen candidates had to be nominated. Since I had no one to nominate me, I walked into the office of the dean of students and asked, "Can people nominate themselves?" I asked. "Why not?" was his reply. Promptly I nominated myself. I saw the stunned looks on the faces of some of the office staff, and for a moment I lost heart, as if I had done something wrong. What would they say about me to others? Would they laugh at me and tell others about how sad it was that I had to nominate myself because no one else would?

Too often in my past I had worried about what others were thinking and saying about me. Waiting for others to nod their heads, smile, and give me permission to step out and live my dreams, I would fall into a heap of discouragement if they didn't.

This time something was different. When the dean of students smiled, nodded his head, and gave me the go-ahead that it was perfectly all right for me to nominate myself, I knew I would never have to ask anyone for permission ever again. As long as what I wanted to do was without any desire to hurt or take from another what belonged to her or him, then I would do it. Let them laugh and talk behind my back. So what!

For a moment I had almost given up my dream of being homecoming queen just because some women in the dean's office gave me the judging eye of disapproval.

Let Them Laugh, and Do What You Want to Do Anyway

People laughed at the Wright Brothers for building a machine that could fly. The critics laughed when the brothers crashed a few times, but they won out and succeeded in their attempt to do what others said was impossible.

Regis Philbin was a television talk show host in Los Angeles, and then he was fired. Regis was the brunt of many jokes and the subject of public ridicule. Not being able to find a job anywhere else, with persistence he finally landed a job as the talk show host of a daily TV program out of New York City. Now Regis is laughing all the way to the bank. This show has been extremely successful nationally for fifteen years and is still going strong. He kept his mind on his goal until he attained it, never allowing the ridicule of others to stop him. Regis is definitely getting the last laugh.

Three Fears Everyone Must Defeat

1. The fear of rejection
2. The fear of ridicule
3. The fear of criticism

These three fears have nothing to do with other people but only with how we let other people control our thoughts, emotions, and actions. Shunning is a powerful way to control people. No one wants to be ignored, unless he or she is a hermit or a very secure and self-reliant person. Being the center of someone's, if not everyone's, attention is the unconscious goal of most. The Old Testament story of Adam and Eve's first children, Cain and Abel, points to envy as a basic flaw in human character. Sibling rivalry caused Cain to kill his brother, Abel. Wanting to be the center of attention, especially the center of our parents' attention and then our mate's attention, is the cause of jealousy, rage, and even hatred.

Looking outside of ourselves for love, we set ourselves up to suffer from these three fears. Fearing rejection, ridicule, or criticism can turn a person into an immovable object. Some fear success even more than failure.

Brenda Was Programmed for Failure

Brenda was programmed to avoid success. Every time she experienced a success in her school and community activities, her mother would ridicule, criticize, and outwardly reject her. She learned through time to fear success, for success meant rejection and the loss of her mother's attention and love. Brenda's mother lavished affection and attention on her every time Brenda had a loss or disappointment. Failure meant love. With each failure, Brenda would be showered with care and concern.

Seeing this pattern manifest over and over, Brenda decided to break the old sick pattern and form a new and healthy one. She programmed her subconscious mind to believe that it was perfectly right for her to succeed. Brenda could see that her mother liked being the center of attention and couldn't tolerate it when her daughter was the center.

Part of Brenda's spiritual therapy was to use the following success mantra: "I do not need my mother's love, approval, or attention, for love is who I am. God loves me and that is enough. It is perfectly right for me to succeed." Saying it over and over many times a day with feeling she planted a new belief in her subconscious mind. Now Brenda could allow her mother to react to her successes and failures however she chose, but she was no longer hurt by her mother's actions toward her. Brenda followed her dream and became a very wealthy business executive.

Success mantra: "God is the unlimited source of my supply."

The root cause of these three fears is the belief that other people are the source of our supply, money, food, clothing, home, happiness, love, and survival. We all have these fears until we see them for what they are: lies. Of course people are our avenues through which money, opportunities, and much-needed things come to us, but they are not our source; God is. Remember: If one person does not want to give you what you need or desire, someone else will. Some people will like you, most likely because you like them, but some will not, especially if they perceive that you present some imagined threat to their enjoyment and plans.

Rachael's Opportunity to Learn

Rachael was a beautiful child who was extremely intelligent, sweet, talented, and positive minded. One day she spoke openly to me, her minister, about how her dance teacher criticized her in class and often would ridicule her with coarse words of rejection. I could tell that this negative treatment was taking something from her and causing her to feel downhearted and unsociable. As I listened to her story, it was clear to me that the teacher was envious of this most extraordinary little girl. Remembering back to my impressionable years in grade school, I too had felt the hurt of rejection, ridicule, and criticism. Thinking something was wrong with me, I developed an inferiority complex, which I had to work to overcome. Once we can understand why we are reacting as we are, we can root out the cause: separation from the love and association of the Divine.

I explained to Rachael that most people are infected with the disease of envy. In their attempt to be happy by getting the attention of others, they will try to rob the one who is getting the love, recognition, and praise by using destructive tools of ridicule, unfair criticism, and rejection. I thought, "I wish that someone had told me this at an early age, as it would have prevented me from having to suffer just because someone wanted something I had." Rachael gained some valuable insight into why people are kind or unkind. She understood that most of the time the way people treat us has nothing at all to do with us, but with them. From this point on she chose to have the attitude of "I am prosperous." Whenever she felt threatened, as if someone could prevent her from getting the love, attention, and good she desired for herself, she would speak the following Success Mantra. The Success Mantra helped to open her mind to possibilities and put her in a positive and optimistic state of mind.

> Success mantra: "There is no scarcity of love. God, the
> source of love, is always with me and I am now aware of
> this endless flow of love coming from God to me.
> I am loved and love is who I am."

PEARL
You are not the target of other people's envy.

We are not the cause of someone else's envy and upset. It may seem to others as if we are standing in the way of their enjoyment, but we are not. Not knowing this fact, people imagine that if they can get us out of the way they will reach their objective and be happier, but this is not true. Happiness and love bubble forth from the wellspring of limitless supply that comes from the Soul of every soul and not from anything outside of this inner Source and Supply. Self-satisfaction is the solution, for within each person is an unlimited supply of love and happiness.

PEARL
No one can reject you, unless you reject yourself.

Self-Acceptance Is Most Important

Once I understood that some people would laugh at me, criticize, and reject me, I made peace with the fact. It is unrealistic to think anything else, and to do so only sets a person up for misery. Not knowing and accepting this one aspect of human nature has ruined many a life by preventing countless persons from expressing their God-given talents to the fullest.

Self-rejection is the worst thing a person can do, especially since it comes only from comparing oneself with others or from believing that the attitudes and actions of others toward us have some basis in absolute truth, which they never do. Self-acceptance and self-honoring are the right and good things to do so that we may become who and what we are capable of becoming. Our work is to let our light shine by fully expressing our god-like nature and our God-given talents and not allow fear ever to defeat us.

Jesus told us to do this with his teaching that states: "Ye are the light of the world. A city that is set on a hill cannot be hid. Neither do men light a candle, and put it under a bushel, but on a candlestick; and it giveth light unto all that are in the house. Let your light so shine before men, that they may see your good works, and glorify your Father which is in Heaven" (Matthew 5: 14–16).

PEARL
Someone will find fault with you no matter what you do or do not do. Do what seems most appropriate for you, as long as you are not intending to cause harm to another or to yourself.

Testing My New Philosophy

Violet taught me to transcend fear by understanding fear to be what it is: a lack of faith in God. My fears behind me, I set out to let my light shine by becoming the new homecoming queen. Jumping right in, I got busy putting up posters and meeting everybody in school. Violet had said to treat others with love and appreciation. Genuinely finding something to admire about each person I met, I came to like everyone without exception. Getting to know as many students as possible was my public relations plan, and it was a good one. As it was the student body who elected the homecoming queen, this was a wise decision.

PEARL
Genuinely liking people is one of the secrets of success.

Confidence Beyond the Shadow of a Doubt

The day came to announce the finalists, and I waited in the student center to hear the news. My name was called, and I jumped for joy. Yes, I was a finalist! My principles of success and positive thinking were working. The queen would be announced at the game on homecoming night.

Homecoming night came and while I was waiting before halftime, one of the other finalists, who was very beautiful, came over to me and said, "I know I am winning, so don't get your hopes up." Not saying anything in reply, I simply took a few deep breaths, held on to my feelings of self-confidence, and refused to allow her to get me down. "Whatever the outcome, at least I am a finalist. After all, God is in charge" was my attitude. She had been a very popular girl in high school and I had been, you know, average. She was certain more people would vote for her than for me. Overconfidence is as detrimental as underconfidence. Real confidence includes humility, knowing that the outcome is up to God. Still, this means we need to be absolutely certain without a shadow of a doubt.

The fear that keeps people from being absolutely confident as they pursue their objectives is the fear that if they fail, they will be disappointed, hurt, and perhaps be considered a loser and failure in the minds of others. The real failure is someone who does not even try. Why should we allow anything that happens, one way or another, to get us down, when the beautiful person we are inside remains the same under any and all circumstances? Driving a Rolls Royce may make you feel important and rich, but if you allow conditions, the opinions of others, and things to control your thoughts, feelings, and conduct, if you must drive an old beat-up Volkswagen, most likely you will feel embarrassed, poor, and unimportant. In either case nothing has happened to you, the soul and person inside the body. One who can maintain an attitude of dignity and high self-esteem at all times is the real winner. Fearing ridicule and criticism, many hide their light and do not share their talents or participate in life at the optimal level. Once we understand that people will criticize us no matter whether we win or lose, we will participate fully in the game of life.

Remaining confident in the face of possible defeat is a challenge, and every champion has learned to do this. Yes, I wanted to be a champion and Nanny always called me her champion. Being competitive by nature, I liked winning. I knew that if I did not enter the game or contest and then play full out until the end, there was no chance of my winning. Confidence takes some time to develop, as people of all mentalities, dispositions, and levels of awareness surround us and have enormous influence over us, if we allow it. Our nature is to be in relationships, so we must learn how to allow others to only affect us positively and never negatively.

Of course we want to be loved, respected, and admired, as this is the basic desire of all people, but we cannot get this from all people and still live our dreams and achieve our goals, because many want us to fail. People are failing just to get love, intimacy, and association from certain people they have designated as important. Remember this: If someone wants you to fail and not achieve your goals, she or he really is not your friend.

Don't Give Up

Some people give up right before the end because they would rather say "I quit" and think that they could have won than to have failed. I read an article that said that most quit right before they would have achieved the goal. Quitting doesn't really exist. At some point, there will be a similar situation and another opportunity either to quit or continue on. Every time we give in to our fears and quit, or refuse to enter the game, we have failed the test. The test is not whether or not you win the race, for there are many variables that are not under your control, but whether or not you were in the race and gave your all. There is no way to escape oneself or the lessons and challenges that each of us must face and conquer. Every person will find himself or herself in the very same spot again and again until the lesson has been learned.

No Place to Hide

In my opinion it is better to face the challenge, be victorious now, and enjoy the treasures and pleasures that come with victory than to run away and hide. Some try to solve their problems and end their suffering with suicide, or the death of the body. But it's not the body that is causing the real problem; it's the person's attitude. Suicide does not end someone's suffering or solve his or her problems. Suicide only makes it more difficult for the person, as she or he must face the exact same situation at another point in time in another body. The person will arrive at the very same spot again and again, lifetime after lifetime, until the lesson has been learned and the test has been passed. The real test involves giving up what we don't need anyway: fear and attachment to people, places, and things as the source of our happiness, wealth, and love. No one was born to hide, but to stand strong and let his or her Inner Light shine brightly and glorify the Father Within. Remaining balanced between success and failure, loss or gain, happiness or distress elevates the person to a place of real transcendental power. Someone who has attained this status is unbeatable.

The one who can keep on keeping on has the greatest chance of achieving victory, but the fear of what people will think is so strong that the weakhearted will stop and not give their all in hopes of preventing the ridicule, rejection, and criticism. The key I realized is this: Be willing to live without agreement and acceptance.

Extraordinary people are those who are comfortable with or without the agreement, approval, and acceptance of others. They have a strong sense of mission and purpose that motivates them and keeps them enthused in the face of adversity. They get tremendous approval and acknowledgement for who they are and what they produce, but they are not controlled by an insecure need to be liked by everyone.

Remember: It isn't the failure or success that is the problem; it is the fear of rejection, criticism, or ridicule. At the core of this is the belief that without the acceptance and approval of others we cannot survive, but we can and we will.

Accepting Validation That the Principles Work

Feeling confident because I was saying my affirmation "I am a winner" over and over in my mind, I walked to the white Cadillac convertible and climbed up above the backseat. The parade of cars carrying the 1957 homecoming queen finalists moved onto the football field amid the sound of thundering cheers and applause. Each runner-up was called and then there was silence, before my name was called. It was no longer a dream or vision but a reality. I had actually become the new homecoming queen. With my eyes filled with tears of great joy I said, "Thank you, God."

Why had this happened to me? I knew it had happened because I had followed what I had learned from my first spiritual teacher. Right after this, I used the same principles to become freshman class president and get the starring roles in the college musicals and plays. Was this fair? This is how things work! The rewards go to those who want them and work to achieve them. The most important work anyone can do is called "Inner Work."

The outer world is the outward manifestation of the inner world of belief, imagination, desire, and acceptance. The visible comes from the invisible as our ideas express into form that we may experience and discover who we are and the creative power we possess. Who are we?

> "I have said, Ye are gods; and all of you are children
> of the Most High." —*Psalm 82:6*

> "Jesus answered them, 'Is it not written in your law,
> I said, Ye are gods?'"—*John 10:34*

Jesus gave this reply when he was accused of making himself God. Human beings are godlike in nature—not God, but godlike—possessing divine rights and qualities that we are using to create a heavenly or hellish existence in the here and now. The principles of successful living are taught in every religion, as these truths are eternal and applicable to everyone regardless of religion, nationality, age, sex, education, or past experience. The choice is ours as to whether we will develop and express our highest or lowest nature or somewhere in between.

How Things Work

No one makes up the principles of success in anything, as the principles already exist and have always been. Our work is to discover, learn, and apply them. Electricity has always existed since the beginning of time, but man's awareness of how to use it has only existed for a short while in comparison. Rightly used, electricity will light up your home, keep your food cold, and run your computer, but wrongly used it can electrocute a person. Is this the fault of the electricity or the person using it?

People blame the Supreme Being for whatever is going wrong. But it is we who are misusing the principles and laws that are meant to bless us and give us the happiness, love, and prosperity God desires for us. God is a loving God, not an angry God, as some would believe. Few take the time to find out about these principles, and this is why there are so few exceptional people living exceptional lives and doing extraordinary work. All this is possible to everyone who has the intelligence to understand.

Three Kinds of People—Which One Are You?

Anyone can tap into the power that is within him or her, if he or she chooses. There are three kinds of people. One: Intelligent persons who learn from the mistakes and successes of others. Two: Less intelligent persons who learn from their own mistakes and successes. Third: Ignorant persons do *not* learn from their mistakes or successes.

Please make a list of the five most important goals you have achieved.

1.

2.

3.

4.

5.

Violet Had Given Me Aladdin's Wonderful Lamp

Having these secrets almost made me feel as though I was cheating. Aladdin's lamp, which I had wanted since childhood, had been given to me in the form of my first spiritual teachings. This is really the meaning behind the story of Aladdin and his lamp. You and I are Aladdin, and the universal creative power of the mind is the genie in the lamp who is willing to grant our wishes. How was the genie to know what Aladdin wanted unless Aladdin asked?

All I had to do if I wanted something was to pull out my notes, study my lessons, and follow the directions, and it would work. No one in my family or close circle of friends knew of my secret lamp, except Nanny. Others wouldn't have believed me anyway! I had tried to tell a few of my friends, hoping they would also receive the benefit, but they showed no interest.

> **PEARL**
>
> *You can't tell everyone everything. They are most likely not ready to listen. It will only give you trouble if you try to convince others of their godlike qualities and the wonderful powers lying dormant within them. Jesus taught us not to throw our pearls of wisdom before those who are not ready to listen. A wise person knows when to share something of great value and when to keep silent.*

Two Frogs in a Well

Once there were two frogs, which had always lived in the water inside a deep, dark well. One day as the bucket was being lowered into the well, one of the frogs was swept up into the bucket by accident and taken to the top. When the water was dumped from the bucket into a large pot, the frog jumped out and hopped away.

You can imagine how overwhelmed and utterly surprised the frog was to see the sun, sky, clouds, trees, flowers, animals, insects, hills, houses, and people. Everything was in living color, with sound, texture, and fragrance. It was almost too much for one little frog to behold, but he took some time and explored this newfound world. Excited to tell his friend so he, too, could leave the dark, cold, and boring well, he jumped back into the well.

Bubbling over with enthusiasm about all the wonders he had seen, heard, felt, tasted, and smelled he told his friend everything. "No, this is not possible. You are crazy," replied the frog who had never been out of the well.

"Come with me and see for yourself," begged the frog, who had seen and experienced another entirely new and glorious reality.

"Don't be a fool. Give up your folly and stay here with me where you belong."

"Good-bye and thank you for all your companionship. I am leaving for another life," said the frog, who had had a taste of something beyond what he had known previously. He hitched a ride on the next bucket.

As far as we know, he is still exploring the wonders of God's unlimited universe.

"Whatever you can do or dream you can, begin it.
Boldness has genius, power, and magic in it. Begin
it now!"—*Goethe, the German philosopher*

This sounded good to me, and why not? Yes, I wanted to explore my possibilities and the wonders of God's great and unlimited universe and beyond. This is my life to live as I choose, and this is your life to live as you choose. Since we are held accountable for what we do by the law of life, called cause and effect, why not do that which will give us the ultimate benefits that are possible for any human being to attain? Our work, should we accept the errand, is to find out just what these ultimate options are and what is required to attain and possess them.

It was from this profound realization that I set out to find and enjoy the spiritual and material riches of life. Somehow I knew that there was much more to life than what those around me knew, or even cared to know was possible. I wanted to have it all, and I wasn't ever going to settle for a common life. Whatever it took, I made a commitment that my life would be an extraordinary one.

PEARL OF WISDOM

The helping hands we are waiting for are on the ends of our own arms. God helps those who help themselves. God can only do for us what He does through us.

Chapter Three

Step One, Desire the Topmost

"Plant the seed of desire in your mind, and it
forms a nucleus with power to attract to
itself everything needed for its fulfillment."
—*Robert Collier, American Philosopher*

Having left the "well" of my former reality for a brilliant new world, I knew something that others did not. I was surprised that no one around me was even remotely interested in finding out what was beyond the walls of their limited thinking and experience. I have come to realize that only a few people seek permanent solutions to problems or take the time to find out how to get where they want to go. For sure, those around me were *not* looking within themselves for the treasures they were seeking, and most didn't even know there were treasures to be found.

Settling for the ordinary and mundane just to maintain the status quo seemed to be the popular state of mind of the people I knew. Somehow I knew that I was different from my friends and family. Whatever it would take, I did not want my life to be like theirs.

"Here's to the crazy ones. The misfits. The rebels.
The troublemakers. The round heads in the square
holes. The ones who see things differently. They're
not fond of rules, and they have no respect for the
status quo. You can quote them, disagree with
them, glorify, or vilify them. But the only thing you
can't do is ignore them. Because they change things.

They push the human race forward. And while
some may see them as the crazy ones, we see
genius. Because the people who are crazy enough to
think they can change the world are the ones who do."
—*"Think Different" advertisement,*
Apple Computers

Buried Diamonds

Around this point in my spiritual quest, I found an old book in the school library that told the story of a hidden fortune. It wasn't by accident that I found this little book, because it was just what I needed at the time. Already I was beginning to understand that there was a higher something at work behind the scenes. Many times it would happen that the right person would appear, just as I needed to see him, or the phone would ring and it would be the person I was going to call. Nonbelievers will call this accident or coincidence, but believers call it Divine right action.

The author of this particular book told the story of a certain person who was seeking wealth. The man in the story sold his undeveloped land in South Africa and took the small amount of money he received and moved to the city, which he thought to be a place of great riches. One day, while the new owner was walking on the property, he saw something shining from what looked like a rock. Further investigation revealed the rock to be a diamond in the rough. Under his feet was an immense diamond mine.

The Potential for Immense Wealth Is Born with Us

The origin and source of all we are seeking is within us. A wealth of invaluable resources is lying dormant in the seed of talent, intelligence, and creativity. When we seek out and use what is within us, what is within us will bless us and produce a beautiful and opulent garden of every good and wonderful thing and experience. Those who are able to bring forth the wealth within them make three primary decisions.

Three Primary Decisions

1. We must decide to find out about the wealth and power that is within us.

2. We must decide to access and use the talents, genius, and power within us.

3. We must decide to set ideals and goals that are far beyond what we have attained in the past.

We come fully equipped at birth with the basic ingredients we need in order to flourish and thrive. Because the whole, or God, is complete, each part of God is also complete. Since we are part of God, we are also complete with nothing missing. Something few people have realized is that the Father has provided for each of His children by giving them talents, intelligence, and creative abilities to be used in exchange for what they need and want. We also have our propensities and inclinations having to do with what we would enjoy doing. These talents, propensities, and inner urging to express are our means to prosper, make a difference, and fulfill our part in God's divine plan.

Most do not know they have an enormous treasure chest of wealth in the form of their talents, intelligence, and propensities. Realizing this, my question became "What can I do to tap into this vast resource of almost limitless supply?"

Give of Your Talents and Your Talents and Wealth Will Increase

The answer to this question came in the form of the Parable of the Talents, which would become one of my most favorite teachings of Jesus: **"And so he that had received five talents came and brought other five talents, saying 'Lord, thou deliverest unto me five talents: behold I have gained beside them five talents more.' His lord said unto him, 'Well done, thou good and faithful servant: thou hast been faithful over a few things, I will make thee ruler over many things: enter thou into the joy of thy lord'"** (Matthew 25: 20–21).

Because the one who was given many talents and advantages took what he had been given and multiplied it, he was rewarded by receiving the joy of the lord, plus he was given 100 percent more to invest and increase. But as the story goes, if you read the entire parable, the one who was given one talent hid what he had been given because he was a miser and afraid of losing the little he had been given. Because of this person's fear, he refused to invest, share, and multiply what he had been given. One of the principles of life is: What you don't use, you lose. Talents and abilities not used atrophy. Therefore what he had hidden away was taken from him and given to the one who had the most. Perhaps this does not seem fair? The law of life is that we must use what we have been given, including our talents, resources, power, and intelligence in service to the greater good of all, and if we do, we will prosper. The more we love, the more love we have to give; but if we hold on to our love and keep it for ourselves, we will be loveless and lonely.

Here is the point of the lesson: **"For unto every one that hath shall be given, and he shall have abundance: but from him that hath not shall be taken away even that which he hath"** (Matthew 25: 29).

> What, if any, talents and abilities have you not been expressing or sharing because of fear?
>
> 1.
> 2.
> 3.

Sharing Brings Great Rewards

Before understanding this teaching on a deep level I had been a miser, keeping everything for myself in fear that if I shared or gave I would forfeit what I had. Now I knew that what we have is not for us to keep only for ourselves, for it is in the sharing and giving of what we have been given that our needs are met and we flourish.

I am sure you have noticed that some have enormous, even colossal, talents, while others appear to be without talents or their talents appear to be pathetic in comparison. Everyone has talents, and this is the point of the parable. Whatever we have is enough, for when we invest it by sharing it with others, that which we have increases and we are given more upon that. Those who hoard the little they have lose what they have and are thrown into lamentation and misery only because of their own unwillingness to give and share of who they are, their talents and resources.

I was thrilled to find out that the most successful are not always the most talented, gifted, or privileged. This meant that with whatever I had I could excel and enjoy a wonderful life in all respects. So what if my parents were not rich or powerful or I had no exceptional talent. I could achieve my topmost goals and so could anyone, if we so desired, deeply and strongly enough.

PEARL
*It never is what we have that is most important,
but what we do with what we have.*

There's Always Enough

Mother Teresa, who did such wonderful work for the poor in India, built her huge organization by starting with three cents, because that was all she had. She wasn't rich, didn't have an influential family or a degree from the Harvard Business School, nor was she beautiful, but she experienced extraordinary success because she desired to help the greatest number of people possible. The secret of any great person's success is that she start with whatever she has. Her kind of giving is rewarded by the Powers that Be, both in this world and the worlds beyond. Whereas I've noticed that many others possessing much more than Mother Teresa never believe they have enough to accomplish their goals, and so they don't. The point being: We all have enough if we begin where we are and start with what we have. Whatever we give—no matter how small and insignificant the gift may appear—if it is given in love, it is enough.

The Ramayana

Another story that makes this point is an incident in *The Ramayana*, a famous legend from India. Hanuman, the monkey man, who was gifted with enormous strength and abilities, was picking up huge boulders and throwing them into the ocean to build a bridge from mainland India to the Island of Sri Lanka in order to rescue Queen Sita from the demon Ravana. A tiny spider was also by the side of the river kicking dust into the water with his legs as thin as strands of hair. Hanuman looked down and saw him. Laughing, he said, "Small spider, what do you think you are doing?" "I am kicking rocks into the water to help build the bridge to rescue Queen Sita," replied the spider, as he continued to work. "Don't be foolish. You are not helping—you are too small to make any difference," retorted Hanuman.

At that moment, King Rama, the faithful husband of Queen Sita, over-heard the conversation and spoke the following words: "Hanuman, the lit-tle spider's efforts are just as great as yours. It is not the size of a person or the greatness of his talent that matters. What pleases me is when he gives whatever he has into service with love and enthusiasm."

Desire Is the Golden Key

Mother Teresa was able to accomplish great works because she had a burn-ing, intense, and all-consuming desire to achieve her mission and fulfill her destiny. Any person can do great things if his or her desire is strong enough. Desire can turn a shy person into a dynamic personality. Desire can take a small talent, and with work this talent can be developed into an extraordinary gift for the world to enjoy.

Desire is the **Golden Key** that opens the gate to the road of personal riches. Everyone has this key with them at all times, but most often they use it to open the door to poverty, heartache, distress, and "the same old same old."

Very few persons, comparatively, know of the power of desire. Desire is the very first step no matter the goal, objective, or dream. Those who de-sire with sufficient intensity can reach the pinnacle of any profession, find the cure for a disease, climb the tallest mountain, have a happy marriage, raise wonderful children, excel in his or her talents and abilities, govern a country, or invent something of tremendous value to humanity.

> "You can have anything you want if you want it
> desperately enough. You must want it with an inner
> exuberance that erupts through the skin and joins
> the energy that created the world."
> —*Sheila Graham, author*

"The starting point of all achievement is desire.
Keep this constantly in mind. Weak desires bring
weak results, just as a small amount of fire makes a
small amount of heat." —*Napoleon Hill, author*

"This gift is from God and not of man's deserving.
But certainly no one ever receives such a great grace
without tremendous labor and burning desire."
—*Richard of Saint Victor, medieval author*

Desire the Ultimate

"Dream no small dreams for they have no
power to move the hearts of men."
—*Johann Wolfgang von Goethe*

Why not desire to achieve the topmost possible to any human being? "If I can see it, then I will believe" is the statement of a materialist. "If I can believe it, then I will see it" is the statement of a visionary. Our desires work like grappling hooks that climbers use to help them to climb to the tops of the tallest mountains. The climber first desires to reach the next higher place and throws the hook to catch on the ledge above. Using the rope hanging from the grappling hook, the climber is able to leave the lower level and reach the higher one.

Flip Wilson's Dream Come True

Flip Wilson, the famous comedian, was one of ten children. His mother had left the family and his father did his best to care for the children. At an early age, Flip performed his comedy routine anywhere there was a crowd. Performing in bars in exchange for donations from the customers, he was often asked to leave since his humor was not appreciated. Having to sleep in the street on many occasions for lack of funds, he never took a second job or gave up his dream of being a world-famous comedian. Flip had a burning desire to achieve the topmost in his chosen profession, and he did.

Without the desire to attain the topmost pinnacle of success, he would not have been able even to come close to using his God-given talents. Flip's desires enabled him to rise out of poverty and mediocrity and attain great wealth, fame, and the love of millions whose lives were made brighter through his enormous talent.

Two Concerns That Rob a Person of Her or His Intrinsic Wealth

There are two main concerns that keep people from setting goals and endeavoring to attain the fulfillment of their heartfelt desires.

1. What will people say?
2. Where will I get the money?

People will be critical of you no matter whether you sit at home and watch television for the rest of your life or win the Nobel Peace Prize. Is there anyone who is not criticized? No matter what you do or don't do, some will criticize you and some won't—and that's the reality.

Fear of appearing foolish to others has kept many a person from fulfilling his or her dreams. Flip Wilson was even physically thrown out of some of the bars where he was performing, but he picked himself up, dusted himself off, and went to the next bar. If one is to carry through and live one's desires, one must have his kind of determination. We must develop a strong taste for victory. Our desires must be stronger than our fears. Fears, for the most part, are simply figments of our imagination and a ploy of the demon-out-of-control-mind to defeat you and keep you its slave. Stop cowering in fear and rise up and take command, for you truly are the Master of Your Destiny.

Money Comes

"Where am I going to get the money?" cry the masses. Everyone worries about not having enough money, as long as they do not understand how money works. Money is an energy that comes to those who offer something of value to others. People who generate big money are those who have big dreams and big ideas backed with well-thought-out plans. Money comes when the person receives money in exchange for goods and services. The key thing to remember is that everyone has something of value to offer, especially you.

Picasso Was Penniless, but He Never Gave Up His Heartfelt Desires

Pablo Picasso, the famous artist, was at times penniless before his art was appreciated. He too never took a second job, because he had vowed to live off the money he made from selling his art. In his early days as a struggling artist, there were times when he missed a meal or two. He could have settled for something other than his heart's desire, but he chose to be true to himself and climb to the top of where his talent and dreams could take him. Picasso never settled for mediocre; he chose the best.

Yes, you say, "That was easy for Picasso for he had tremendous talent but, what about the average person possessing little talent in comparison?" If Picasso had not thrown the grappling hook of desire to the highest point possible, he too could have been an obscure and unappreciated artist.

The fear is "What if I desire the ultimate of what is possible to attain and I do not make it?" Embarrassment is the concern of the weakhearted. Again we come back to the same thing: the opinions of others. Just because you are famous and rich does not mean that everyone will love and respect you, for there may be many who are envious of you and even hope for your downfall. If you fail to attain your goal, there is no embarrassment, for at least you made the wholehearted attempt. It's not always the goal that's most important but what you will learn and who you must become in the process. Living in fear of what others will say is the mark of a coward. Only the brave and the strong can achieve victory. Because we must become strong and courageous in order to achieve our topmost goals, the value is not just the attainment of the goal. In our attempt to reach for and attain something beyond where we are at the present time, we will need to grow in our understanding, develop our skills, and build our confidence—and these qualities of being are the real treasures.

Desires Come Before the Money

As far as where are we going to get the money is concerned; we need to know that money follows after a project has been started. Don't wait to get the money before you desire to attain something, or you could be waiting forever. Desire first, set the goal, start with what you have, and you will see that as you progress, the money or whatever you need will come. Too many people give up before they even set a goal because they believe they will never get the money. Globally speaking, money exists in abundant supply, but a person with a poverty consciousness of there never being enough will limit the amount of money that will come to him or her. At the present time we may not have the full amount we need, but there are enormous amounts of money available in the world, and we can tap into that supply if we have the right consciousness and attitude. Money is not the goal. The goal is the experience, product, or service one can get in exchange for the money. Often a person with a prosperity consciousness will get what he or she needs without the exchange of money.

Millie Had Little Money, but She Had a Big Dream

Millie wanted to travel, but she had no money to do so. She made a list of the places she desired to visit. Then she prayed and asked God, as she knew God to be, to give this to her. She had absolute faith beyond the shadow of a doubt that it would happen, but she didn't know how or when. To help her increase her desire, she made a "dream map." Looking in magazines, she found pictures of the places she wanted to visit. After cutting out the pictures, she pasted them on a poster board and put the board up on the wall in her bedroom. Every day at least three times Millie would look at the pictures and see herself actually in the places she desired to visit. Millie was increasing her desire to travel to these far-off and exotic lands by seeing, sensing, and feeling herself as already there. Her seeing, feeling, and sensing herself to be in these desired locations also set in motion the universal law and power of manifestation.

Soon, as if from out of nowhere, she was hired as a tour guide and entertainment hostess on a luxury liner. Millie traveled to every place she had written on her list and placed on her map, all her expenses were paid, and furthermore, she made good money. She even fell in love with one of the passengers, and they were married.

Set Your Goals Before You Know How You Will Achieve Them

We do not need to know how desires or goals will be obtained before we decide on our goals and dreams. Desire is like a seed that has the completed plant inherent in it. A watermelon seed contains the entire plant plus many watermelons each containing hundreds of seeds for more plants, more watermelons, and more seeds, etc. I started thinking of my desires as seeds, and I had a lot of seeds to plant. My dream was to grow and enjoy a bountiful, opulent, and beautiful garden of every good and wonderful experience and thing.

Carol's Dream

Carol was only eight years old when her mother saw the crayon sketch of a whale she had drawn and put up on the windowsill. Carol's mother asked her about her sketch, and Carol replied, "We're all going to Sea World in San Diego to see the whales." The family had no plans to go to Sea World. "Mommy, will you please take me to Sea World," begged Carol. "Carol, I am sure you will go to Sea World because this is a strong desire, but don't look to your father and me to be the ones who will pay for you to go," responded the mother.

Carol's mother was a Sunday school teacher, so she proceeded to give Carol a lesson on the power of manifestation. She said, "Carol, remember that God is your source of supply, not me. Sometimes I may be your avenue, but not always. People are your avenues and the agents who deliver to you that which is coming directly from God though the laws of the universe. It is important to remember this. If one person is not able to give you what you need and hope for, then it will come through another person and avenue. People are limited, but God's unlimited. Therefore, when you pray to God, be open to your desires being fulfilled through expected or even unexpected avenues. God may use us, your parents, or someone else."

Carol's mother concluded by explaining, "No one can take your good or has the power to prevent you from achieving your goals. Remember that God is your source and people are the avenues that God is using to help you to get what you need. If one avenue is closed to you because that person does not want to give you what you desire, someone else will."

A couple of months after that the family was given an all-expense-paid trip to San Diego, as a business perk for Carol's father. The trip included free passes to all the amusement parks, including Sea World. Her parents weren't her direct avenues, someone else was. On a higher level, Carol and her mother knew it was God fulfilling one sweet little girl's heartfelt desire.

Shoot for the Stars

The ultimate for you may be different than for your closest relatives and friends, but this is your life you are living, not theirs. Ultimate, meaning the best, topmost, finest, zenith, excellent, or most seemingly impossible to achieve. Set your sights high beyond what appears possible to attain easily. To accomplish things beyond the ordinary one must call in the Power of God, and this is where one's faith will grow. When there appears to be no chance because of overwhelming odds against something happening and then it does happen all in perfect order, as it will, you know that God is real.

My experience with my great-grandfather had taught me there were two worlds, the spiritual and the material. The visible and material world is created from the invisible spiritual world. Those who do not know this live as slaves to the material world in fear of dying, not having enough, or losing what they have. Knowing the laws of life allows any person to shoot for the stars, and with enough desire and effort she or he will attain them.

PEARL

If you shoot for a star you may hit the moon, but if you shoot for a small hill you may hit a rock in the road. Why not shoot for the stars? You just may reach the stars, and if not, you will most certainly attain that which is way beyond anything you could have imagined or acquired had you settled for that small hill.

What Is Possible For One Person To Attain?

Buckminster Fuller, a freethinker, inventor, humanitarian, and architect, chose to use his life as an example of what one person could do without a formal education or without government or corporate financial support. He chose to accomplish the topmost of what he was capable of achieving on his own as an experiment, and he did wonderful things. One of his books, *Operating Manual for Spaceship Earth*, is priceless if you want to read a simple explanation of how the political and business worlds work. He invented the geodesic dome as an ideal living space and discovered the power of the tetrahedron, the shape of the basic building block of the universe. He tapped into universal intelligence and was able to accomplish more than most who had far more to start with than he.

Ned Chose a Higher Existence

Ned was in prison serving time for drug-related offenses after an attempted suicide. Determined to start and live a new life, Ned contemplated his possibilities. We all know the high incidence of those who are released from prison returning again and again. Ned could have been another statistic, but instead he chose to desire the topmost of what was possible for any human being. To accomplish this, upon being released from prison he took spiritual classes, read positive-thinking books, and volunteered for spiritual organizations. Why not desire the ultimate? He was a person, wasn't he? And he possessed the same God-given creative abilities as others. His desire was strong, and from this opportunities came to him.

One of the things he did was to use a success mantra to reprogram his subconscious mind. Because deep-seated beliefs stored in the subconscious produce our thoughts and feelings and motivate our actions, if we want a better life we must change those beliefs. He spoke this success mantra over and over every day with feeling until he believed it. Soon his old belief of unworthiness had disappeared. Whereas before he had been using mind-altering drugs to avoid pain and feel pleasure, he now knew that the reservoir of pleasure was within him. He used a success mantra to turn his attention to his inner source of real and lasting pleasure, peace, and prosperity.

Ned's success mantra: "I keep my mind focused on the peaceful presence of God within me. I know that all is well with me and in my world because God is with me in this moment. Divine bliss is around, in and through me, now."

Day by day things changed for the better and today Ned is a teacher, minister, and seminar leader who has helped thousands of people around the world to change their lives for the better. He is a respected citizen, husband, and successful human being because he desired to achieve the topmost of what he could conceive of as being possible. You might say Ned was a sinner who became a saint through the power of choice. Ned refused to dwell on his mistakes or allow the thoughts and judgments of others to make him remain a criminal. He realized his mistakes and was intelligent enough to recognize how he suffered from them. Ned had a burning desire to live in a heavenly state of mind, and he does.

How Barbara Reached the Top

Barbara was married to an abusive man, who drank, womanized, and was lazy. Barbara was the main breadwinner for the family of four boys. Her husband kept the money he made for his drinking and to support his playboy lifestyle. Besides all this he was unkind and disrespectful to her even though she was a chaste and good wife in every way. Over time things became intolerable. She took the time to delve deep into her subconscious mind, and there she found an inferiority complex that had started as a child.

Her mother had been the one who was disloyal to her father, having left him and her children on numerous occasions in pursuit of her extramarital affairs. Barbara believed that love meant taking this kind of treatment. After reading some spiritual books, however, she understood that this was not the way it had to be. Barbara realized that she deserved to have a loving and mutually supportive marriage. She worked to reprogram her subconscious mind to suit her new goals and desire for a healthy, loving, reciprocal marriage. She repeated her success mantra over and over almost continuously, and the old pattern was replaced. As her consciousness changed, her faithless and useless husband moved away to be with another woman who had an inferiority complex. Soon after this the most wonderful man moved in next door, and they have been married for over thirty-five years. It all started with the desire for something better. She didn't even need to go out and look. God brought her perfect mate to live in the house next door.

Her success mantra: "I deserve to have a faithful, loving, and prosperous husband who is my best friend and lifelong companion."

Barbara had a deep and compelling desire to have the topmost relationship possible according to her ideals and heartfelt desires. This is exactly what happened—and not by chance or luck. When she changed her consciousness and inner world, the outer world naturally changed to reflect the inner. The remarkable thing was that simply by changing her beliefs and consciousness she didn't have to do anything as the negative moved out, and she was free to be peaceful and loved.

Enthusiasm

"Every memorable act in the history of the world is a triumph of enthusiasm. Nothing great was ever achieved without it because it gives any challenge or any occupation, no mater how frightening or difficult, a new meaning. Without enthusiasm you are doomed to a life of mediocrity, but with it you can accomplish miracles." —*Og Mandino, author*

Intense desires have much more power than lukewarm ones. Enthusiasm is the fuel for our desires. Somewhere along my spiritual path I realized that if I wanted something it was up to me to generate an intense desire, as well as the appropriate amount of enthusiasm to keep me going. Enthusiasm moves the world, and without it one's desires will diminish to lukewarm wishes. Excitement is short-lived, but enthusiasm is generated from within, as the sustaining power and force that can harness the support of millions of people and dollars, if necessary.

Extraordinary people who make enormous contributions to humanity are driven by their obsession to fulfill their mission and achieve their goals. They think about what they want, envision the achievement, and work to attain it. Really great people are focused and not scattered in their thinking, and this is why they can produce extraordinary results. Most people rob and cheat themselves of the wealth of love, happiness, success, and prosperity they desire because they allow distractions, lack of enthusiasm, negative thinking, anger, resentments, lack of faith, lamentation, and doubts to drain away their power and energy.

Imagine creative energy flowing like water through a garden hose. Think of your life as a garden of possibilities. If you want your garden to grow, the water will need to reach the plants. What if the hose is full of holes? Instead of the water going full force to the garden, it will be lost through the holes and not much if anything will be left to water the garden. The result would be an abundant crop of weeds rather than an opulent and bountiful garden of delicious fruits, grains, and vegetables. We're the ones who decide what will be in our garden by where we focus our creative energy, and we focus our energy through desire, positive thinking, and enthusiasm.

GEM

Increasing desire to boiling hot is the way to build
the steam to manifest a dream.

One of the ways to intensify your desire is to envision its attainment. See, sense, and feel that your garden, your desires, and goals are real. An architect envisions a structure in its completed form. Then the architect makes an artist's rendering and next a model so the ideal structure is tangible and not just an abstract idea. Thoughts produce form when backed by intense emotion, faith, and action.

Another way to build intensity is to envision and get a sense of the benefits you will obtain when you reach the prize. Athletes work long hours and must endure rigorous exercise to become champions. Their thoughts and desires for honor, distinction, money, fame, satisfaction, and appreciation motivate them to continue even in the face of pain, loss, and sacrifice.

Extraordinary people throughout time have achieved the impossible because they chose to dare to dream and accomplish what others would not think was even possible.

What Do You Desire?

I invite you to take a little time and make a list of your **Ten Most Heartfelt Desires**. Perhaps you would be so bold as to aim twice as high as you believe it is possible for you to reach. Why not desire the topmost and ultimate of what is possible for anyone to attain? There is no good reason not to, so I suggest you shoot for the stars, and dare to dream a big dream.

> Please make a list of your Heartfelt Desires. Contemplate that which is the ultimate of what is possible or has ever been attained by anyone. Choose that for yourself. There is nothing to lose and everything to gain.
>
> 1.
> 2.
> 3.
> 4.
> 5.
> 6.
> 7.
> 8.
> 9.
> 10.

Silence Is Golden

Keep silent about your goals and desires. The precious energy you need to manifest your goals and desires into reality can be scattered and dissipated if you tell others who are not intimately involved with you in the project. There is great power in the sacred/secret. Telling others about your goals and dreams sets you up for ridicule, criticism, and direct confrontation with those who are envious or committed to limited thinking. If you want to share with someone, share with those who are already being, doing, or having what you desire to be, do, and have. They are the most likely ones to encourage you and give you some good advice, unless they are afraid you will take what they have.

Desires Do Not Cause Suffering

Some believe that desires cause people to suffer. People suffer not from their desires, but because they are too attached to the outcomes. No one knows exactly how anything will turn out, so it is foolish to be attached, as this kind of an attitude only sets us up to suffer. Suffering starts in the mind as a thought. The thought goes something like this: "This is not what I want, therefore I cannot be happy." Detachment is actually one of the secrets of happiness because we are able to maintain a positive mental attitude regardless of what is going on around us. By maintaining a positive mental attitude, we can stay calm and direct our intelligence to find the best solution and action possible; whereas someone who is a victim of his or her own state of mind is a slave to people, places, things, and events. Faith in God is the ultimate detachment, for one who has faith knows that whatever the outcome it is in his or her very best interest. Right here is the very essence of positive thinking. Without faith a person lives in hell suffering from fear, insecurity, envy, and worry. Having faith means knowing beyond the shadow of a doubt that what you desire will come to you in the right time and in the right way if it is for your highest good and, if not, something better will come along.

Our answer is not to eliminate desire, as this is impossible, for everyone desires. No one can stop the flow of desires, as there are countless things to see, hear, taste, touch, smell, feel, and sense. This constant flow of desires can depress us if we believe we must taste them all. Anyone who does not use his or her intelligence to discern his or her most important desires can be run ragged in the attempt to be, do, and have everything. Advertisers want you to desire what they are selling, but if you let the advertisements control your mind, desires, and actions, you are a slave to others rather than in control of your own life. An addict is someone who cannot control his or her desires to taste, see, hear, speak, feel, or experience certain physical or mental sensations. Our work is to select only those desires that fit with our goals, ideals, values, and dreams and reject the rest. Selective desiring puts you in the driver's seat instead of making you a slave to your senses.

Being a Broadway Star

I too had many desires, so I made a list of my favorites. Most important, I wanted to be loved, serve God, help others, and be famous and rich, but I did not know how any of these would come about.

One of my early desires was to be a singing star on the New York Broadway stage. Being a Broadway star seemed like great fun. When I was in college, I started toward my Broadway goal by auditioning for the starring roles in the college musicals.

Standing in the wings, I prepared myself to audition for the starring role of Sharon in the school's first musical of the season, *Finian's Rainbow*. I was nervous, of course, not yet having learned to be confident when performing or speaking.

My fear of rejection almost kept me from auditioning. There was only one way to get that part: to audition in front of the director and all the other students who were also trying out. The alternative was to sit in the audience and watch others live the life I desired to live and wasn't.

PEARL
If you don't sign up or audition, it's a sure thing you won't get the part.

Hearing the director call my name, I walked boldly onto the stage of the 1,500-seat auditorium. The school pianist was playing the introduction to my song, and it was "now or never." Taking a deep breath, with a big smile on my face I opened my mouth and began to sing "Look to the Rainbow."

Talk about uncomfortable. I was literally shaking in my shoes. "Please, Lord, don't let the director hear my knees knocking and my heart pounding," I begged silently. But I kept on singing anyway, shaking and all. There was no other way to be the star of the school musical.

Describe something you made yourself do even though you were afraid.

What I did was to:

How did this courageous decision make a difference in your life?

Because of this, I was able to:

PEARL

Do what needs to be done, and your power will increase. Don't do what needs to be done, and you will lose power.

Expand Your Comfort Zone

I was learning one of the most valuable lessons in life. Do the thing you desire to do even if you are afraid. In time, with practice, you will be comfortable and confident. On the contrary, if you honor the fear you can just forget your dreams. I got the part, nervousness notwithstanding, as well as all the other parts I went after. No venture, no gain. And because I wanted to gain, I ventured out beyond my comfort zone—nervousness and all—to achieve my heart's desires. Extremely nervous and afraid at that time, I almost did not audition. Now I speak before thousands and have not one ounce of fear or nervousness, but I don't even want to think of what the consequences might have been, if I had let my fears control me.

My true life's work was not to be a star on the New York Broadway stage, but this desire was most important in my being able to eventually do my life's work. Sometimes our current dream is just a stepping-stone to something that is much more important and valuable to us. This high school and college dream of being a singing star on Broadway led me not to the New York stage but to speak to audiences from the stages of some of the most beautiful theaters and churches in the world. Theater training helped me to become an inspirational and motivational speaker, but at the time I had no idea what my life's true work and mission would be. Never judge your strongest desires, for if there is something you feel you must do, even if it is not the ultimate step for you, it will be one of the steps that will take you to the ultimate one.

Too often to avoid feeling uncomfortable people will kill their dreams. We must learn how to tolerate disturbing feelings and new situations if we want to fulfill our heart's desires. We must realize that mastering the fear of rejection, humiliation, and criticism is an absolutely necessary part of anyone's journey to the spiritual and material riches of life or we won't make it. Auditioning terrified me, but unless I did audition there was no way to get the part. If I couldn't tolerate the discomfort of an audition, how would I be able to sing before a theaterful of people? Simply overriding my fears, rather than giving in to them, prepared me to eventually speak before millions through the medium of television. All this would come about because I was willing to tolerate the feelings of being uncomfortable in order to get where I wanted to be.

Jim's Comfort Zone

Jim was used to making around thirty thousand dollars a year. No matter what he did, his income would stay around thirty thousand dollars. Desiring to increase his business, buy a home, send his children to private school, and help more people get value from the vitamins he sold, he sought help. Jim learned that he was attached to being comfortable with struggle and poverty because he had been raised in poverty.

Meditating, he requested his subconscious mind to reveal to him the belief that was blocking him from earning one hundred and fifty thousand dollars a year. Right away came the thought "Dad will feel like a failure because you are making more than he ever made." This was it! Jim did not want to hurt his father's feelings. His father was proud of his struggles to raise his boys with so little money, but with lots of love. His belief was "If I make more money than my father, I won't have love for my children and my father will be proven wrong."

Jim had connected money with love and happiness. Happiness and love are independent of money. Jim set his goal at one hundred and fifty thousand for the year and proceeded to attain it. In order to expand his comfort zone, he used the following Success Mantra.

> Success mantra: **"It is perfectly right for me to prosper, own a home, and send my children to private school. My success is a validation of my father's love and support."**

With his new belief system everything opened up to him, as he no longer feared financial success. He has associated money with a loss of love. Jim realized that he was not in charge of his father's beliefs or responses to how much money he earned. Not that there weren't challenges;

there were, but Jim overcame them to go on and reach his goals. Yes, his father went into a slight depression when Jim's income began to climb, but soon he got over it and was pleased with his son's efforts.

Being at cross-purposes with our desires does not work. Whatever the desire or goal, we must expand beyond our present comfort zone if we want to access more of our divine potential.

Developing Confidence

You expand beyond your comfort zone by first noticing where and when you feel uncomfortable. Also, notice exactly what you do to again reach your comfort zone. Ask yourself this question: "What am I losing by not reaching beyond my comfort zone?" "What is keeping me stuck within the confines of my comfort zone" is the second question to ask yourself. The third question is: "Am I willing to reach beyond my comfort zone and tolerate any uncomfortable feelings in order to attain my goals?"

Once you do something new, you will gradually feel more comfortable each time you do it until soon your comfort zone will have expanded.

My challenge was that I lacked confidence, and it was this lack of confidence that created my nervousness. In later years I developed the following technique, and to this day it matters not to me who is in the audience or how many. What is the secret? Instead of trying to get love and acceptance, it matters not to me because I am there to give love and acceptance plus something of value.

MY CONFIDENCE TECHNIQUE IS THIS

Think only of the message and gifts you have to contribute to your audience or client. See their beauty. Desire to enrich them with your knowledge, talents, skills, and message.

Obviously we want the job or the part or we wouldn't be interviewing or auditioning. We really do need the approval of whoever is making the decision as to who will play the part or get the job. But concentrating on obtaining the approval does not work to get the approval. In fact, it works to the contrary.

The greater the fear of rejection, the worse will be the audition or interview. Focus on finding something to like about others. It also does not help to be arrogant, acting as if you don't care, when you really do. What to do? Love is the answer.

People respond to love and appreciation no matter who they or who we may believe they are. Everyone wants to be liked and appreciated. Everyone responds favorably to being treated well. When you radiate acceptance and appreciation and you are wrapped in the garment of expertise in your subject, your audience will gladly welcome you with open arms. People want to feel good and to receive value. There is not much in their world that gives them the feelings they crave nor are there many who are committed to helping them get what they want. Giving naturally gives the giver what she or he desires, for our needs are met as we help others to meet theirs.

The Simple System for Being Confident Before an Audience or an Interviewer

First: Be prepared and know your material.

Second: Be clear on what you want to accomplish and the response you desire.

Third: Before you get up to make your presentation, take some time to get ready mentally and emotionally. Genuinely like the person or persons in your audience or the interviewer. Send love and acceptance to them by thinking, "I love and accept you."

Fourth: Focus on giving them what you believe is the valuable gift you have to give.

Fifth: Give your gifts with love and enthusiasm with the desire to help and benefit them and their organization.

"A desire to be observed, considered, esteemed,
praised, beloved, and admired by his fellows is one
of the earliest as well as the keenest dispositions
discovered in the heart of man." —*John Adams,
Second President of the United States*

You Are a Star

Stars radiate light, energy, and warmth. People love to bask in the glow of a star. When what is called "charisma" is present in someone, others want to be there and they will pay handsomely for the privilege. We are all stars if we let our light shine brightly.

I love the Bible quote in which Jesus told his students in his Sermon on the Mount, **"Ye are the light of the world. A city that is set on a hill cannot be hid. Neither do men light a candle, and put it under a bushel, but on a candlestick; and it giveth light unto all that are in the house. Let your light so shine before men, that they may see your good works, and glorify your Father which is in Heaven"** (Matthew 5:14–16).

How to Generate Charisma and Let Your Light Shine

Be aware of your self, the soul within your body. From the center of your heart extend love, energy, and awareness to each corner of the room and fill all the space with your presence. Focus on extending your presence to and through everyone, and it will happen. Most people withdraw and hide somewhere inside their bodies dimming their brilliant light. Charisma occurs when the people let their awareness and presence emanate beyond the body, as they extend their energy to all the corners of the room. Simple, but very effective.

I applied this knowledge about how to generate charisma, and it worked. Later on I applied the same to my work as a minister and it also worked, for it is the truth. We are here to give of ourselves, as a contribution to God and others. As we give of ourselves and release our Inner Light, we are flooded in return with rewards, blessings, appreciation, and wonderful experiences.

Riding on the wave of success I achieved one desire and goal after another until a single undesirable event pulled the rug out from under me.

Something Happened That I Did Not Desire

I was twenty-three at the time and gaining confidence in myself and my positive-thinking philosophy, when something happened that I had not planned on that knocked me for a loop.

> **PEARL**
> *Some things happen that we do not desire and not everything works according to our plans.*

Nanny's Departure

My great-grandmother, Nanny, and I had made a pact. Whichever one left her body first would come to the remaining one and share the experience of what it was like "on the other side." It happened just as we had promised.

I looked up at the clock. It was precisely 9 P.M. Instantly I was lifted up above all my problems and concerns, feeling lighter than a feather, without a hint of anxiety and blessed with the "peace that passes all understanding." "Everything is fine. Don't worry," spoke a voice out of nowhere. It was Nanny's voice and her lavender perfume was everywhere, surrounding and embracing me. "Nanny is gone, but she is in a wonderful place and she lives on" was my thought. With tears of joy and sorrow streaming down my face I rushed out, got in the car, drove home, and ran into the house. A relative was waiting for me when I came into the house to tell me that my beloved spiritual partner, Nanny, had left this world at exactly, 9 P.M.

Leaving this world, she was continuing on her path, but I missed her. Gone was my spiritual buddy, and now I desperately needed spiritual support. One door closes and another door opens. Her departure left a void in my life, and this caused me to desire to have this void filled.

What appears to us as the most terrible event has a gift in it if we will look. Nanny's departure meant it was time for me to grow spiritually. I had some knowledge, but not much, and there was more. There is always more, and this is the beauty of sacred knowledge: it is infinite.

The Gift of Crisis or Loss

I had not desired to grow, but I was suffering so much pain from the loss of Nanny that I had to have some help to go on. Crying day after day for weeks, I prayed to God to help me. My crying was selfish, for Nanny was fine, as it was her time to move on, but I missed her so very much. This crisis served to encourage me to question the purpose and meaning of life. In my deep sorrow, the only one I could ask for solace was God.

If You Feel Separate From Your God, Who Has Moved? was the title of a little booklet I had found in the laundromat. Yes, I was feeling very separate from God—in fact, isolated. Nanny had left me her estate, and part of her fortune was her metaphysical library. Not having her as my inspiration, I did have her precious books. Opening up one of the books I read, "The Chinese symbol for crisis means both danger and opportunity." "Problems," it stated, "can help us or destroy us and the choice is ours." Losing a loved one is an opportunity to grow, or to hide out and feel sorry for yourself. Growth seemed a much better alternative than hiding out and wallowing in self-pity. Very soon after I started praying to God for help a neighbor came over and invited me to her church, and I agreed to go. The philosophy of this church was the same as had been Violet's teaching, so I felt right at home.

Using Adversity to Build Strength

Descartes, the French philosopher, wrote, "That which doesn't destroy you will make you strong." The church and its teachings became my strength and sanctuary. Why do we wait until we are almost destitute to seek God's help? Who knows, but we do.

THE LESSON OF SUFFERING
Seek to discover what you need to know and do that will give you meaning and happiness, and do that. Stop doing that which makes you suffer.

Sitting in the congregation my first Sunday I listened intently, as Reverend Mark spoke right to my mind and heart: "There is no death, only a transition going from one experience to the next. Everyone is eternal and, yes, we miss our loved ones when they pass on, but their love is still with us. With the loss of a loved one, we must turn within to the One Power and Presence that will never leave us. The only one we can truly surrender to without fear of loss or exploitation is God Within. Think of death as a person getting into a boat, and as they leave this shore we wave good-bye, and as they approach the next shore there are those who are waving hello. Your happiness did not die with the loss of a loved one, for your happiness is always with you. Your work is to go on, live your dream, and give your gifts in service to God and others."

After the service, I stopped at the door to thank the minister for helping me to see beyond my grief. "Reverend Mark, you must be psychic. How do you know to say exactly what I need to hear?" were my words to him.

Trying it again, I went the following Sunday and again he spoke to my heart as if he had been reading my mail. His powerful message went something like this: "Perceiving the unseen hand of God behind everything, we realize that nothing happens by accident. God brings the right person to us at the right time, the right book or the right job. Those happenings we call coincidences are His workings and never an accident.

"The atheist sees and believes only in atomic and subatomic particles of matter as their god. Choosing *not* to recognize a higher authority of divine intelligence as the creator and maintainer of the universe, they will never know the bliss, prosperity, peace, and joy that only come with faith, trust, and love of God.

"'It is we who are responsible for things happening as they do. We deserve the credit, and there is no God,' brags the atheist. But the theist says, 'God did this' and 'Thank you God.' Behind everything is the loving, supernatural intelligence of the Supreme Being, orchestrating all perfectly, solely for the purpose of bringing the greatest happiness, prosperity, and love to His beloved children.

"But atheists have no desire to know God, so God blocks their understanding and inner vision in order to grant them their wish. Free will gives each the choice to believe or not. 'It is done unto us as we believe,' said Jesus. The only way a person can come to know God and His wondrous ways is to believe, apply His principles, and observe the results. Atheists seek to prove that God does not exist. I say to them, 'Prove to me He doesn't.'"

His sermon put everything into place. We can prove anything we desire to prove. Why bother to explain my faith or try to get those who don't believe to believe? Who cares! That is their problem, not mine. I made a commitment to myself that my life would be about knowing and serving my unseen God. No one else needed to agree with me or even understand. "This is my life to live as I choose" was my newest "Success Mantra," and I said it over and over with conviction.

Divine Revelation

Later that Sunday, while working in the garden, these words poured into my mind as a beam of white light: "God is a real person with unlimited spiritual form. He exists in His eternal spiritual body of pure bliss, beauty, and sweetness. In this material realm governed by Mother Nature, He lives in the heart of every person in the form of the Super Soul or Holy Spirit. He exists in the center of each atom and in the fragrance of a flower and the taste of pure water.

"God is everywhere present and the substance and cause of all existence. Eternally nonexistent for those who believe only in what they can see, hear, taste, touch, and smell, He remains hidden from their view. Faith in God, when no god can be seen, is the coin of spiritual advancement. Faith is the golden key that unlocks inner doors of spiritual riches forever closed to one who chooses to have faith only in what is seen and can be explained by the physical senses and the theories of science. Just as you cannot see the wind but only observe its effects, so it is with God.

"Supernatural experiences, faith healing, unexplained and miraculous occurrences, sacred scriptures, self-realized knowledge, exalted states of consciousness, and answers to prayers are just some of the methods God uses to awaken, build, and strengthen faith in Him. There is more to life than what appears." As quickly as the experience had come upon me it was gone, but I was different.

Obviously, I had been asleep and somehow I had awakened. Now I knew for certain that I was on the right track. Everything I had just been told felt true at the core of my soul. Standing there for a few minutes, I allowed the message to sink in and become part of my consciousness. "Terry, you are glowing. What happened?" remarked Betsy, my neighbor. What could I say? Betsy wouldn't have believed me anyway. I just smiled and said, "I had a lovely day."

The Number-One Most Important Thing I Ever Did

Under Reverend Mark's guidance and encouragement I regularly gave a portion of my time, money, and talents to the church. Taking classes, teaching Sunday school, and volunteering for everything I could, I immersed myself in the living waters of spiritual life and what I call sacred service. Sacred service is called Seva in the Eastern religions and volunteering in the West. Above all else, sacred service is the single most important thing I have ever done and continue to do. Reverend Mark was right! I was getting the taste of something indescribably sweet and precious that was impossible to communicate to someone who had not had the same experience. Nanny was with me in spirit, and I knew she was pleased.

The First Stages of My Prosperity Philosophy

Thinking about what I needed and desired, I came to the conclusion that it was more money. Lack of money had been a source of argument and suffering in my family. Rooting out self-defeating subconscious beliefs and replacing them with the right ideas and beliefs was necessary if I wanted to be wealthy, which I did. Reverend Mark would constantly remind us, "We attract or repel through our attitudes, beliefs, thoughts, and actions." My question was "How can I make myself a money magnet?"

"Giving back to God a portion of what He is so generously and lovingly giving to us is the most important action, above all others" was his answer. Each and every book I had read on spiritual economics and prosperity taught the law of tithing—tithing and joyfully giving to God's service a portion of our God-given talents, money, and resources as taught in the scriptures of every religion. Everything I had been reading pointed to tithing as the single most important thing a person could do if he or she wanted to prosper and be happy. I wanted to prosper and be happy, so I decided to try out this law to see if it really worked.

The Law of Giving

Each time I went to church I gave some money, even though I did not have much. I gave what I could, sometimes only fifty cents. Giving to the cause of God's work had brought prosperity to many throughout history. Would I prosper as well?

It wasn't just money I was giving but time, talent, energy, and love. Prosperity means an overflowing abundance of ideas, energy, time, love, happiness, money, and every good and wonderful thing we need and desire. The law of prosperity states: Give that which you desire to receive. I wanted to receive every good and wonderful thing possible, so this meant giving on every level of life. It was a simple teaching, but a challenge to practice. Having been so steeped in the belief in poverty and scarcity, I had to begin by changing my belief system at the core.

Because we are so steeped in the fear of there not being enough, major work is required to change our beliefs and concepts having to do with prosperity. Giving is a spiritual quality that must be developed. Selfless giving helps people to awaken and develop their spiritual nature of pure love and bliss, as well as opening them to the flow of all good fortune.

Miserliness is based in poverty and fear. Someone at church had made an acronym of fear: false evidence appearing real. This fear of giving was coming from my subconscious mind and not from the spiritual truth of my greater possibilities. I could honor my subconscious fears or honor the principles I was learning. I decided to honor the Truth from here on out. Otherwise, how would I ever know if these principles worked?

Repeating my prosperity mantra quietly to myself until I felt more peaceful, I was then able to place my humble offering in the collection plate with gratitude, love, and anticipation of the prosperity that was mine.

> Prosperity mantra: **"Whatever I give is returned to me multiplied ten times or more. God is my unlimited source and supply. Thank you, God, for receiving and returning this gift to me increased by the law of tenfold return."**

This affirmation was my constant companion, and I repeated it whenever I had the opportunity to give money to the church. Throwing away my old belief, "There is never enough," I created my new belief, "There is always enough." This new belief of sufficiency automatically shifted my awareness from scarcity to prosperity. Sure enough, as I gave to the church my money and good fortune increased, just as the scriptures said it would. The fear I had always felt in the pit of my stomach was subsiding.

Discovering the Value of Volunteering

Something very significant was happening to me. "Engaging in volunteer work at the church is making me happier than ever," I realized. "Why?"

Giving a portion of my talents, time, money, and energy to my church work seemed to be improving the quality of my life, and I was beginning to actually prosper. Money was coming to me from expected and unexpected avenues. Not much, mind you, but some. Every so often, someone in the church would walk up and hand me a twenty-dollar bill and say thank you. Friends would invite me out to lunch and pay the bill when, before, this was out of the question. I would find the dress I really liked but couldn't afford at another store on sale. People were giving me gifts for no reason at all, and I was winning door prizes at luncheons. It was working!

PEARL

Necessity really is the mother of invention.

It was time to get serious, because I knew I would need to support myself and I also wanted to be wealthy. The money wasn't the important thing; it was what money could bring. The necessity to obtain money got me to thinking about my life's work and right livelihood. I knew I didn't want a job. At this time in America women were usually nurses, teachers, and secretaries, and I didn't sense that I fit in any of those positions. What I really wanted was my right livelihood and Life's Work, something that was my destiny. Having a job seemed like a dismal idea, but the idea of having my Life's Work was thrilling.

Finding Your Life's Work

I listed Life's Work at the top of my list of desires. At this point, I had no idea what it was. I picked up a book in the church bookstore on right livelihood and read every word like a hungry person. What was I going to do for the rest of my life? The words in the book read, "Everyone has his or her right and proper place in the divine scheme of things. For each person there is a right career that exactly fits the talents and abilities he or she possesses. Their right work desires them as much as they desire their right work. Think of yourself as a piece of a puzzle with a right and proper place where you exactly fit and belong. Trying to place yourself where you do not belong creates an empty place and hole in the puzzle where you are supposed to be. Doing someone else's job takes the space belonging to another, and now she or he is displaced. Perfect harmony exists in the universe and when we know who we are, and we use our God-given talents, we are happy and prosperous and order is established. Each and every person has a role to play in God's divine plan and play. Our greatest joy will come when we have found our niche and are busily performing our part with love and enthusiasm. No two people are the same; therefore, there is no competition. God knows where you belong and if you want to know, pray and ask God to reveal your work to you. Have faith and in the right time and way you will know."

I found this wonderful little book on how to manifest your dreams into reality by an obscure Chinese mystic. He wrote: "Do your inner work first. Don't ask other people for their advice as to what you should do. First you decide what you desire to manifest. Write out the benefits you would like to obtain, and also the specific criteria you want included in your ideal manifestation. Start with your ideal, not by looking to see what others have done or what is available, but what you really want in your heart. Begin in the future at the end result giving no attention at this time as to how or when it will happen, as this is up to God and the universe. Do not be limited by the world of appearances, what other people do or have done or your own past experience. Work with God the Supreme, All-knowing, All-powerful and everywhere present Power of love."

Wanda Got Married

A woman I knew in church had used this process. Fifty at the time and never married, she was advised by her friends to give up hope. But she really wanted to be married and refused to listen to the doubters. She stated her goal in prayer: to be happily married. Having no idea of who this person was or where to find him, all she could do was list qualities she desired her future husband to possess. Visualizing herself happily married to the unknown man of her dreams, she felt confident. Her wedding dress was being made and she started preparing for the wedding, even to the point of putting aside money to pay for the ceremony and reception. Others laughed at her, but she kept her faith. Yes, one day it happened. She met him in church. They are married and love to tell their story.

Discovering the Power of Universal Intelligence

Similarly, most people who are looking for work first go to employment agencies or look in the classified section of the newspaper to find out what is available rather than looking first to their God-given talents and heart's desires and what they really want. I couldn't have gone to an employment agency, for I didn't have a clue as to what I could do. The place to find my life's work was with the One who knew it, Universal Intelligence otherwise known as my Higher Self.

The same holds true for finding a mate. List the criteria for your ideal mate and God, who is in the heart of every person, knows exactly who perfectly fits the description. You may put an ad in the paper and he or she will come to you in that way, or you may meet him or her in the market. Be assured it will happen in the right and perfect way in the right and perfect time, if you really desire to have a mate.

MY GOAL
To know and be fully engaged in my life's work as my ideal livelihood.

Since I didn't know what my life's work was to be, I made a list of the benefits I desired to receive from this unknown career.

The Benefits and Criteria for My As-Yet Unknown, Ideal Livelihood

1. This work uses all my talents in service to God and others. (At the time I didn't know what all my talents were.)
2. I do this work my entire lifetime and no one, including the government, can force me to retire or fire me.
3. I make unlimited amounts of money. (Why not?)
4. I work my own hours. My time is my own.
5. I love my work.
6. I travel to the most beautiful places in the world as part of my work.

7. I meet, associate with, and make friends with the most important, inspiring, and successful people in the world.

Make a list of the benefits and criteria that you would like to obtain from performing your life's work.

1.

2.

3.

4.

5.

6.

7.

8.

9.

10.

If you know your life's work, please describe it below.

My life's work is:

"You are not here merely to make a living. You are here in order to enable the world to live more amply, with greater vision, with a finer spirit of hope and achievement. You are here to enrich the world, and you impoverish yourself if you forget the errand." —*Woodrow Wilson, Twenty-eighth President of the United States*

Desire is the first step in anything that we do. It begins with that first step as an infant and continues throughout our lives. If only people everywhere knew just how powerful they are and how important it is for them to desire the best that is possible for them to attain. Ordinary people waste their lives running after every little desire that floats across their minds, but ordinary people who become extraordinary are selective when it comes to their desires. They desire the topmost that is possible for any person to attain, and why not? Achieving a small goal takes about the same amount of energy as achieving a big goal, if the desire is strong enough. Once I was clear about everything I wanted to attain from doing my unknown life's work, it was time to pray to God and ask to be given my heart's desire.

Chapter Four

Step Two, Pray and Ask for What You Desire

"Therefore I say unto you, What things soever ye desire, when ye pray, believe that
ye receive them, and ye shall have them."

—Mark 11:24

Success mantra: **"It is okay for me to ask God
for what I need and desire."**

Success mantra: **"It is okay for me to ask
others for what I need and desire."**

There is no harm in asking" was the judge's ruling in my friend's court case. She had sued someone for asking her for a large amount of money, which she thought was unfair. He added, "Everyone has the right to ask for whatever they want; whether or not they get it is another matter."

Jesus instructed us to ask in this quotation from scripture: "Ask, and it shall be given you; seek, and ye shall find; knock, and it shall be opened unto you: For every one that asketh receiveth; and he that seeketh findest; and to him that knocketh it shall be opened" (Matthew 7:7–8).

Asking is necessary, because we have free will and even God won't intrude where He or His help is not wanted. Asking for what we desire and need is the key that unlocks and opens the door to the fulfillment of our desires.

GEM

When you ask for what you desire you never know the form it will take, how it will come to you, or even when, but it will.

"Pray and ask for what you desire" is the natural, second step on my "Seven-Step Sacred Treasure Map." Something wonderful always happens when we pray. Because of the miracles that I have seen happen for others and for myself as well, praying is something I do whatever the situation, challenge, or desire. Seemingly impossible obstacles have instantly dissolved, bodies have been healed when the diagnosis was terminal, money has come out of nowhere, people have purchased homes with no money down and bad credit, marriages have been saved, and losers have become winners.

Can people achieve what they desire without praying? Yes, a person can achieve some of what she or he wants without prayer through struggle, sacrifice, manipulation, anger, fear, violence, thievery, great difficulties, extra-hard work, constant vigilance, or by exercising enormous control over the minds and actions of others. By great endeavor results can be attained without prayer, but through prayer results can easily, quickly, and miraculously be attained. People live in fear and strife because they are not aware that a Higher Power, who loves them, is with them and ever willing to help them should they ask. Without God and prayer, life is a struggle at best; but with God and prayer, all things are possible with love and ease.

Twenty-Four-Karat Gold Plates

Throughout history there have been rulers who ruled by inspiration, empowerment, love, and fairness because they saw themselves as servants of God and guardians of the people. In ancient India there were kings such as King Rama, King Ashoka, and King Yudisthira who were pious rulers. Under their leadership their fortunate subjects all lived in opulence, even to the extent of eating off of twenty-four-karat gold plates. Besides everyone flourishing, there was no crime, very little illness, the people were protected from hostile attacks, and harmony and cooperation prevailed.

Today this sounds like an impossible fantasy because world leaders are often the faithless who only exploit the people to their own advantage. Because we cannot expect our leaders to look out for our best interests, we must and we can. Just as these ancient wise rulers understood and worked in harmony with the laws of God and the universe, so can we. Regardless of whether or not someone else is practicing the spiritual principles of successful living, we can and therefore we will receive enormous benefits. The same universal laws and principles that worked for the royalty of yester-year work for us commoners today. Often this knowledge that you are learning here was hidden from the masses out of fear that if the people knew this then all people would be powerful and not just a privileged few. In truth all of us have the same power, but some know it and some do not.

The Principle of Abundance

One of the first, and most basic, of all principles is that of abundance. God created everything in perfect working order so that all His children throughout time could have their needs met, if they lived in harmony with the laws of life. But if they did not, they would know poverty and insufficiency, not because God wanted them to be impoverished but because they brought it upon themselves. The world is a perfect ecological system of balance and ever-renewable abundance, and in the terms of prosperity we call this the principle of circulation. Circulation means to give back to what is giving to you and when you do, by the law of increase, you will prosper. By giving the soil the remains of our food and the waste from cows and such, the soil is replenished. This same soil because it is fed will continue to feed us vitamin- and mineral-rich delicious food forever. If we do not pollute our water, the water will recycle by the law of circulation and give us ever-fresh, clear, and tasty water. Lack does not exist in God's universe. There are so many stars we cannot even count them. If there is any lack, it is only in the minds of those who are not aware of the spiritual and material laws of life.

Four Million Dollars a Year for Life

Buckminster Fuller found in his research into global sufficiency that there are enough renewable natural resources in the world for every man, woman, and child on earth to receive four million dollars every year for life. That is a lot of money. But it isn't the money that is important; it's the idea that there really is enough for everyone to have what they need to survive and thrive. In Mr. Fuller's book *Critical Path*, he explains his whole theory. Of course his theory works, as it's the natural order of things. Prosperity is natural because it operates on the basis of giving and receiving as a continuing cycle. The foundation of the ideal loving intimate relationship that everyone is seeking is giving and receiving. Because most live in fear when it comes to relationships, one or the other doesn't give back and the cycle is broken. When we honor the law of circulation by giving back to who and what is giving to us, everyone involved prospers and will continue to prosper as long as the cycle is honored. If we took care of our natural resources and gave back to Mother Earth there would always be enough, for God created a perfect system of regeneration through recycling. All we need do is observe how nature works and this will tell us how we are supposed to function if we want to be materially successful.

But the only way His theory can work, which He did not know or at least if He did He never mentioned it, is that the people need to be God-conscious and committed to the greater good of the all. A God-conscious person is one who is certain that God, as they know God to be, is the source and substance of their eternal supply of whatever they will ever need or desire. God-conscious people know that there is an endless supply of love, happiness, peace of mind, ideas, energy, creativity, and whatever else they need now or will need in the future so they can afford to give back to those who are giving to them. There are two kinds of people: those who place their trust in things and other people, as their source of supply, and those who place their trust in a Higher Power and act accordingly.

Misplaced Faith

As the story goes, a woman prayed to God to help her pay her rent, buy her groceries, pay the utilities, and make her car payments. She was praying to God, but in truth she was depending upon her boyfriend to pay all these bills. One day he walked out and never came back. There she was without any money and destitute. In the silence she again spoke with God, but this time she was angry, as she said, "God, I prayed to you to help me pay my bills, but you didn't, and now I have nothing and I am out on the street." She was surprised to hear a still, small voice from within her say,

"My child, I know you asked, but you had faith in your boyfriend and not in me, and since I was not needed, I did nothing."

Faith in a Higher Power

Many place their complete faith in the government, the stock market, big business, their boss and company, bank accounts, family, etc. All these can fail, but God never fails. Of course we can work with each of these avenues and use them to help us prosper and meet our needs. With faith in a Higher Power, however, we are certain that if one door closes or one avenue dries up then another door and another avenue will also open up.

Powerful people put their faith in the source of intelligence, love, bliss, energy, peace, and wealth; work as if everything depended upon them; and trust in God to bring the right results at the right time and in a way that is best for all concerned. The most intelligent concern themselves with God and the application of the Spiritual Principles of Successful Living, for there is nothing more exalted, higher, or better.

Those who are not aware of God as real, present, and available are like people who are thirsty but go to the river with an eyedropper with which to obtain the water. They could take a bucket and, better yet, they could hook up a hose and receive an unlimited supply right from the source, but they don't. The choice is ours. The size of the container we use to receive that which the Almighty is giving is the size of our faith and acceptance. Do you want more? Then accept more.

Success mantra: **It is perfectly right for me to thrive and prosper in all ways.**

How to Be a Ten

People talk about being a ten, meaning the best, but without a conscious connection with a Higher Power, they are actually zeros. When you add the one God and Power next to a zero, what you do get? With God we all become a majority for we have the Force of the Universe with us, around us, and for us; but without the Force as an ally, we are a minority and must struggle for whatever we get. Real prosperity begins by knowing who we are: children of the Almighty. This means we are now and always will be, by divine inheritance, royalty. Knowing this, we can be certain that God loves each of us, and therefore He desires that each of us receive the bounty of the spiritual and material riches of His opulent and limitless Kingdom. But this is not a passive, one-sided relationship in which we sit back and wait for good things to drop into our laps. We can be, do, and have whatever we desire when we work together with the Supreme Intelligence.

Know that you are never alone but always in the company of the One Creator of all. This Creator loves you unconditionally and never has even the slightest thought to harm or hurt you; on the contrary. His desire is for you to live in a constant state of bliss, opulence, beauty, peace, and love. If we suffer, it is only because we do not accept His gifts.

Those who know of this co-creative relationship have the advantage of being able to operate as one-half of a dynamic duo called God and Company. Why not be partners with the creator of the universe? Think of all your possibilities when your willing partner is the most wealthy, powerful, strong, giving, and intelligent of all. Without God, every person is a zero. With God, as each understands God to be, adding the one in front of the zero, everyone instantly becomes a ten. Many tens together will create a heavenly state of affairs, wouldn't you say?

Help Is Only a Prayer Away

We are told in the scriptures that God is closer than breathing. What this means is that everyone has immediate access to universal knowledge, help, guidance, ideas, solutions, beauty, opulence, power, love, happiness, and every good and wonderful quality, experience, and thing. Because we are part of God and in Him we live, move, and have our being, each can draw from the totality whatever he or she needs and desires.

To work with this unlimited Presence and Power and direct it toward fulfilling our desires we must make a request or, as some say, place a demand upon the law. This little-known fact, if known, would save people from having to endure every kind of hardship.

Dial One for God

Prayer is the telephone that unites the caller with the Almighty, and sincere desire makes the connection. Unlike other parties, this One is always home, always available, always kind and loving, always giving; and He always answers and responds, personally. Inconceivable as it may be, this is the Absolute Truth. Lack of faith in God, for whatever reason, is the cause of all misery, poverty, and strife. But it is not easy to have faith given the fact that one must overcome the world of appearances, the opinions of others, his or her past conditioning, plus a good measure of fear, greed, and miserliness.

What Prayer Is, and Why It's Important

Prayer is the most important way in which a person can dispel doubt and consciously connect with the Holy Spirit and Divine Presence Within. The reason we need to ask is that we have free will, so if we want something we need to ask for it. Some do without simply because they are expecting others to know what they need and want, but it is we who need to ask. Because we have free will, we must even ask God. God does not enter in where not wanted. Once we pray and ask, things will change, often instantly. As we witness the results of our prayers, our faith will grow until we will have enough faith to literally move mountains, if need be. There are two kinds of faith: blind faith and faith that is backed by experience. Obviously, we need to begin with blind faith. Faith by direct experience will come as we witness the results of our prayers and supplications.

Success mantra: **"It's okay for me to ask God for whatever I need and desire."**

Success mantra: **"It's okay for me to ask others for what I need and desire."**

Estranged Husband Came Back Home

Patricia's husband had left her after twenty-five years of marriage. She still loved him and wanted him to come back home, but no matter what she said he was unbending in his resolution to get a divorce. He had bought another home, had a new set of friends, and was living a totally separate life from Patricia. Patricia never gave up hope. She found a wonderfully supportive spiritual group, and along with their added prayer support she prayed every day that her husband would return to the marriage. Within a few months the divorce was final and it looked as if all hope was gone, but Patricia was determined to save her marriage. She remembered a story that Jesus told about the woman who was persistent. Because the woman in the story was persistent, her requests were finally fulfilled. The scripture is Luke 18:1–5, if you are interested in reading it. One day her now ex-husband called to talk with her about something, and she invited him over to her home. One thing led to another, and a miracle happened: he agreed to marry her a second time. That was fifteen years ago, but this time they serve God together.

Prayer Is a Supernatural Activity

To pray means to make a fervent request, to beseech, and urge. Just as children know that the more persistent and imploring they are the more likely it is that they will get what they want, the more we are sincere the more likely it is that we will be given what we need and desire.

Some feel it is not okay to bother God with prayer, but actually it is the right and proper thing to do. Not praying and asking in each and every moment and situation of the day compares with having a houseful of costly appliances but refusing to turn them on.

Prayer is an act of communion with God, as a confession, praise, or thanksgiving. Besides asking we can share everything within our heart, express our gratitude for our many blessings, praise God, and confess our faults, mistakes, and errors. When we open our hearts and share our deepest secrets, fears, doubts, and errors, we are relieved of our burdens and set free.

The word *communion* means "to communicate," and communication is a two-way flow of giving and receiving, outflow and inflow. God is the Supreme Servant and Provider of all. So who better to ask?

There is a principle operating for all of us, and that principle is "If you want something, you need to ask for it." Why? Because we have free will; even God respects our right to choose. Even though God, who is in the heart of every person, knows what we have need of before we even ask, we must exercise our free will by asking for what we desire.

C.D. Was Picked Up

C.D. was sailing with a friend off the coast of Honolulu, Hawaii, when a brisk wind came out of nowhere and tipped over the boat. Both C.D. and her companion were thrown into the water. The wind swept the boat away so quickly that C.D. was not able to grab hold of it. Watching her companion and the boat being taken farther out to sea, C.D. was now alone in possibly shark-infested waters. The shore was too far to reach by swimming and, with no other boats in sight, she decided to pray. "Lord, please save me and help me to get safely to shore right away" was her plea. Within moments, a helicopter was above her. A kindly lifeguard let down a ladder, and she climbed up to safety. C.D.'s prayer had been answered by an unseen Power.

Linda Was Saved from Disaster

Linda's husband had died three weeks earlier, and she was still grieving. Today was the day for her squad to practice jumping out of airplanes, as part of her military training. Both she and her husband were in the Marines, and now that he was gone Linda had lost her heart for even serving. Full of anger and resentment that he had been taken from her, she had also lost the little bit of faith she had in God.

The doors of the plane opened, and each Marine took her or his turn jumping. Linda lifelessly stepped up to the door and stepped out into the open space. Falling freely, she remembered it was time to pull the rip cord and open the parachute. She pulled the rip cord and nothing happened. "This is not good," she thought. Keeping calm, she pulled the second rip cord and again nothing happened. "This is really not good," she cried to herself.

Falling toward the landing strip at full speed Linda made a lifesaving decision. She pleaded, "God, I want to live. I let go of my anger and resentment toward You for taking my husband from me. Please save me; I want to live." In that instant, a wind came up and blew her away from the landing strip and over a lake. She landed in the lake feetfirst, and the water broke her fall. To this day she has only a slight problem with her knee, but she lives on, as a woman of profound faith.

Desire What You Want and Then Pray from Your Heart to Receive It

Just as burning desires are the most powerful desires, sincere, direct, and heartfelt prayers are the most powerful prayers.

Ann's Miracle Healing

A young woman in her late teens took a ride with her boyfriend to the local airport. Walking from their car to their friend's plane that had just arrived, Ann didn't see that the propellers were still spinning and she walked right into one. Instantly her arm was severed and thrown across to the other side of the plane.

Ann was stunned, but she kept calm and prayed immediately to God saying, "God, I want my arm. Please let me keep my arm." She thought, "What man would want to marry a one-armed girl?" There was no question that she intensely desired to keep her arm.

While praying, she also directed everyone as to what she wanted them to do. An ambulance came, and she made sure her arm was with her packed in ice as she and her arm were rushed to the emergency room of the hospital.

Her mother, at Ann's insistence, called all the prayer counselors at their church and asked each one to pray. Each of the prayer counselors volunteered to call and ask others to also pray.

One of the only doctors in the world who could perform the type of surgery needed just "happened" to be at the hospital, and he rushed to Ann's side. The surgical procedure was performed as Ann stayed conscious, praying steadily. Everything worked out, and Ann was able to have almost full use of her arm, even to the point of being able to earn money as a waitress in the summer between college semesters. Her mother wrote a book called *The Miracle of Ann*, which was all about the power of intense desire and heartfelt prayer.

Instantaneous Response

A woman in the church called me and related to me the difficulties she was experiencing with her eleven-year-old daughter. Confused and distraught, she didn't know what to do. I suggested she pray and ask God to help her solve her problem. Right after we hung up, she sat down on the sofa and prayed for the understanding of what she could do to help her daughter. When she opened her eyes, you can imagine how surprised she was to see a book her friend had suggested right next to her on the sofa. Because the friend had suggested buying it, she did so, but she hadn't paid any attention, even to the title. Right then and there she opened the book, and after reading only one chapter she had her solution: stop constantly criticizing my child. Yes, this was the answer to her prayer. She had been criticizing her daughter for every little thing, so no wonder her daughter was feeling so dejected and unhappy. With her new awareness, she stopped criticizing and was more accepting and appreciative of her daughter.

Every night after this she would sit at the edge of her daughter's bed and see her as a beautiful and perfect child of God without flaws. She rubbed her daughter's back, asked her about her day, and listened to whatever her daughter said without being judgmental. Of course her daughter did not trust her at first and wouldn't say anything at all. Little by little the daughter softened up and their relationship improved in every way, thanks to a simple but heartfelt prayer.

Delayed Response

Some say God does not always answer prayers, but this is not true. A delay never means a denial. God works in mysterious ways, and we have to be alert in order to receive the blessing. We get what we desire, ask for, and earn in the right time and right way according to God's Divine Plan. It all works together in some inconceivable way, and for it all to work we must do our part.

A good example of a delayed answer to prayer happened recently. Some thirty years ago I was a regular attendee of a certain beautiful church. I thought, "Someday I would like to be the minister of this church." Then I said a silent prayer. Having forgotten this desire and given that I was no longer a member of the parent organization with which this church was affiliated, it was really out of the question. Due to some challenges in the church, however, the president of the board of trustees called and asked me to be the minister, and I accepted. Here I was the minister of this beautiful church just as I had requested. I had not been denied my prayer, but there was a thirty-year delay until it was the right time for everything to fall into place.

Request and Response

The universe operates by the process of request and response, otherwise known as outflow and inflow. For an inflow to happen, there needs to be an outflow. Would you go to the travel agent and stand in front of the counter without saying anything? No, you would ask the salesperson to sell you a ticket. Would you say, "Please give me a ticket to anywhere—it doesn't matter"? Of course not; you would request a ticket to your desired destination. Human beings request and the Supreme Being fulfills those requests for the purpose of awakening each of us to our partnership and our eternal, loving, reciprocal relationship.

Of course any sincere prayer works, but there is a wonderful way to pray that puts us in the right consciousness and helps us to understand and feel the connection with the One Power, Intelligence, and Presence we call God. After reading many books on the subject of prayer and experimenting with prayer, I discovered that there are six basic steps to effective prayer.

Six Steps of Effective Prayer

Step One—Speaking to God, as a friend who is right next to you in the region of your heart, say, "Beloved Lord, I know that You are All Powerful, Everywhere Present and All Knowing. I know that You are the Supreme Source and Supply of everything and everyone." This helps us to focus on God within and to remember that all of life is contained within God, who is also right here with us.

Step Two—In order to remember that you are part of God and that God is present with you, say, "Divine Presence, I know that I am part of You and that you are hearing my every word and responding to my requests."

Step Three—Share your mind and heart with God. Talk with God, as you would talk with your best friend. You may be thinking, "If God knows what I am thinking, why should I talk with God and tell Him what I am thinking?" By sharing your heart and mind with your true best friend, you are developing a very powerful personal relationship with the Supreme Being.

Step Four—Now is the opportunity for you to ask for whatever it is you desire and need. Be specific when you ask. Instead of saying what you do not want, remember to say what you do want. At the end of your request add the statement that if God has something better for you than what you are requesting, then this is what you desire.

Step Five—Thank God for hearing your request and for answering your prayer. It's important for us to be in the mood of appreciation and thanksgiving even before we receive the answer to our prayers. By being thankful before you have received your answer, you are developing your faith beyond a shadow of a doubt. A grateful heart is a receptive heart, and we must be receptive and appreciative, if we are to receive the bounty of God's gifts.

Step Six—Once you have said your prayer, it is time to release it into God's hands. Release your prayer and let go and let God. Here it is appropriate to say "amen" or, "and so it is." Don't worry and have absolute faith that you will receive what you have requested or that you will be given something far better.

Danny Saved His Sister's Life

Danny and a couple of friends were in the front car and Danny's sister Christa was driving the car behind. Danny was going a little faster than necessary, and soon he couldn't see his sister's car. Looking out the rearview mirror searching for Christa's car, he was shocked to see flames shooting into the night sky. Turning the car around, he sped as fast as he could to find it was Christa's car and she was trapped inside. He tried the window and door but neither would open. "God, please help me to get Christa out of the car, please God, please," he begged.

Without waiting for an answer, Danny grabbed the car door and tore it off the hinges and pulled Christa out to safety moments before the car exploded. Danny was stunned and in shock. How could he have pulled the car door off its hinges? But, he did. Divine Intervention was the only answer. Danny was given extra strength in order to save his sister's life. Did Danny need the Six Steps of Affirmative Prayer? No, of course not, because his faith was strong. He acted on his faith before he had the time to even think that it wouldn't work.

A Snake Story

I remember reading about a remarkable incident that took place in a room in a hospital in a tiny jungle village in South America. Twelve or so men were in the room, and each man was paralyzed and bedridden. Suddenly through an open window slithered a huge snake. Within moments not one man was left in bed or in the room. How did this happen? Obviously the fear of snakes is such a primal fear than not one of the men had time to remember his body was paralyzed. Somehow each one got out of bed and escaped from the room. Were they really paralyzed or faking it? I have no idea, but I remember how the story made such a strong impact on my thinking about the power of mind over matter.

No Hard-and-Fast Rules for Prayer

There are no hard-and-fast rules when it comes to prayer except that we must believe in God, ask for what we desire, have faith that it will happen, and then act on our faith with confidence. I am sure those men in that hospital bed prayed something like "Oh my God, get me out of here!" And that is exactly what happened.

My experiences were not so dramatic and I needed to learn and use the Six Steps of Effective Prayer. These steps became very important to me, as I worked to gain spiritual knowledge and increase my faith. Another tool that works for developing both an intense desire and strong faith is visualization. Once you can see it, the body and mind will respond and do it.

Athletes mentally and visually practice making perfect scores. Because the subconscious mind cannot tell the difference between what is real and pretense, it accepts the mental image as real and true. We are creatures of habit. Every time we imagine something and feel strongly about it, this makes a deep impression in the subconscious. The deeper the impression, the greater its influence upon us. Because of their mental imagery the players do much better when it comes to playing the real game, for they have the memory of making perfect scores.

If You Can See It, You Can Have It

Vincent van Gogh, the artist, wrote that before he ever painted even the first brush stroke, his painting was already complete in his imagination. The great singers have already sung the note in their mind before the sound comes forth. This is making a "mental equivalent," the pattern for the finished product. Blueprints and patterns are essential if a person wants to build anything, especially a life.

By asking in prayer and then by visualizing and seeing the result we desire already manifested, we are setting a Universal Creative Process in motion that must respond to us by fulfilling our request. There is an impersonal law that is always in operation. Some are using this potent law unknowingly to create poverty, misery, limitation, and strife. Those who know about it are using this same law intelligently to bring them love, happiness, wealth, and success. This impersonal creative process will work for or against us, depending upon how we use it.

Those men in the hospital, no doubt, saw themselves out of the room. Because of the state of emergency they had no time to think, and their bodies simply responded to the command.

Visualization helps to give the command we desire to our subconscious. Mental imagery can be used to help us increase desire, build a mental blueprint of our completed goal, and also to produce faith. People are visualizing all the time anyway, but for the most part they are visualizing that which is harmful and negative. When we watch movies and television we often use the power of visualization to produce similar events in our life. Imaging something sorrowful from your past brings you sorrow in the present and sets you up for more sorrow in your future.

Manifesting My Right Livelihood

Having made a list of the criteria for my life's work, including some of the benefits I wanted to receive, I made a habit of praying and visualizing two times a day, morning and evening.

Sitting in my favorite chair, I closed my eyes and prayed. Then I pictured myself telling my mother about how happy I was to be doing my life's work. In my mind, I saw and heard her respond with "Terry, I am very happy that you have your ideal work and are prospering." No, I didn't know my work as yet, but I had been instructed in the little book by the Chinese mystic to create the feeling, as if I did.

The important effect of this mental imagery was, besides seeing myself in a situation where I was explaining the benefits I was getting from my right work, to generate the feeling I would have if I already had my life's work and were doing it. Feeling, I had been told, would project this image out into the universe, setting up a sort of force field that would draw to me the right situation and circumstance for my work to be revealed to me.

Emotion is a powerful creative energy that helps us to magnetize what we desire to us. By the law of attraction our emotional state draws to us that which is also at that same frequency. Those who are angry or weak attract violence, and those who are peaceful and strong attract peaceful and harmonious people and situations.

Part of the miracle of prayer is that because God, as the Super Soul of every soul, lives within the heart of everyone, He knows who the right people are to come together at the right time and place. Therefore, He could whisper my name to anyone he desires or tell me what my ideal life's work and sacred mission are. He can bring together any combination of people, situations, and events simply by His will. Knowing each of us better than even we know ourselves, the Divine Presence within us is aware of each and every one of our talents and desires and those of all others, as well. And we have a say in this whole happening.

No Answer Yet

Faithfully I continued with this process for a couple of months and then I stopped. My faith was strong and I knew when the time was right I would know my true life's work.

My ideal livelihood did not manifest itself right away. That was also part of the teaching: to be patient, have faith, continue to study, and apply the teachings. When a prayer request is made sometimes the result is immediate, but other times we have to wait for the various necessary ingredients to be made ready so everything can come together at exactly the right moment.

Friends and family would ask, "Terry, what exactly are you going to do for work?" Then they would add, "Don't you think you should get a job?" "I am visualizing and I know my right work is coming to me," was my response. Their usual reaction was to laugh at me, utter some smart, condescending remark, or out-and-out call me a dreamer and fool.

I had chosen my path. Anyone can prove the way of the world, the way of doubt, fear, anger, greed, and scarcity. I wanted to know for sure that God existed. The only way I knew to find out was to have absolute faith and put into practice what I was learning. Other people can come on strong and push us off our path. If we are not careful, weak-mindedness on our part will let them, for they always have good arguments in favor of fear, lack, and limitation. "Argue for your limitations long enough, and they are yours" read a sign on the wall in the church bookstore. They could argue for theirs but I was arguing in favor of God and me together, as a great team.

Learning the Secrets of Manifestation

The church bookstore was a treasure chest of riches. Never having liked to read in school, now that I was out of school I found that reading was one of my most favorite things to do. Because I was reading about something that fascinated me, I couldn't get enough.

Manifesting Out of Thin Air

I came across a collection of books that really peaked my interest in the possibilities of mind over matter. The books contained stories of holy men who lived high in the Himalayan Mountains. Because of their devotion, knowledge, desire, and hard-earned mystic abilities, they were able to produce gold, jewels, food, and clothing; heal bodies; and obtain whatever they needed on the spot. They could also travel anywhere in a moment, or so the book said. That was for me!

This sounds as if I was very materialistic, but the desires for wealth and happiness are bona fide paths leading to higher understanding. There are four doors that open onto the path of a spiritually directed life:

1. desire for wealth and financial independence
2. desire to be happy and end distress
3. desire to gain knowledge of higher truth, including the laws and workings of the universe
4. desire to love and serve God

Each of these four doorways was of great interest to me. Learning about mystic powers suited me perfectly because of my childhood fascination with hidden treasure, Aladdin's lamp, and mystic powers. I wanted to know the secret science behind miracles and the unexplained.

Checks in the Mail

"I wonder if I could just see something happen and it would happen, instantly" was my thought after one of minister Reverend Mark's classes one night. I had hoped that by praying for and visualizing the money in my mailbox, the money would come automatically without my doing anything else. Visualizing every day for a few weeks, I would imagine my mailbox full of letters. Inside of every letter was cash or a check made out to me. I would make the visualization real by generating the feeling that it was actually happening.

Seeing my mailbox full of letters all containing checks made out to me was casting a die, an ethereal prototype, that would eventually take form in the real world.

> My money mantra: **Money, in large quantities of cash and checks, is flowing into my mailbox, purses, and bank accounts. I am wealthy in every way, including financially, and my wealth is increasing daily.**

Creating the Future in the Present

Everything happened, just as I imaged and affirmed. First one and then two checks in the mail, until years later there were thousands of letters, and almost all contained money, in fact millions of dollars every year. Actually, there was so much mail that the post office had to deliver the mail to the office in large gray bags, just as I had visualized.

All this came to pass, as I preached and taught my message of love, happiness, and prosperity in the church, in the business community, and on television. Yes, every check had my name on it, just as I had envisioned so many years before. But the money did not go to me personally; it went to the Terry Cole-Whittaker Ministries to pay the ministry expenses, as it was intended. My visualizations had worked, even though they took seventeen years to manifest fully. Time is relative, and some goals and dreams may take years—and others, less than a moment. Between my first visualization and the manifestation of my dream there was action to take, service to give, and people to help; but it all came true just as I had desired. At the time of my first visualization and prayer on this subject, I had no idea I would become a minister, teacher, motivational speaker, and business consultant.

A Lot of Cash in My Hands by Tonight

Another such "money miracle" took only a few hours to happen. Many years later at a time when I was on a sabbatical and doing research for one of my books, I had a need for a lot of cash. Being real estate rich but short on the cash I needed for a project, I prayed one morning for God to help me. Mind you, this wasn't the usual kind of prayer because I was feeling very alone, not knowing if God even existed. "God," I prayed, "if you exist, then put a lot of cash in my hands by tonight and I mean a *lot* of cash! And my neck feels out of alignment and sore, so please have my neck adjusted, also." What was about to happen would touch me at the deepest level of my soul.

Late that afternoon, I got a call from a couple of old friends who were passing through on business. "Sure, stop by for dinner and spend the night" was my response to their call. Given I had a large, abundant organic garden and they were also vegetarians, we would have a feast. Upon arriving one of them asked me to go in the house and sit on the floor, which I did. With a big smile on his face, he opened his suitcase and dumped $150,000 right into my hands. Just as I had requested, God had sent me the cash before the evening. Amazing!

With my mouth wide open I just sat there, not knowing what to say. In moments my neck was put back into alignment, as my friend was a chiropractor and he gave me an adjustment. Everything I had asked for came to me in a matter of a few hours. Yes, I got exactly what I had requested from God, but I had forgotten to ask for the money to belong to me.

The $150,000 belonged to my friend, and he had wanted to give me the experience of having that much cash in my hands. God had answered my prayer, and right on time. He let me know he was real and present with me, and it wasn't about the money; it was about my faith and trust in Him. Totally beyond coincidence or chance, this was an absolute personal message from God to me. The Lord had heard me and responded exactly according to my prayer request, and in a way that got my attention. This was a miracle in itself. I found I didn't need the money to do my project after all, and soon something better came along.

The Wrong Answer Is Really the Right Answer

Sometimes when it seems as if our prayers have not been answered, they really have been. God gives us what we need, and it is not always what we think we need. Knowing beyond a shadow of a doubt that God had heard and responded to me gave me the gift of absolute faith and trust in God, which is worth far more to me than any amount of money. To this day, I have no fear for I know that everything is working out for my highest good. I know I am being protected and maintained by the Loving Creator of the universe and this is called real security.

G E M

Serendipity is another way to say divine right action.

God Works in Mysterious and Roundabout Ways

How was I to know that the Mrs. America contest would play such an important role in God revealing to me my life's work? How had things worked out so that I would be in the right place at the right time? God only knows!

Mrs. America at Vacation Village

Having lunch one day at Vacation Village in San Diego, I noticed lovely and sophisticated women wearing banners across their chests reading MRS. FLORIDA, MRS. ALASKA, MRS. WYOMING, etc. "What is this?" I asked one of the waiters. To which he replied, "They are contestants in the Mrs. America Contest."

"The Mrs. America Contest? I didn't even know that there was one," I responded. At the time the Mrs. America title was not widely known, as it was a homemaking contest and not a beauty contest. "That's for me," I thought to myself. But I didn't say anything to Lynn.

"Mrs. America is a contest that could open many doors and also yield some valuable prizes. I wonder how to enter?" were my next thoughts. Asking seemed appropriate, so I approached a couple of the contestants, and they gave me phone numbers. I couldn't wait to get home to call and request that I be sent an entry form for the next year's contest.

Finally, after a couple of weeks, the letter arrived. As I held the letter, I felt excited. I had a premonition that something wonderful was going to happen to me on account of this contest.

Becoming Mrs. California was the first step. I took my time and filled out the entry forms conscientiously and answered all the questions as truthfully as I could.

PEARL
Don't let a rock in the road keep you from your destination.
Move it or go around it, but keep on going toward
your destination.

It took some months before I got a letter back from the Mrs. America Pageant. Imagine how excited and nervous I was to read, "Congratulations, you have been selected to be a finalist in the Mrs. California Pageant." I was invited for an all-expenses-paid weekend in Concord, near Oakland, for the finals, and there I became the new Mrs. California and a contestant in the Mrs. America Pageant.

Visualizing Myself Winning

With only three months to get ready for the Mrs. America Pageant, I worked to prepare myself. First I did what I had done before the Mrs. California contest, and that was to pray and visualize.

Instead of praying and asking for a particular title, I listed the benefits I wanted to accrue from the pageant. I left the title up to God.

The benefits I desired were as follows:

1. I would get to travel, all expenses paid, and stay at first-class hotels and eat at the finest restaurants.
2. Whatever I won would help me to discover and succeed in performing my life's work.
3. I would receive money and clothes.
4. I would be able to serve God and help others.

5. I would meet wonderful and successful people from whom I could learn to also be successful.

Daily Ritual

Each day in the morning and evening I would sit in my place of meditation, close my eyes, and pray. Then I imaged myself winning and receiving everything on my list. I saw myself telling my mother about all my good fortune, as I had in my visualization for my, as yet unknown, life's work. Then I finished my manifestation process, in gratitude, with the feeling of my having already received the fulfillment of my prayer.

Act As If, and You Are

Act as if you are, and you are. This means that you have to be who and what you desire to become before you will be. A dancer must identify him- or herself as a dancer first before he or she can actually be a dancer; a singer must think of him- or herself as a singer before he or she can act as a singer. Lessons don't make anyone a dancer or singer unless they consider themselves as one already. Lessons can only help those to develop and express their talents who are already singers and dancers first in their own minds.

I was working to convince myself that I was a winner, knowing that if I did then the rest would fall into place.

Disciplining Myself to Win

The pageant directors sent me a list of the events that would take place over the ten-day period in August of 1968. Flower arranging, driving, interior decorating, talent, public speaking, psychology tests, cooking, meal and party planning, efficient grocery shopping, inventing and cooking a pancake, modeling, clothing selection, etc. I set out to learn what I did not know and to get in shape by disciplining myself to exercise every day. Previously I had been fairly undisciplined but I knew that if I was to win, I had to prepare myself.

Now I know that everything of value has to be worked for through some form of discipline.

PEARL
Discipline is the difference between a wish and a reality.

The time came. I boarded the plane for Minneapolis/Saint Paul, the Twin Cities. Excited and nervous I leaned back and went through my prayer and visualization process. "Terry, you just have to be positive and confident, no matter what," was what I said to myself. I took a few minutes and wrote a "Success Mantra" for the occasion.

Silently, as the plane headed for Minneapolis/Saint Paul, I repeated it again and again until I was confident. Yes, I wanted to win, but I was going to have a wonderful time, whatever the outcome.

Success mantra: "I am a winner and I know that whatever comes to me will be perfect and part of God's perfect plan for my life."

Everything wasn't totally rosy, for there were people close to me who tried to discourage me. Whenever they got the chance they ridiculed me and felt it was their duty to let me know that I was a big loser. "Terry, you're a failure and you have no chance of winning, so you may as well stay at home and prevent yourself from looking like a fool." My confidence was being built from within, however, and I was not going to let any negativity or fear take this from me if it was meant to be mine.

LESSON
If something is yours, no one can take it; if something is not, there is nothing you can do to keep it.

After seven out of the ten days of competition, my name had not been mentioned even once. Determined not to give up, two or three times every day I would go to my room and lie down on my bed. Relaxing as well as I could, I would then silently speak my success mantras and do my visualization. When I felt calm, confident, and assured, I would get up and go back downstairs and participate in the next event.

I never quit. I kept affirming: "I am a winner, and everything is working out according to God's perfect plan for my life."

Mrs. Pancake of America

Finally came the talent event, the pancake competition, interior decorating, and meal planning, and I won them all! We were in the final stretch, and I was catching up and moving into one of the lead positions.

Mrs. Pancake of America became my new title. I had invented the winning recipe. But, it really was not I alone who had invented the recipe. It was Divine Intelligence and I together as a team.

My Winning, "Tangy Strawberry Roll-Up" Recipe

Pancake:
   1 cup of Aunt Jemima Pancake Mix
   1 cup of milk
   1 tablespoon of vegetable oil
   1 small package of lemon pudding-and-pie filling: regular, *not* instant.

   Mix with a whisk and cook as you would any pancake
   Yield: 8 pancakes

Filling:
   Wash and slice as many strawberries as desired. Reserve 8 strawberries with stems to use as garnish.

Topping:
   Mix one small container of sour cream with two tablespoons of sweetened condensed milk and lemon juice to taste.

   Fill half the cooked pancake with sliced strawberries. Fold it over, crepe-style, then spoon the sweet-and-tangy topping over the pancake.
   Top with a whole strawberry including the stem for beauty.

How I Got the Winning Recipe

Back home before the pageant, I had prayed to God and asked for the winning recipe. I used a special system called the **Percolator Process** to tap into universal mind, the reservoir of all ideas, inventions, and knowledge. I did my part by reading pancake recipes, experimenting with recipes, and then, "out-of-the-blue" in a flash of awareness the winning recipe was given to me in perfect detail. I will share this marvelous process with you in the next chapter, as it is a wonderful way to seek and receive knowledge, ideas, inventions, and solutions for every kind of challenge.

The Big Night

The night of the coronation of Mrs. America 1968 came. As our names were called in alphabetical order, each of the contestants walked out on stage and took her place accompanied by applause from the grandstand. First the name of fourth runner-up was called, followed by my name, Mrs. California, as third runner-up in the Mrs. America Pageant of 1968. I didn't get to be Mrs. America, but the title of Mrs. America would not have given me what I had prayed and asked God to give to me. Mrs. Pancake of America did, however. All I had desired, written down, prayed about, and visualized had come to pass, without exception.

I received an all-expenses-paid, nine-week television, radio, and media tour of twenty-six major cities in the USA and Canada, promoting and cooking my winning pancake recipe as a representative for Quaker Oats and Aunt Jemima Pancake Mix. I was also given a new wardrobe of my choice, spending money, and the opportunity to stay free in first-class hotels. What I didn't know was that the experience of doing television, radio, and newspaper interviews would prepare me to have my own television program and to travel on book and promotional tours as a minister and author in the years to come. I had asked that whatever I won would help me to know and succeed in my Life's Work, of which I had no awareness at the time, but God did.

Off I went touting the benefits and importance of grains, especially pancakes, in a person's diet. More than the value of pancakes I talked about positive thinking, goal setting, and all the things that I had been learning and applying. People were fascinated and wanted to know more. Most had never heard of any of this positive-thinking philosophy, and they loved it.

I was speaking, motivating, and teaching, on television and radio and through newspaper articles throughout the United States and Canada. I felt I was in heaven because I was doing what came naturally. Speaking about positive thinking and spiritual matters and inspiring and motivating people to have better lives gave me great pleasure and satisfaction. Still it had not dawned on me that this was or had anything to do with my Life's Work.

PEARL

Our talents are natural to us and so much a part of us that we often do not consider them as having anything to do with our Life's Work. These talents are tradable commodities we can exchange for money, goods, and services.

Realizing Your Life's Work

What do you like to do?

What do you find yourself doing quite naturally?

What do others tell you they appreciate about you?

What would you do if you could do anything at all?

When the tour was over, everyone at church congratulated me and celebrated my victory. It was their victory, too, and a validation of everything we had been learning in church and our classes.

The Big Day

One momentous Sunday morning after church Reverend Mark called me to his office and said, "Terry, would you please give the sermon for the Wednesday noon service? I want you to share your Mrs. America Pageant

Serving Others and Receiving Money from What You Love Doing

Brainstorm and list 20 services or products you could produce, offer, and deliver to others using your talents, propensities, and abilities.

1.	1.
2.	2.
3.	3.
4.	4.
5.	5.
6.	6.
7.	7.
8.	8.
9.	9.
10.	10.

and media tour experiences. Because you applied the spiritual principles that we are teaching in church it would be helpful for others to hear about what you did to achieve your goals, so they can do the same thing and achieve theirs." Being taken by surprise I didn't know what to say, thinking I had never given a talk or speech before in my life. Being completely oblivious of the fact that I had just completed nine weeks of extemporaneous talks speaking on national and international television and radio shows across the continent, I felt inadequate.

Reverend Mark wouldn't take "no" for an answer, and I finally agreed. What to do? Thumbing through my favorite spiritual books, I cut out the teachings of others that appealed to me the most. Placing these statements in some kind of order, I taped them to three yellow legal-sized pages and read over them aloud a few times.

PEARL
It is more important to start, no matter how humble the first step, than not to start at all.

Wednesday came, and I had invited one of my dearest friends to be a guest at my talk. Pretending to be confident, I stepped up to the podium and looked out at the audience made up of my fellow students. I proceeded to read every word of my borrowed talk.

After I finished, there was a definite and profound feeling of the presence of what people call the Holy Spirit. No one said anything for a few moments, and then many burst into tears and others into applause.

Something spiritual and out of the ordinary had taken place, and it had something to do with me. Even though not one word I spoke was mine, everyone was moved, inspired, and uplifted, including my friend.

As I stepped away from the podium, my friend walked right up to me and, looking directly into my eyes, she said, "Terry, your calling is to be a motivational speaker and preacher." I was stunned. This had never entered my mind, but it felt so very right.

PEARL

Our talents and gifts often go unnoticed by us, and it takes another to point out the obvious. This is one of the blessings of friendship.

Everything I had desired, prayed for, and visualized having to do with my Life's Work" was contained within my two new professions: minister and motivational speaker. When I told the news to Reverend Mark, he exclaimed, "Congratulations, Terry! Being a minister and working for God is the greatest work in the world!"

Chapter Five

Step Three, Seek Knowledge of How to Attain the Ultimate

"And ye shall know the truth, and the truth
shall make you free."—*John 8:32*

"Today knowledge has power. It controls
access to opportunity and advancement."
—*Peter F. Drucker, author and business consultant*

Don't Wait; Jump Right In

Positive Thinking for Women Only, a four-week class taught by Terry Cole-Whittaker, 1968 third runner-up to Mrs. America" is how the ad read in the YMCA newsletter. My friend JoAnn had suggested that I call the director of the "Y" and ask him if I could teach a class and he had said "Yes." No one knew that, although I had a great name for the class, I didn't know precisely what it was that I was going to teach. My only teaching experience had been as a Sunday school teacher.

Even though I had no prior teaching experience, I was certain that there was a Presence and Power within me that knew everything, including how to create and teach a dynamic class. There wasn't time for me to spend years in school in order to learn what I needed to know for myself and to teach. Since my subject of interest wasn't being taught anywhere else, except in my church and in my precious books, I had to train myself. The universities of the world teach about worldly things, but my interest was in the unseen power and intelligence behind the outer world of appearances.

The Unseen Power

There is a sixth sense, which is superior to the other five. Because I wanted to know the formula for creating my life, as I desired it to be, I sought out the knowledge of the infinite and of this special sixth sense. With this knowledge I was certain I could make things happen and not just let things happen. With this superior knowledge I could be a co-creator with God and not a victim without hope for something better. This knowledge was giving me the tools to build a beautiful garden of love and opulence in my heart and in my outer world, and I wanted more of it.

I didn't have time to wait until some unknown future time, because I wanted to live my dream, as a motivational speaker and minister, now. My new philosophy was to simply start with what I had and then get ready and improve, as I went along. Already I had gained some knowledge from my two years of study at my church, from the numerous seminars I had attended and the books I had read. What I already knew about my subject was sufficient to begin.

You Are Richer Than You Know

People are actually much richer than they realize. Each and every person has a wealth of experience and knowledge that someone else would love to know about and be willing to pay for. I was certain that what I had already learned and experienced would be of value to others.

Tom Was Rich in Experience

For years Tom had been the chairman of a local nonprofit charitable organization. Under his guidance the organization had raised literally millions of dollars through donations and from various fund-raising activities. He loved his work, and all of it was done as a volunteer. As time passed Tom realized that because his children were growing he needed to get a job that paid more and even though he would no longer have the time to do his charitable work, he had to move on. What was he to do since his actual job was as an auto mechanic and his income was limited? Tom's father had been an auto mechanic before him, so Tom naturally followed in his footsteps.

Visiting a career counselor, Tom was surprised to realize that he was actually suited to be a corporate executive. Tom's years of successful fundraising had prepared him to get a high-paying job, without a college diploma, based on his track record of success in his charitable work.

Homemaker Turned Domestic Executive

Joan had raised three boys, helped her husband to succeed in his business, run the household, given dinner parties, handled the family finances, plus volunteered in the community. Suddenly her husband passed away at the same time as their youngest son graduated from college. What was Joan to do, as her husband had neglected to provide an insurance policy for her security?

Joan sat down and made an inventory of her talents, skills, and experience and found she was rich and could take care of herself and others. She marketed herself as a domestic executive and helped families to succeed as hers had under her care and management. Her work became so successful that she was able to build a company that found similar career opportunities for other displaced homemakers who had a wealth of experience and knowledge.

Inventory Your Personal Resources

List your knowledge, experiences, talents, and abilities that can be turned into services or products that can help others to get what they need and desire.

1.
2.
3.
4.
5.

Have Faith in Yourself

Clear that I had something to offer others that they really needed, I took a leap of faith before being completely ready. Later I found out that the practice of jumping into a project before being prepared and ready is advised, and it is actually the preferred system used by extraordinary people in all walks of life.

Many with enormous talent wait for years until they are ready and still they never do much, if anything, with their talent. Others, who have an obsession to get to work, express their talents, build their empire, and make their mark see no reason to wait, nor do they allow others to destroy their creativity and enthusiasm.

College Dropout Becomes a World-Renowned and Wealthy Architect

Barry wanted to be a world-famous architect, as this had been his dream since childhood. Enrolling in the school of architecture of a major and well-respected university, he proceeded to take the courses. Finding the teachers limiting, he felt that his creativity was being stifled, so he quit school.

His dream of being an architect was even stronger than ever. Barry believed that if he remained in school and conformed to meet their standards he would have had to squelch his unique ideas in order to graduate. He knew that if he did this, his spirit would die and so would his genius and talent.

Barry set up his architectural office and hired architects who were graduates of bona fide schools of architecture. Barry designed his structures and sought the help of his employees when needed and used their credentials to get his most creative and unusual work accepted by his clients and the state.

Over time, after Barry was already globally recognized for his genius as an architect, he did get a degree. He never let his not having the credentials stop him from giving his gifts or from prospering. Barry was already an architect in his mind and heart, and he didn't need anyone to validate him or give him permission to do his beloved work. He lived his dream before he was qualified, and so can anyone who is willing to step out beyond the crowd. Those who are waiting for permission may never get it.

PEARL

Don't wait until you are ready or it may never happen. Be afraid, if necessary, but go forward anyway.

Everything starts small, and even the giant redwood began as the tiniest of seeds. In our day and age when there is so much opulence, power, and excellence around us even the most talented can be frightened and prevented from following their heart and living their dream. Do not be afraid, for even IBM and Microsoft were at one time tiny seeds and before that simply thoughts in their originators' minds.

Look around and find all the things that were first a thought in someone's mind. If you look outside you will see the wonders of Mother Nature. Each and every one of God's creations was first a thought in His mind. Your thoughts will also manifest if you take action and begin, ready or not.

Don't Wait Until All Your Problems Are Solved or the Time Is Right

One of the reasons we may wait too long before we begin is because we are waiting until all our problems are solved. That day will never come, as there will always be challenges and problems to solve. Problems are not bad; they are opportunities to invoke our creativity and achieve our goals. Go toward your goal, and I guarantee your problems will be solved along the way to your desired destination.

Say Good-bye to Procrastination, the Killer of Dreams

Here are the ten main excuses and reasons people use to cheat themselves out of the fulfillment of their dreams.

Ten Worthless Excuses

1. It will be too difficult and I will have to work like a slave. I will have no time to relax and enjoy life.
2. There are already other people doing the same thing, so I am not needed or wanted.
3. I don't have enough money to live my dreams or achieve my goals, and I don't know where or how I will get the money.
4. Others will criticize, ridicule, and reject me.
5. I don't have the talent and I am not qualified.
6. It will take too long to achieve.
7. I don't have the time, as I am already too busy.
8. Others say it can't be done.
9. I could fail.
10. I can't be really great, so why try at all?

Anthony Robbins Got Up and Out and Made Hundreds of Millions of Dollars

Anthony Robbins, the world-famous motivator, tells the story of how for months he stayed at home, slept, lounged around, and watched television. Wasting his life, he became increasingly listless, bored, and dejected until one day he had had enough. He got up and out and got back into the motivating business and the rest is history. Tony would sit in my Sunday morning church services with some of his students, as he listened to every word I said.

People believe that Tony is different from them and that somehow he is special. Everyone is special, and just as everyone is different and unique we are also the same. The formula for success is the same for everyone. Success means reaching your goal and arriving at your destination, so success is different for everyone, but the steps are the same.

Action Is the Cure for Poverty and Unhappiness

Action and continuous action toward your goal destroy all excuses. One either has results or has the reasons why they didn't get the results, but no one can have both. You get reasons or results and you choose. My father taught me this lesson early when he said to me, "Don't give me your excuses. You either did it, or you didn't."

Procrastination leads to fear, but action cures fear as it produces desirable results. We can only get the results we want if we get up and go. By taking action in the direction of our goals, we develop our character and talents, become stronger, and receive the tasty fruits of our labor.

Action Produces Wealth and Fulfillment

Here's a simple trick that I know you will love, especially if you are ready to dump the self-defeating habit of procrastination. Procrastinators are basically lazy, and sloth is one of the seven deadly sins or errors that we must avoid if we are to receive the treasures of God's opulent kingdom. God is giving us the treasures of His kingdom in each and every moment, but it is up to us to receive these riches by doing the right things and avoiding the wrong ones. Laziness is to be avoided.

Laziness, if not averted, will cause depression, discouragement, and eventual poverty. Never be discouraged, and always keep a positive state of mind. The mind is the gateway between heaven and hell. It is our choice as to which way the door swings open, depending upon our thoughts and behavior.

As a former procrastinator, I used to avoid doing what needed to be done. Choosing to do as little as possible, and for sure postponing whatever I could for another time, day, year, or lifetime I found myself overburdened with the heaviness of the mountain of what needed to be done. One fine day it dawned on me, as I sat there not doing much of anything, that if I kept up this lazy behavior I might as well kiss my dreams good-bye.

Procrastination was my way of protecting myself from rejection, criticism, and ridicule. An out-of-control mind will convince you that you have something or someone to fear and that your fear is actually your protector. Once you have surrendered your will and power and are cowering in fear unable to take positive action, your mind will imprison and torture you until you are miserable. The only solution is for the real, fearless person to rise up and take a stand in favor of life. One must commit to the attainment of one's goals and dreams, no matter what, and then do it.

Here is a key point: It is not our thoughts alone that create but our actions. Thoughts cause us to act, and positive thoughts cause us to take the positive actions that manifest our goals. You can think and dream all day, but unless you do something toward creating the reality of it in the here-and-now, real world, it will remain a wish and fleeting desire, and that is all. Someone said, "The road to hell is paved with good intentions." You might even say the road to personal riches is paved with action after action.

Activity is the true nature of every person, but somehow we have been led to believe that the goal of life is to be inactive and, in fact, useless. Perhaps we are afraid of being overworked as slaves of an evil master. The real evil master is an out-of-control mind that would defeat us at every turn if we allow it to. The difference between a winner and a loser is that the winner does not listen to his or her mind but keeps the mind steady and consistently positive and a reliable servant of the true divine self.

Work is a good four-letter word. Work is our vehicle to attaining and enjoying prosperity, vitality, and happiness. Right livelihood, which means work done in the mood of love and service, brings us the greatest satisfaction and fulfillment possible. The idle rich and the idle poor have something in common: boredom.

Stamp Out Procrastination

Because I had a strong, even overwhelming, desire to achieve my higher goals, I knew I had to find a way to eliminate procrastination, the famous killer of dreams. The trick I developed was to fool my mind by making a commitment to accomplish something bigger than my normal tasks. If need be, I'd promise others that I would perform this great task just to give me some added incentive and to box myself into a corner. To avoid doing the larger tasks, I get busy doing all the smaller ones. By the time I have finished with the smaller tasks, I am on a roll and it's easy for me to accomplish the greater ones.

Getting started is half the battle and, once you start, all you have to do is keep the ball rolling and you will gain momentum. Most people defeat themselves in their minds, but remember that action cures fear. Take your fears with you and don't wait for them to go away before you move forward. Moving forward and facing your fears will get rid of them, one by one.

I had fears, but my obsessive desire to attain my goals was stronger than those fears. When your desires are mightier than your fears, you will achieve your goals.

PEARL

Do the thing and the power is yours, but don't do it and you won't get the power.

Like Barry, the famous architect, I also had a burning desire and heart-felt dream. My dream was to help others to attain the spiritual and material riches of life, and my way to do this was as a minister and motivational speaker. Having done neither, but knowing this was truly who I was, I got started with what I had. I took action to set up my first motivational seminars for the public, and I also enrolled in the seminary of my choice.

What, if anything, do you desire to be, do, or have but because you believe you are not ready or qualified, you have not?

I want to _____

My dream is to _____

My burning desire is to _____

Something I have always wanted to do is _____

There Is Always a Way, If You Are Bold Enough

The story goes, that Steven Spielberg, as a young and unheard-of producer, director, wanna-be, walked onto the Universal Studios back lot in Holly-wood, California, and found an empty office. Offices were in trailers, so he went in, set his work on the desk, and put the name plaque he had brought with him on the door. He always carried a briefcase, looked like someone important, got to know the people who really worked there, and wove himself into the fabric of the studio life.

In time others were sufficiently impressed to include him in some projects, and the rest is history. Is this dishonest? No! He didn't steal or harm anyone, but he was courageous enough to do the fearless thing and it worked.

Goethe, the German philosopher, said, "Genius has boldness in it." Much of what we call genius is simply the courage to do what others are afraid to do or even attempt. Extraordinary people are not usually more talented than others, but because they have an overwhelming desire to express their talents, be rich, famous, appreciated, and fulfill their mission, they are willing to overcome enormous obstacles and tremendous fear.

Fear of what others will do to us is one of our greatest fears. Remember: Whatever you do, some will love it and some will hate it—and this is the way it is. Once this issue is resolved, the person is free to live her or his dream.

What the Extraordinary Have in Common

Michael Childers, a world-famous photographer of many of the most celebrated artists, actors, and musicians of our time, invited me to come to his palatial home in Palm Springs for a visit and to pick up some photos. Michael took me on a tour of his photo gallery, and there on the walls of his home were many of the famous pictures he had taken of the greatest stars and legends of the movies and theater. What struck me the most, as I looked at the pictures of these people whom I had admired over the years, was that all of them had attained the ultimate of what was attainable in their fields of endeavor because all fully expressed their talents and uniqueness. Paul Newman, Andy Warhol, Marilyn Monroe, Clark Gable, John Huston, Georgia O'Keeffe, John Travolta, Dustin Hoffman, Marlon Brando, Ava Gardner, and so many others were there on Michael's walls of fame.

I thought, "Critics had both hailed and denounced them, gossip columnists had bad-mouthed and slandered them, audiences loved and hated them, and most likely there were others far more talented who had resented their fame and success, but still each one of these legends persevered and prevailed." The fainthearted do not survive the attacks of the envious, but the strong willed do and actually become stronger in the process.

Each "star" had an obsessive desire to give his or her gifts and live as he or she chose, and did. We revere them because of this. They fascinate us, as if they have something special, but they don't. If they had succumbed to rejection, ridicule, and criticism and given up, as many wanted them to do, their great talent would have been wasted and they would have been relegated to a life of "could'a," "should'a," and "would'a."

It takes courage to live your dreams and to leap out onto the center stage of life. You cannot control the minds of others, and you never know what "they" will do, but you can control your own mind.

The Queen's Dilemma

Once there was a queen who enjoyed walking around her realm, but she was barefooted and her feet became cut and bruised from the rocks and thorns. She asked her prime minister to solve the problem by carpeting her entire realm but the prime minister, being particularly intelligent, had a pair of shoes made for her instead. Imagine how happy the queen felt as she had the freedom to walk anywhere and be comfortable and happy. The prime minister received a huge bonus for solving the queen's problem and saving her so much money. Plus, the prime minister set up a new royal business: shoes. Any employee who can problem-solve as well as offer valid suggestions for moneymaking and money saving will be the one who makes the big dollars.

Many of our problems can be solved in the same way. Erecting a wall of protection around our own higher minds will keep us from being harmed, discouraged, or stopped by the thoughts, beliefs, actions, and opinions of others. Everyone has two minds: the higher and the lower. The higher mind is linked with Divine, Universal Mind and the lower is linked with the false and fearful self. The false self is created when we believe we are separate from God and God's limitless good, when we are not. "As a man thinketh in his heart, so is he."

Of course the rocks and thorns will be there as we travel in our search for spiritual and material treasures, for it is impossible to change others so that we may be comfortable and happy. The solution is to change our perception and act as we desire in each situation rather than react to the actions of others. This can only happen when we have control over our own mind by keeping it steady, calm, and elevated.

Over time, unless released, the pain caused by the rocks and arrows slung by others will cause us to carry the heavy and painful burden of bad feelings. Bad feelings destroy our chances for happiness and for the success we desire. It is best to let this burden go as quickly as possible and resume our forward motion with enthusiasm.

The Healing Art of Forgiveness

Forgiveness makes a practical pair of shoes. Someone who tries to harm or hurt you in anyway either on purpose or by accident cannot, and there is no harm done when you are wearing your forgiveness shoes. Some call this having thick skin, but I prefer to be softhearted, alert, and aware of human nature.

Our work is to rise above our fear-based animal nature and achieve what some call Christ Consciousness, our true divine nature. The word *Christ* is not the last name of Jesus but an adjective used to describe a God-realized and therefore self-realized person. The choice is ours in every moment, as to which nature we choose to recognize and honor. Even Jesus, while on the cross, offered forgiveness to his attackers when he prayed to the Father, "Father, forgive them; for they know not what they do" (Luke 23:34).

Fear, anger, resentment, shame, guilt, and the desire for revenge keep people stuck in the rut of hopelessness and the quicksand of misery. Imagine yourself wearing a Teflon coat and a suit made of a miracle material of super strength, abilities, and power. The amazing suit-and-coat combination lets you accomplish anything your heart desires while at the same time repelling the envy, anger, and hostility of foolish people who do not know that God is also their source and supply.

You don't need to slow down or give up your dream just because of a few rocks and thorns on the road on the way to your destination. People are only hostile to you if they believe that you are preventing them from being, doing, or having something they want. True pleasure is an inner experience, and no one can take this from another.

Those who have what I call a poverty consciousness are not aware that there is more than enough for everyone, especially when it comes to love and happiness. Believing that another's good fortune is a threat to theirs, they may attempt to rain on someone else's parade and give him or her some uncomfortable feelings. Hoping to feel better themselves, they will try to bring someone else down. A knowledgeable person does not do this to another or allow this to happen to them.

Contained within the Soul of every one of us is an unlimited supply of happiness, love, intelligence, ideas, and peace. All anyone need do is draw from this reservoir of God-Within and therefore meet all his or her needs. No one can take away our inner peace and joy no matter what they do, for it is always our choice as to how we shall respond to any person or situation. We respond to others as we do because of our beliefs and habits. Once we have the knowledge, we can change our beliefs and habits and train ourselves to act from confidence, peace, and positivity, whatever the situation.

How to Change the World in One Easy Lesson

Preparing for my Positive Thinking classes at the YMCA, I developed my "Act not react" technique as the solution to this problem of rocks and thorns in the road. Drawing from my own experience of what was helping me, I knew that others needed the same kind of knowledge and encouragement as I. Changing the world to suit us is impossible, but changing the way we respond to the world is possible.

Because I was supersensitive to the negative and even cruel actions and words of others, I developed a system that my students and I could use to rise above the attacks or negative words and actions of others. Not that everyone wants to hurt us, but sometimes even the slightest well-intended criticism can demolish a fragile "people pleaser." Instead of reacting to others' words and actions in the same old self-defeating manner, it serves us to train ourselves to remain calm and self-assured. Anyone can respond in a positive manner from choice rather than react in a negative manner from habit. There are three steps to making a new habit: desire, knowledge, and action.

View from the Top

Until we desire to have a different response, we will continue to respond as we have been responding perhaps since childhood. Robots have no

---

"Act Not React"
This is role-playing and a wonderful way to make a new habit.

Get a friend to be the other person who is causing you difficulty. If you cannot get a friend, either do this exercise in your mind or use a plant, pillow, or chair to represent the person or type of person. By practicing your ideal and chosen response, you are creating a new memory in your subconscious. This new ritual when done enough times will become a new wanted habit that has replaced the old unwanted habit. You are using the same system that programmed you years ago to reprogram you now, as you desire.

1. Decide on the person or type of person with whom you are having or have had difficulty. Face the actor or pillow playing the role of this person or close your eyes and see the person in your mind.
2. Have her or him say or do the thing that has previously evoked a negative, self-defeating, or unwanted response from you. Have her or him use the exact words, tone of voice, and mannerisms that have engendered these unwanted responses from you.
3. Respond as you desire to respond. Say what you would like to say, act as you would like to act, feel as you would like to feel. Do this as many times and with as many different statements that evoke a negative response from you as you can, until you feel comfortable in your automatic new response.

What you will find is that as you change your pattern and habit, you will no longer be as affected by others and you will be in greater control of yourself.

---

choice and neither do we, until we actually recognize that we do have a choice. People relive the same troubles over and over simply from habit, like stimulus-response machines. Spiritually intelligent people realize they have options and they exercise them, and it's at this point that we actually have choice. Spiritually intelligent people seek knowledge of what to do to make their lives better, and then they do that. By doing the same thing over and over, a new habit is made. Making new patterns of thinking, feeling, and behavior takes work, but the rewards are well worth it. My "Act

Not React" technique is a worthwhile tool to use to build the habits you want. So many of my students have used it with great success.

Joan's Mother Could No Longer Get Her Upset

I first taught this technique to one of my friends to see how it worked for her, before I taught it to my students. When Joan's mother started her usual, hour-long criticism of her over the phone Joan said, "Mom, I can't talk any longer, as I have to go because I have an appointment. Talk with you later, and remember, Mom, I love you." Then she hung up.

Joan was recreating a new and more pleasant and productive ritual between them by changing her own behavior first. Her plan was to continue talking with her mother, as long as the conversation was pleasant and mutually enriching, but if the mother veered off into hostile territory she would find an excuse and politely hang up. By reinforcing good behavior, her plan worked. Almost effortlessly her mother became more and more pleasant on the telephone, and their enjoyment of each other increased.

Peace in the Family

A neighbor confided to me how her daughters argued around her just to get her engaged in their fights. She didn't like being part of their squabbling, but when she told them to stop fighting, it never worked. I shared with her my technique, and she loved it. After practicing her response a few times, she was ready for them. Her use of the new strategy of Act Not React went like this: When the girls came into the room fighting and each complaining how the other one was causing trouble, she would say, "You two can fight, if you choose. Just do it in your part of the house. This argument involves the two of you, therefore you will need to solve it between yourselves."

The next few times when either they started their argument in front of her or had brought it to her, she told them the same thing. How simple it was. She never said to stop fighting, but only that they would need to fight in their part of the house, as her part was to be peaceful.

As she refused to get involved, they fought less and less, for much of their arguing was simply to get her attention. Along with this, she gave each of the girls more personal time and attention.

It Also Worked on Her Husband

She used another version of the same technique on her husband. Something would irritate him, and then the war would start. Yelling and sometimes screaming at her, he would use every foul word, accuse her of every ugly thing he could think of, and then threaten to divorce her and cause her every kind of trouble. After practicing with a friend who played the role of her husband, instead of crying, yelling back, and threatening him, as she had so many, many times before, she just stood there breathing deeply and listening. Rather than taking what he said too seriously, she realized he was overreacting to something she had done and was out of control. She remembered that she was wearing a "Teflon coat" and nothing was sticking.

PEARL
There is no reason to accept the unacceptable.

Remaining calm, she'd excuse herself after a while and go outside and take a walk. Coming back home, she would find that her husband had calmed down sufficiently so they could better understand the real problem and look for a solution. After a few times of her responding and acting in this new way, his radical behavior slowly changed, until at the onset of trouble they were able to view the real problem and work for a solution without a war.

When one person in a family or group changes, everyone around him or her is forced to make changes. For a while the other members of the group will work to keep things as they have been, but if you are persistent, in time everything will make a shift for the better. Of course at first they are likely to resist change even though the old ways aren't working. It takes an intelligent person to see the error of his or her ways and change his or her thinking and behavior. Most are committed to continuing on as they have been, even if what they have been doing is not working to give them the love, prosperity, and pleasure they are seeking. Be patient and give it some time, and you will be very happy with the results.

PEARL
*Everything new and uncomfortable
becomes comfortable in time.*

PEARL
*Genius doesn't mean knowing everything; it means knowing
where to find whatever you need to know.*

Finding the Third Step On My Treasure Map

Time was running out, and I needed to absorb myself in my studies to prepare for my upcoming classes. What else could I teach that would be extremely valuable to my, as yet unknown, students? To answer my question
I sought knowledge from the books in the church bookstore, libraries, and
used bookstores. Reading had never appealed to me until now. Because I
so loved what I was reading, I felt myself filling up and bubbling over with
priceless treasures of my heart, soul, and mind. I was getting food for my
hungry soul as well as a practical philosophy by which I could live my life,
solve my problems, and also succeed in business and prosper.

Indeed, knowledge is power. Step Three on my Sacred Treasure Map to
the Spiritual and Material Riches of Life had to be "Seek Knowledge of
How to Attain the Ultimate."

> "The trouble with the world is not that people
> know too little, but that they know so many
> things that ain't so." —*Mark Twain*

With the right knowledge, a person can achieve the ultimate available
to human kind. Without higher knowledge greatness can never be
achieved, nor can peace of mind or happiness—let alone wealth. Without
knowledge, not much is possible at all. With the right knowledge one can
restore a lost kingdom, build a good relationship, gain health, become a
child at heart, reach beyond this universe, or own a small farm in the coun-

try. Whatever your desire, there is a formula to attain it. Even though I didn't know it at that time, the basic formula for achieving my heart's desires was being given to me step-by-step.

> "Seeking Knowledge of How to Attain
> the Ultimate" is the third step of this
> remarkable formula.

If someone else has attained what you want, so can you. Start by finding out what they did to attain it. You can be certain that knowledge exists that will lead you to the priceless treasures of your heart and soul, but you have to have an open mind and be willing to learn. Are you willing and open?

> "To know that we know what we know, and that we
> do not know what we do not know, that is true
> knowledge." —*Henry David Thoreau*

PEARL
It matters not the goal; the steps are the same.

There are five sources of well-founded, valid information. Seek your solutions, answers, and guidance from each of the five following sources of knowledge. A sure way to know the best decision for you to make is when all five sources give you the same answer.

Five Main Sources of Authoritative Knowledge

1. Scriptures from the world religions
2. The wisdom of the ages including stories, legends, and myths brought to us in great works of literature or passed down to us through the teacher/student relationship
3. Experts and the leading examples of those who are being, doing, and having what you desire to also be, do or have

4. Your own experience of what works and what doesn't
5. Divine revelation and knowledge given to you by Infinite Intelligence

"Knowledge rests not upon truth alone,
but upon error also." —*Carl Jung*

Knowledge is twofold: knowing what to do and what not to do. The most valuable road maps point out both the best and fastest ways to get you to your desired destination, as well as the dangers and problems to be avoided. One thing to avoid is learning only by the slow and dangerous method of trial and error. There are so many possible errors, there aren't enough lifetimes for one to find the right formula for success. The truth is the knowledge of what works already exists and has been given to us in each of the five main sources of authoritative knowledge.

PEARL
If you want to attain the finest, then seek advice from the prime authorities in your particular field of endeavor.

For me, absorbing higher knowledge meant taking classes, listening to experts, and reading books and articles on the subjects of success, motivation, spirituality, presentation, and marketing. There was so much I did not know but others did, and I could learn from their experience and do what they had done before me. I wasn't the first person to become a minister or to be a motivational speaker, nor was I the first person to desire to find out the secrets of the universe and beyond.

When We Need Something, It Appears

I found an extraordinary book hidden in a dusty corner of a used-book store. By now I had come to realize that nothing happens by accident. Behind everything is the unseen hand of God. Finding this book was a huge miracle, and these kinds of miracles are happening every day if we pay attention and see God's handiwork.

This find proved to be a gold mine. People hope to find a real gem in a pile of cheap costume jewelry at a yard sale, but if they want riches they would do well to visit stores specializing in used and out-of-print books.

The title of the dusty, out-of-print relic was *Genius and Your Subconscious Mind*. It contained priceless information that transformed the way I approached any problem or challenge from the moment I read it. The knowledge in this little book, which never made it onto any best-seller list, gave me access to the vast resources of knowledge banks of the universe and beyond.

Tapping into the Wealth of the Cosmos

I became totally absorbed in the book and immediately applied the knowledge I gleaned from it. I was amazed at how easy it was to be a genius. For instance: If the television was broken, I closed my eyes and visualized it working. Then I requested my subconscious to give me the knowledge to fix it. Next, I set about finding out what was wrong, and an idea would come to me that worked. If the problem were the picture tube or something big, I obviously would take it in to be fixed by an expert. Generally speaking when things went wrong by using the percolator system, I got things to working, or rather the Power of the Universe put things in order through me. So many times simple problems around the house or in my work were solved in moments, as the plan to fix them or the knowledge of what to do flashed into my mind in full detail. Sometimes the solution would come in a small voice or a knowing, I would follow the directions, the thing would work, and whatever I needed to know would be made known to me.

"Genius is awareness and the ability to access universal knowledge beyond a person's own experience" was the gist of what I was reading in my newfound book. Using the remarkable creative answer-giving power of the subconscious mind, I found myself permanently able to invent new products, find lost articles, solve problems, be artistic, create successful businesses, and navigate the world with ease.

God has given everyone this ability, but few know anything about this marvelous ability. You might say our intelligence can be compared to a super-deluxe Swiss army knife, but most of us never use more than one blade.

Einstein is a good example of someone who tapped into the secrets of the universe. His knowledge did not come from his inert brain made of dense matter, but from his Spiritual Intelligence. He somehow knew how to access universal knowledge.

Everyone has intelligence, but because of his or her past desires and actions there are various levels of intelligence. Some use their intelligence for finding limitless numbers of sex partners, some in pursuing other addictions, and some like an Einstein or a Stephen Hawking use their intelligence to seek out the knowledge of matter and the various aspects of the physical universe. My interest was and has been not in finding out about matter, but in finding out about spirit, God, and the unseen realms that create the outer visible worlds of matter.

Great inventors, scientists, artists, and musicians use their intelligence to access and process information that has always existed and is available to anyone who knows how to open the door to the vast resources of the mind and universal intelligence.

How It Works!

Those who are extraordinary, ultrawealthy, and talented and those who have genius have much in common. By studying the creative techniques of inventors, artists, and geniuses in many walks of life, the author of my new, favorite book had discovered that these special people had taken similar steps to access talent, knowledge, and genius. From the findings of his research he put together a list of common strategies used by these extraordinary people. From reading his list I put together a system that I termed the "Incredible, Genius-Producing, Percolator Process."

The Incredible, Genius-Producing, Percolator Process

1. *They had an intense desire.* Each had an intense desire to invent something or to create a solution to a problem or challenge. An example of this is Thomas Edison, the inventor of the lightbulb, whose desired outcome was to light up the dark.
2. *They had faith.* Each believed that he or she would find a solution without fail.

3. *They sought help from a higher intelligence and power.* Many actually prayed to God and others, who were not spiritually inclined, simply made the request to their subconscious mind or to the Universal Higher Intelligence for the perfect solution or invention.

4. *They did extensive research.* Each did his or her part, which was to do extensive research and learn as much as possible about his or her subject. They analyzed the problem, brainstormed, and called in the power of Infinite Intelligence to bring forth the solutions and answers they sought. All this was naturally stored in the human computer called the subconscious mind.

5. *They released the problem, so the answer could come.* When they felt overwhelmed with information or frustrated, they would abandon the project for a while and take a break. Each had a special method for relinquishing the task by focusing his or her mind on something else, totally unrelated. Some would take long walks and enjoy the scenery while others would take a nap, read a story, work on another project, take a boat ride, etc. Whether they knew it or not, they were letting go and letting God do the work through the phenomenal power of Infinite Intelligence.

6. *They were given the solution and invention in a flash of inspiration.* Now the percolation could begin its marvelous process. When the subconscious was finished in some unexpected moment, in a flash of insight, intuition, and awareness the perfect solution was revealed to them, down to the smallest detail.

This Power Is Available to Every Person

Each inventor or genius found a way to tap into the secrets of the Universe. Allowing the universal creative intelligence and the power of their subconscious minds to work for them, they took their ideas into the marketplace and thrived mightily.

The Wondrous Capability of Your Subconscious Mind

The subconscious mind is the model for the computer. Enter everything you can find on a certain subject and give it a goal in the form of a request. It will, as computers do, give you the correct answer, using the knowledge it contains. Because our individual minds are part of a greater, universal mind, by adding prayer in our request we are given access to higher realms of knowledge, inspiration, and help way beyond what we could ever know or do on our own. What is known in one place is also known in all, given the fact that we are all swimming together in a sea of consciousness. Some stay within their own bubble of experience, and others know how to open up to virtually the whole ocean.

The Man Who Wrote Six Books at the Same Time

Isaac Azimov, the famous scientist and science fiction writer was able to write six books at one time using the "Incredible, Genius-Producing, Percolator Process." I don't know if he had read the same book as I had read or how he knew to use this system, but in reading about him and how he wrote books I was impressed with the similarities.

Whenever he felt dried up or frustrated with one book, he would leave that book and transfer to one of his other typewriters and write for a while on another book, etc. His subconscious would process or "percolate" and deliver the next chapter to him, one story after another, even when he wasn't consciously working on any of them. Of course he was well educated in his field of science. But he also knew the system of tapping into his subconscious mind and the universal mind.

Azimov didn't possess some special, unique-to-him-only quality that others cannot also develop. He had discovered how to use an ability that, in others, often remains dormant. A genius is someone, anyone, who knows how to tap into and access the knowledge of the universe and beyond.

Million-Dollar Idea

Sue was tired of being poor and having to struggle to make ends meet. One evening after reading about the marvelous capabilities of her subconscious mind, she decided to try it out. Her request was for Infinite Intelligence to give her an idea and plan for a product she could produce that would give her and her husband millions of dollars in revenue. Following the steps of the percolator process, she was delighted when in a couple of days she was awakened from her afternoon nap with the idea clearly in mind. Something as simple as a large brass key chain made them millions of dollars, just as Sue had requested.

Opening the Door to the Temple of Wisdom

People who have activated their Spiritual Intelligence are able to communicate with Infinite Intelligence through the creative imagination of their subconscious mind. These people have turned themselves into "receiving sets" through which ideas, thoughts, and plans literally flash into their minds. Some call these flashes intuition, others, illumination or inspiration.

One is only able to access this ability through prayer, meditation, and a sufficient amount of mind control—just as knowledge of God is only made available from God and given to a person with strong faith.

There Are Laws Beyond the Physical

We all believe that Mother Nature never deviates from the established laws of the universe. We can count on gravity working, as this is a law of the universe, but there are actually times when even gravity can be altered by an act of divine intervention.

Here I was standing at the very top of an ancient Mayan Temple in Telum, Mexico, on the Yucatan coast. The steps of the temple were extremely steep, and one had to pay attention to keep from falling. Ready to go back down, I felt overly confident and decided to skip down the almost straight-up-and-down stairs. Right away I tripped and found myself falling headfirst down the side of the temple to an almost certain horrible, if not fatal, accident. "No!" I cried out in my mind. "I am not falling! Please help me, God!" Staying conscious I pulled myself up as high as I could, and then in a moment I found myself in another dimension.

Gravity had altered its laws for a few seconds. Everything was now in slow motion and one second became ten, giving me enough time to straighten my body into an upright position. I was sure I was experiencing levitation, which was only possible through the help of the unseen power. Finally time and gravity returned to normal, as I set foot on the step below right where I had been. I had only bruised the bottom of my foot from the pressure of the fall, and that was all. Finding it very difficult to walk, I wondered how I was going to make the one-mile hike back to the car. Just as I arrived at the bottom of the temple, a young man rode up on a bicycle. He agreed to take me to the car.

This ancient temple was in the middle of the jungle and there were no people or villages to been seen, but right at the exact right moment Infinite Intelligence brought everything together at the right time, even altering gravity, because it was necessary. Here's one more interesting bit of information: Legend, as I was told later on, warned of the dangers of taking pieces of the temple. Right before I tripped I had picked up a small piece of the temple to take home as a souvenir. As soon as I heard the legend, not because I am superstitious, but because I know to respect the ideals, religious rights and beliefs of others, I took the stone back to where I had found it. There is more going on than only that which we can see, hear, taste, touch, and smell, and I honor the unseen even more than that which we can see.

Unseen Protection

By placing a demand on Infinite Intelligence we can also be warned of impending dangers, alerted to advantageous opportunities, and reminded of what we need to know and do at exactly the right time. Soon after I had read about these powers I put the system to work. I instructed Infinite Intelligence to guard and protect me at all times, warn me of any problems, and get me out of danger should something unforeseen occur.

One afternoon my friend Lynn and I were having a picnic in an isolated part of a community park. We chose this spot because it was quiet so that we could discuss some projects we were working on for the church. I felt a negative presence behind me, and immediately I turned around to see two unsavory-looking men approaching us. "Lynn, get in the car, right now," I demanded. "Why, what's the matter?" she replied in her slow southern drawl. "Don't ask questions. Just get in the car. We are leaving, now," I pleaded. Jumping in and closing the door, I turned on the ignition, put the car in gear, and drove away, as the two men lunged for the car doors. After this I always paid attention to these kinds of warnings rather than thinking "Oh well, this is just my imagination."

Why not use invisible protection because it is available to everyone if they will ask and then listen and follow the guidance? We live and move and have our being in an ocean of pure love and consciousness. Available within this ocean of knowledge, energy, bliss, and love is everything we could ever possibly need or desire. How much and exactly what we are given depends entirely upon what we request, accept, and use.

My eyes were being opened to literally infinite possibilities. Beethoven was deaf, yet he composed the most magnificent music because he heard the music, not from his own imagination, but from the celestial music of the spheres.

There Is Perfect Order

The Presence, Power, Love, and Intelligence of God permeates every atom and is the life force that transforms an acorn into a huge oak tree in perfect divine order. This same intelligence directs the rain to fall and the water to be lifted once again to the heavens, only to fall again in a perfect cycle of giving and receiving. Night always follows the day, just as spring always comes after winter. This same intelligence is working in us and through us and it can, through the Universal Principles of Successful Living, be moved to help in converting our heartfelt desires into concrete forms.

Creating My Seminar and Motivation Business Out of Nothing

Over the years this percolator process method of tapping into the creative and problem-solving power of Infinite Intelligence continues to be the single most useful information I ever received on the subject of creativity. This process and method of accessing knowledge, answers, solutions, inspiration, help, and levels of God consciousness has been my companion and ever-ready friend in every possible kind of situation. "Ask and ye shall receive" is the truth on all levels.

Having personally experienced the creative power of Infinite Intelligence as it had given me a winning pancake recipe, guided me to the perfect book and teacher at the right time, protected me, and solved my problems, I decided to call upon it again and again, because the process worked.

State your problem, and it can be any simple problem such as "I cannot find my car keys, and I want to find them right now." This is a wonderful process for business. State the problem, such as "I am going into an important meeting and I want them to buy my ideas and product." Now ask Infinite Intelligence to help you solve your problem.

You can solve complex problems such as "How do I become president of my country, heal an illness, know God, mend my marriage, or get a multimillion-dollar idea for a product or service?"

This is a type of prayer, of course, but it is the kind of prayer—or rather communication process—that activates our own natural ability to access the wisdom of the ages and universal knowledge. God has given us natural abilities and intelligence. Too often we do not use what He has given us. Making the most out of all you've got is the intelligent thing to do, and those who use this power are applauded and rewarded abundantly for their brilliance.

This process is the right use of our intelligence. It gives us access to the resources and knowledge of our own subconscious mind, the knowledge of others, and the rich treasures of Infinite Intelligence. Infinite Intelligence gives us access to knowledge beyond what is known in the world at the present time.

All knowledge, ideas, inventions, and solutions exist eternally at some level of cosmic intelligence, but it isn't until there is a need and demand for a particular piece of knowledge that it will precipitate through the dimensions and into this world to a willing and qualified receiver.

Those who know how to use this process operate from their higher Spiritual Intelligence and are able to remain connected and in communication at all times.

Solving My Problem and Creating a Successful Class

State the problem. My problem or challenge was to create and fill my classes and to be a successful motivational speaker and minister.

I had never created, taught, or promoted a seminar or a class before, but I knew that others had and that I could draw from their experience and knowledge and also tap into Infinite Intelligence. So many people believe

---

State Your Problem or Challenge

My problem or challenge is:

they cannot do something merely because they have never done it before. My answer is "There is always a first time for everything and the knowledge exists somewhere, and because it exists I can get it."

Writing a Book by This Wonderful Process

Years later when I decided to write my first book, *What You Think of Me is None of My Business,* I didn't know how to write a book, as I had little if any experience as a writer. What I did know was that others had written books and I could draw from their experience. I was certain that God knew how to write a best-selling book that would be helpful to others. I had faith that God, as Infinite Intelligence, would write through me and make the appropriate arrangements for the book to be completed and sold throughout the world.

I had had the title for six years, but no book. It dawned on me that the only way to have a book was to write it, word for word. Deciding to use a combination of the Five Steps of Prayer, visualization, and the percolator process, I began by stating my problem. My problem: I wanted to have a best-selling book that would help millions of people to be victorious over their life's challenges. Also, I wanted the publisher to come to me and offer me a deal, as I did not want to go to New York and pound the pavement in hopes of getting a publisher.

Sitting down in my meditation place and getting quiet, I centered on God within my heart. After saying my prayer with intense desire, I visualized myself autographing books in bookstores. Everything happened just as I had requested and visualized. The unseen hand of God through the supernatural power of Infinite Intelligence arranged everything perfectly in the right time and in the right way. All I had to do was my part and then witness what I call the miracle take place.

Creating My Ideal Class

Clarity is power. We have to know what we want before we can give clear direction to Infinite Intelligence. Taking step one on my "Treasure Map," I spent some time figuring out exactly what I desired to create and achieve. I had purchased a notebook, and in it I wrote my purpose and the desired goals for my four-week class.

I. My Purpose:

to provide the opportunity for each participant to learn the principles of successful living and thus achieve her heart's desires

II. My Goals and Desired Results:

1. The room is full of women who are enjoying the class and getting great value.
2. All the women who are participating achieve their goals and improve the quality of their lives and those of their family members.
3. The class members sign up for more classes with me and bring their friends to class.
4. I am teaching and speaking throughout Southern California, the nation, and the world.
5. Money is coming to me in ever-increasing amounts from my ongoing classes and lectures as well as from expected and unexpected avenues.
6. I am one of the top motivational and inspirational speakers in the world, drawing huge speaker's fees because what I have to offer is so valuable.
7. All this work leads to my being a successful minister.

Applying the second step on my treasure map, I sat down in my "quiet place," closed my eyes, and, in prayer, asked God for His Infinite Intelligence, guidance, and direction to come through me and help me to create the class and fill it with students.

MY PRAYER WAS
"I know that You, God, are with every person and You are with me. Even though I have never created a class, I know You know everything. Therefore, you know what I should teach. Please guide me in preparing the class material. I ask and know in faith, believing that the women who can get value from my class will hear or read about it and attend. I ask for this all to transpire in perfect order for the highest good of all. Thank you, God, and so let it be. Amen."

Knowledge of What Is Wanted and Needed

"Find a problem, then look for a solution. Don't develop a solution, then spend your life searching for a problem for it. Pull through an idea from the marketplace; don't push it through from inception toward some intangible market." This is a quote by Jack Ryan, the inventor of the Barbie Doll and the Hawk missile. Jack owned more patents at the time of his death than any other person in the United States.

One of the Topmost Secrets of Wealth

I had read that helping others to get what they want is the secret of success in business, so I asked myself, "What do women want and need?" Women complained about their husbands and wanted to have happier marriages. Mothers desired to help their children overcome the abuse of other children and to be happier and more successful in school and life. Every woman was hoping to increase the amount of money she was getting, and many wanted to have a more beautiful home. I also noticed that most women, even if they had everything, still wanted more.

Fear, stress, and worry were high on the list of "don't wants." "How can I cope with everything that's going on around me?" "What could I do to eliminate stress and be more peaceful?" were the questions of many I interviewed.

Almost every woman wanted to lose weight, exercise more, and be beautiful and desirable to her mate or men in general. "I want to have meaningful work and help others to have better lives" was the heartfelt desire of a few. Some said, "I want to own my own business, be extremely successful, and make and control a huge fortune." Basically every woman was seeking happiness, love, and wealth and to also make a difference in the lives of others, especially their families. I could relate, for their desires were mine and their suffering had also been mine.

Success mantra: **"My classes are full to overflowing with students. The popularity of my classes is growing daily. My success is guaranteed in every way and I am confident."**

> ### Market Research
>
> What are the needs, wants, desires, and problems of your clients, customers, or family? Before you can help others to get what they want, you need to *know* what they want so you can direct your products, services, and advertising directly to meeting their needs.
>
> 1.
> 2.
> 3.
> 4.
> 5.
> 6.

Sixty women attended my first class, to my great surprise. I was so overwhelmed that I stayed in the kitchen at the YMCA for a few extra minutes, before daring to walk out and address the group. I wore my best dress, checked my makeup in the mirror, and got ready to face the test. "Confidence" was the topic of my first class. Now was my chance to practice what I was going to be teaching.

Repeating my success mantra over and over to myself to stop my mind from defeating me, breathing deeply, and praying, I turned the results over to God and walked out confidently to teach my first class, as if I were an expert.

Success mantra: "God is the perfect teacher of this class, and I am His instrument. God is teaching through me and giving each woman exactly what she needs. Thank you, God. And so it is."

Women from every walk of life and age group had enrolled in my class. Even though we had vast differences, we had yet more in common. To start with, every person in the class had a woman's body, so we understood what each had been through.

It was as if these women were my children to guide and console, and also my dearest friends with whom we could celebrate our victories. I was their guide and cheerleader. Some of these women were battered wives or widows. Others were happily married, and a few were single. Each class had a couple of lonely seniors who wanted to grow spiritually, find some happiness, heal an ailment, and make some extra cash.

Still others were ambitious and passionate like me. Many wanted to know their life's work and achieve profit, distinction, and adoration, while making a positive difference in the lives of others.

Each woman was interested in having an abundance of money, love, happiness, inner peace, and good fortune. Yes, I had something they could use to get what they wanted.

PEARL

Good fortune is more than money. It is a state of mind, an attitude of possibilities beyond having or not having money and beyond one's past or current situation.

I taught them from the outset to abandon the belief that money was the only form of prosperity. Prosperity meant possibilities beyond a person's pocketbook, expectations, or prior experience. "Prosperity" is the concept of an unlimited abundance of love, inner peace, money, knowledge, energy, time, ideas, happiness, and intelligence. The abundance of knowledge I had received from my teachers through classes, books, and lectures had opened up the doors to a whole new and enormous world of opportunities. Seeking knowledge from those who had achieved what I wanted to achieve gave me the information I needed to also accomplish the same things and more.

Prosperity Is Everyone's Divine Right

My favorite topic, prosperity, was now to become my focus. I felt that a prosperity consciousness was essential for those who had a heartfelt desire and obsession to fulfill their mission and live as God intended them to live. To me, prosperity meant absolute trust and faith in God as one's perfect protector, provider, partner, and friend. During this time of study and preparation for my life's work, I had become even more committed to sharing these life-transforming principles with as many people as I possibly could. People struggle and do without not because they can't do anything else, but because they are not aware of their possibilities. I had found my niche where I could be of service and prosper at the same time. Thank you, God.

Chapter Six

Step Four, Do What Works, and Don't Do What Doesn't

"If you have built castles in the air, your work
need not be lost; that is where they should
be. Now put the foundations under them."

—*Henry David Thoreau*

PEARL

*With a goal in mind, do what must be done in each moment, and
you will reach your destination.*

You Were Born to Prosper

Raise your hand if you would like to have more love, money, happiness, peace of mind, and self-expression" were my opening remarks to my very first class. All hands were raised, and some raised both hands. Cheering them on, I continued, "It's time to say good-bye to poverty, fear, distress, and worry and hello to prosperity, happiness, and love. Do you agree?" "Yes!" they shouted. What a thrill! I had a roomful of women who were enthusiastic and gung-ho. I challenged them again when I said, "Are you ready to dump poverty and imitation and accept prosperity, as your Divine right?" In one unanimous voice they yelled, "Yes!" These were my kind of people and I was in my right place, doing my life's work.

I paused a moment and silently sent my gratitude to God for answering my prayers and giving me this most wonderful opportunity.

It's Perfectly Right for You to Prosper

"Prosperity is the basis of life" were the first words of my lecture. Enthusiastically I explained, "Everywhere we look in God's creation we see beauty, opulence, abundance, magnificence, majesty, and perfect order. Human beings can live abundantly or they can trash what God has given them and turn a sweet dream into a nightmare. There are two fundamental realities; one is true and the other is false.

The true one is based on love and abundance. The false reality is based on a lie and the belief in scarcity, poverty, and separation from God. Those who separate themselves out of arrogance or ignorance must live a life of struggle, worry, strife, fear, and emotional desolation.

Those who recognize their eternal connection and oneness with God have a prosperity consciousness. Regardless of appearances, past experience, age, sex, nationality, education, color, religion, or current situation, they are certain of their connection with God, and they will always have what they need.

Prosperity-minded people are absolutely confident and positive that there is an eternal wellspring of every good and wonderful thing, idea, and experience residing within them, as the Super Soul. They know that the invisible is the creator of the visible and when they need something they go to the storehouse of all riches and treasures, God within.

Move Out of Scare City and into the Land of Plenty

Yes, it is just this simple! Because we have been led to believe that what we want we cannot get or if we get it we can lose it, most of us live in fear in the City of Scare. The word *scarce* has the sound of scare in it. A person in fear or Scare-city is like a small, frightened deer running here and there in a forest that is on fire not knowing where to hide for protection. The only medicine that can get rid of worry for good is trust in God. "In God we trust" is the motto printed on our money. Notice that our motto is not "In money we trust," or "In government we trust," or even "In others we trust."

What Is Prosperity?

We are prosperous to the degree that we are conscious of our connection with a Higher Principle of Infinite power and possibilities. One who honors his or her eternal connection experiences a continual supply of love, happiness, inner peace, plenty, career satisfaction, good health, compassion, and enthusiasm. True wealth comes from knowing that you are a beloved child of God and that it is your Father's good pleasure to give you the kingdom.

Dispel the Lie That It's Spiritual and Virtuous to Be Poor

Throughout my years of teaching I gave my students everything that I was learning and applying, and they ate it up. They especially appreciated the knowledge that God did not want them to be poor or miserable. Many had come from fundamentalist religions where they were taught about an angry God who caused people to suffer.

The truth is, we bring about our own troubles when we do that which carries with it unwanted reactions. If we run out into the oncoming traffic, it is more than likely that a car will hit us. But this is not God's fault or anyone else's; it's our own. Everyone has the gift of free will and the freedom of choice. Failure to understand and correctly use this law excuses no one, including children. Each person will suffer or rejoice depending upon his or her consciousness and actions. This is what needs to be taught in school, but for some reason the masses are never taught what can really help them to succeed.

Poverty Is Degrading to the Soul

While I was teaching others the principles of prosperity, happiness, and successful living, I was learning and applying them. Just like most people, I had some beliefs that were founded in lack and limitation that I needed to dump. Every spiritual book I read and class I took was teaching the same knowledge. Through the process of repetition, I was able to build a consciousness of prosperity: one of limitless possibilities.

Repetition is a most valuable tool for learning anything, because one of our greatest handicaps is doubt. All the holy books of the world are for one purpose, and that is to eliminate doubt about the existence of God and to give us the steps we must take in order to reach our spiritual and material goals and objectives.

Poverty is a habit because it has been practiced generation upon generation. Those who are born into wealth are taught the principles of prosperity, so it seems as if wealth is natural to them, but it is still a habit that anyone can learn.

Poverty is a type of hell caused by man and woman's ignorance of God's laws and the Principles of Successful Living. Each of these exact laws and principles exists for the specific purpose of bringing intelligence, prosperity, love, health, beauty, strength, and happiness to each and every one of the Lord's beloved children. No one can force us to do that which is for our own good, and no one can deny us the treasures and riches we are seeking if we claim them.

A poverty consciousness is the cause of every kind of misfortune. Some religions have made poverty a virtue, but this has robbed people of their right to know that God will care for and maintain them when they do their part. Keeping people in fear and ignorance is a powerful way of controlling their minds, actions, and purses.

Prosperity has its roots in reciprocation, and poverty has its roots in miserliness. Surprisingly, many who are financially rich have a poverty consciousness, and no matter how much they have they are still afraid, untrusting, greedy, and stressed. In their mind there is never enough, for they have never solved the problem: lack of faith and trust in a Higher Power. True prosperity brings with it a peaceful mind and a deep and abiding faith in God and their own sufficiency. "I am enough" and "I always have enough" are two powerful success mantras.

Mike Todd, the movie producer who was married to Elizabeth Taylor, was asked if he had ever been poor. He replied, "No I have never been poor, but I have been broke. Poverty is a state of mind and broke is a temporary situation."

The lie of poverty fills jails with men and women who are seeking to get what they need and desire from everywhere except from where it really is, within. No, money is not literally stored within, but you could say that the golden energy of money and wealth is stored within one's awareness in the form of one's beliefs, desires, intelligence, and habits of thinking, feeling and behaving.

The Qualities of Consciousness

As one's body is a manifestation of one's consciousness, so is everything else in the personal world a manifestation of one's consciousness. Change your consciousness and awareness, and everything in your outer world will also change.

Judy's House

Judy was a friend of mine who had the heart of an angel, but when it came to housekeeping her consciousness lived in the city dump. Each time I visited her I would refuse anything she offered me to eat or drink, including coffee, as her kitchen was extremely dirty. Thinking perhaps the reason why everything was so dirty was that she didn't have nice furnishings, I went around to friends and collected some lovely things for her home. Judy was very appreciative. Sounds as though I was interfering and perhaps I was, but she was a cousin and we had always been close.

I helped her place the new things in her home. At the end of the day her home had been transformed into a lovely cottage. The next time I came to visit, I was shocked. All the new things looked exactly like all the old and unclean things she had before. This was a good lesson, as consciousness is superior to matter. A person's consciousness will always determine his or her conditions and surroundings. Unless the consciousness changes, no matter what anyone else does for that person, everything will remain the same. I decided to just love her as she was, but still not eat at her house.

Harvey Couldn't Do Enough for His Son

Harvey's mother had been the strongest influence in his life, since his father had passed away when Harvey was a young boy. Harvey was taught to work hard, do community service, and strive to reach his goals. He had been an honor student in school and went on to be a respected lawyer. Harvey's problem was his son. Because Harvey wanted to give his son everything he himself had never had as a young boy, he lavished gifts on his son and protected him from the challenges of life.

His son got into trouble early on in school. This pattern continued way past high school. Every time, Harvey was there to bail him out of jail and pay the bills. He never let his son suffer the consequences of his own actions. Instead of his son being appreciative or showing any kind of love and respect to his father, he was cruel, angry, lazy, and discourteous.

The most difficult decision Harvey would ever have to make was the one to release his son and let him live his own life and reap the good or bad results of his own actions. The one thing that Harvey had neglected to understand was that the reason he had grown into such a successful, wealthy, and respected man was that, through the love and wisdom of his mother, he had had to earn his every advantage.

Within time Harvey's son began to make some advancement, but it took awhile for he had to make his own way through the real-life school of hard knocks, having to pay for his every mistake. Within time, though, he was ready to learn and apply the principles of successful living.

Harvey knew that God was his opulent source of infinite supply, but his son believed that his biological father was his source; he wasn't, but God the Father was and is.

The Principle of Attraction

Unless people willingly change their consciousness, it is business as usual. Through the magnetic quality of consciousness they will continue to draw to them the same circumstances over and over until they change their mind and behavior.

Through the law of attraction we can all draw to ourselves the most desirable people, things, and circumstances by creating the right mentality, force field, and mental equivalents. In essence, develop the attitude, habits, and actions that are appropriate for who and what you desire to be, and you will be able to achieve your goals and live your dreams. By creating a shield of discernment, we are able to accept the favorable and reject the unfavorable.

What We Can Do to Experience Greater Prosperity

My students were hungry for the truth of what exactly they could do to prosper in every area of their lives. I would tell them, "Anyone can prosper by following the laws of prosperity. The laws of prosperity are the primary laws of life. The Supreme Being created them for the very purpose of providing for our every need and heartfelt, well-intended desire. These laws apply not only to money and tangible things but also to love, satisfaction, health, joy, and all the invisible treasures.

This Is a World of Action

It's simple! Do you want more love? If you do, then *do* that which will increase your love and do *not* do that which will decrease love. Do you want to be a happier person, perhaps even blissful? Do you want and need more money? Do you desire to travel to exotic lands, but have a limited income? Whatever your need and desire, the system is the same.

I gave them the three basics steps of the system of progress, which I had been using with great success. **1. Do what works. 2. Don't do what doesn't work. 3. Gather knowledge of whatever else works and do that.**

Do What Makes You Happy, Loved, and Wealthy, and Avoid the Rest

Doing *only* what makes you happy, successful, and wealthy, and not doing what makes you miserable, unsuccessful, and poor is the fourth step on the treasure map. I know this seems obvious, but very few pay attention to the obvious. This is why "common sense" is not common. God is present within us all and acting as our conscience, but we have to pay attention and follow our guidance. Our problem is that we want to do what we want to do when we want to do it, and it takes a wise person to question his or her desires to make sure they are in his or her best interest.

The key here is that if you want the best life possible, it is up to you to be responsible for getting it. Whatever action one takes causes a reaction to take place. If you want the best, you will need to *do* that which is in your ultimate best interest.

"Why would anyone do something that wasn't in his or her best interest?" was a question someone would always ask. To explain I would share the story of the tight shoes.

Shoes Too Tight?

For years, buying shoes that were too small was a foolish habit of mine. I'd try to wear the shoes, but because they were so painfully uncomfortable,

I'd take them off and go barefoot. Eventually I would give the practically unworn shoes away to a friend.

It finally dawned on me to buy shoes that fit and were comfortable. When I stopped doing what didn't work and started doing what did, I saved money and eliminated my suffering. You might be thinking, "Why would you have ever purchased shoes that were too tight?" This bad habit started when I was a child. My grandmother took me shopping to buy a pair of black patent-leather party shoes, but they didn't have my exact size. That day we walked empty-handed out of the only shoe store in town.

Nanny forgot about the shoes and we didn't go shopping again that season, but I didn't forget. The pattern was set. After that, even if the shoes were too small, I'd get the ones I liked. Finally, the error of my ways dawned on me. I had established a belief based on scarcity and fear. Stored in my subconscious mind was the memory of my disappointment. No one likes to be disappointed. I had made a decision to avoid disappointment. This is how it works. We work to protect ourselves from pain and to gain pleasure.

My solution to avoid the pain of disappointment was to buy the shoes I really liked, even if they were too tight. Most people are still making present-time, adult decisions based on incidents that happened in childhood.

People do this all the time when it comes to choosing a mate, taking a job, renting or buying a house, taking a trip, or planning a life. Out of the belief that there is not enough, the belief in scarcity, a person will take whatever presents itself, even if it is wrong, foolish, and perhaps even dangerous.

Those who have developed a prosperity consciousness simply choose that which is in their best interest. This is the right thing to do.

The Laws of Prosperity

Prosperity has two main aspects: giving and receiving. Both giving and receiving must be fully operational for love to flow.

My students were always enthusiastic about learning the Laws of Prosperity. I would hand them a list of the Ten Laws and go over each one. "Keep this in mind," I said. "Knowledge has two aspects: consciousness and action. The purpose of knowledge is to know what to do that works and what to avoid because it doesn't work."

1. The Law of Desire
2. The Law of Abundance
3. The Law of Acceptance
4. The Law of Good Fortune
5. The Law of Tithing
6. The Law of Exchange
7. The Law of Love
8. The Law of Communication
9. The Law of Appreciation
10. The Law of Investing

The Law of Desire

Desire is always the first step, for it is up to each person to decide what she or he wants to obtain and achieve. No one can do this for another. A desire is different from a wish: wishes are hopes without a plan to make them come true.

Albert Was Passionate about Prospering

Born in a poor family, Albert had had few advantages. Tired of being poor, he was determined to prosper and have all the advantages that rich people had. Being spiritually inclined and the son of a Baptist preacher, Albert wanted to prosper by doing good works. He spent his free time reading books and taking seminars on positive thinking, success, and prosperity.

Something Albert had that others who were also attending these same seminars did not was his strong commitment to applying everything he was learning. Besides being a listener, he was a man of action even to the point of tithing 10 percent of his time, talent, and money to where he was getting his spiritual knowledge and support. Religiously he applied everything that was supposed to work, and it paid off.

In time he found a partner who was also committed to living a God-filled and prosperous life, and the two of them worked together. First they would build one business and find competent people to run it, then start and operate another business until it too was successful. They had found their system, which they used over and over and built an empire. Owning many businesses, properties, and investments, they both prospered beyond their fondest dreams. Daily they would remind each other that all they had really belonged to God and they were God's grateful caretakers.

Prosperity Action Item #1

Write down your desires in a special book. Make a plan having to do with what you can do to achieve each of your desires. Read your list over each day in the morning and evening. Follow your plans. Every day do at least one thing that will help you to achieve your goals and desires.

Make a plan to achieve your most heartfelt desires.

What is your ideal finished result? My ideal result is:

Write five actions you can take that will produce the result you desire.
1.
2.
3.
4.
5.

Brainstorm

On a separate piece of paper brainstorm using the percolator process and list thirty things you could do that could possibly bring you the desired result. This will stimulate your subconscious and assist you in tapping into Infinite Intelligence. Let the ideas flow even if some seem foolish or impossible. Act on the ones that seem most right.

The Law of Abundance

Recognizing the limitless bounty and goodness of God's creation is the premise of the Law of Abundance. Everywhere we look we see abundance. The Spirit is absolutely without boundaries, and everywhere there is endless variety. Spirit is the essence of life, as well as the Intelligence that is guiding and directing the course of the stars. Abundance is really the outpouring of the Infinite All-Giving Spirit of Love. "The Lord is my Shepherd, I shall not want" is the opening statement of the Twenty-third Psalm, which promises that all our needs will be met.

To believe that we please the Supreme Being by living in unhappiness and lack is to deny the abundant life, which Jesus spoke of when he said, "I have come that they might have life, and that they might have it more abundantly."

If we would pray and prosper, we must believe that the Spirit is both willing and able to give the gift from the wellspring of infinite potential and the unlimited wealth of possibilities. Do not try to place limitations on what God can do. Always know that with God all things are truly possible. Because the Spirit can give us only what we can take, we must convince ourselves to believe and accept that our desires can and will be fulfilled regardless of appearances to the contrary. Train yourself to know this truth as a basic operating principle that many call "principle."

The world of things and the world of our affairs are merely the out-picturing of yesterday's thoughts, desires, and actions. For new conditions, start with new ideas and ideals and place no limitation on Spirit.

Joyce Chose Prosperity

Joyce was a primary school teacher, but she was unhappy with the public schools' system of teaching and working with the children. As a teacher she felt stifled, for she had to conform to a system that was devoid of spirituality and didn't foster the true creativity and genius of the children. Her dream was a school that was spiritually based and taught the principles of successful living and creativity right along with reading, writing, and math. She didn't have the money to start her own school, and she needed the job she had to pay her bills. What to do? Praying to God over and over, she asked that a door be opened for her to step into her ideal work and make a difference in the education of many children. Instead of believing it couldn't be done, she believed it could.

Talking with her minister one morning after church, she shared her idea for a school. Immediately the minister, who had also been thinking along the same lines, invited her to present her ideas to the church board of trustees. Joyce did her homework and prepared a plan, including how much it would cost. The board agreed and Joyce became the principal and teacher of a spiritually based school, just as she had desired.

Prosperity Action Item #2

Observe the Abundance

1. Look at the abundance of stars in the sky. If the sky is not clear get a video on the universe and see the abundance of life that is everywhere.
2. Notice all the leaves on the trees and how many creatures great and small, seen and unseen there are in only one acre of land.
3. Drive through a wealthy neighborhood and realize the people who live in these houses are just like you. They are drawing their ideas, energy, and Creativity from the same source as you, Divine Intelligence
4. Notice the similarities in all people. Where is the love coming from?
5. Read from the scriptures or from your favorite spiritual books every morning as soon as you get up and every evening before sleep. This activity will place your mind upon the limitless potential of Spirit.

Don't Buy the Lie of Scarcity

If Joyce had believed the lie of scarcity, she would have never even thought it possible for her to have her school. The belief in scarcity bars the door of opportunity, whereas the belief in prosperity swings it wide.

Those who know that God is their limitless, forgiving, and giving Source and supply live in harmony, peace, prosperity, and love. The choice is ours. This does not mean that we must work to accumulate a great fortune, but we can if we so desire. A person of inner wealth may choose to live simply, free of worry, anxiety, or money problems.

The Law of Acceptance

Accept Your Good

One of the first questions I asked all my students was "Are you really willing to prosper and be happy, loved, and successful? Of course everyone said, "Yes." The truth of the matter is, if we are really willing to prosper and be happy, we will be.

Sharing with them the immense importance of the subconscious mind, I said, "Stored within the memory banks of our subconscious mind are many emotional decisions that become etched-in-stone beliefs. Beliefs control and bring forth our thoughts. Thoughts and words have a vibration and this vibration attracts people, conditions, and things at that same frequency. Thoughts cause us to act, and actions produce results. That's how it works. Some of what we have stored in our memory bank is working against us and destroying our chances to live happily and abundantly.

"We need to recognize and pull out the unwanted and self-defeating weeds in the subconscious, much as the gardener pulls out weeds and cultivates the soil to make it ready to receive and nurture new seeds. Our thoughts and desires are our seeds. If we have new ideas, thoughts, and desires we would like to manifest, we must prepare the soil of the subconscious mind to accept these new ideas and nurture them to fruition."

Preparing Yourself to Prosper and Flourish

The subconscious is like a giant iceberg with the majority of it, over four-fifths, being beneath the sea and out of sight. The sinking of the *Titanic* came about because of the four-fifths of the iceberg that could not be seen. Subconscious sabotage sinks people's dreams all the time, and they do not even know why. Many good people who have every right to have happy marriages, beautiful homes, and satisfying and fulfilling careers don't, only because something within them is sinking their ship.

I strongly suggested that my students take some time and analyze the contents of their subconscious minds. When they found a thought or belief that was working against them, they were encouraged to root it out with logic by seeing the lie of poverty and then reprogramming their subconscious with the desired belief using the tool of a success mantra. Repeating these new concepts over and over with feeling made a positive impression on the subconscious, which changed their thinking, feelings, and results. Repetition is very important when it comes to learning.

Prosperity Action Item # 3

Q. & A. with Your Subconscious Mind

Filling in the blanks on my questionnaire gave my students an idea of what was hidden within their subconscious minds. Successful people analyze themselves, not to beat themselves up over their flaws or faults or even to blame those who perhaps hurt them, but to know their strengths and weaknesses. Pogo, the comic strip philosopher, said, "We have met the enemy and it is us." The purpose of the questionnaire is to act as a beacon of light shining into the recesses of one's memory bank. With the light of awareness we can observe obstacles and dangers and get rid of what we don't want or need for good.

Once we have reached agreement on the conscious and subconscious levels of awareness, there is smooth sailing toward the achievement of our goals and the fulfillment of our dreams. Personal alignment is the end of self-sabotage.

Questionnaire

(Be very honest and write down the first thing that comes to your mind.)

1. Money is _____.
2. My parents believe that money is _____.
3. I believe that having large sums of money will _____.
4. It is _____ for me to have great sums of money, because _____.
5. With a continuous flow of great sums of money into my bank accounts I will _____.
6. If I have a lot of money, I will _____.
7. My number-one fear in receiving all the money I need to do my projects and attain my goals is _____.
8. I have been withholding my goods and services because _____ _____.
9. The more I succeed in my work, the _____.

10. If I am true to myself and follow my inner guidance, then _____
_____.

11. As my wealth and success in my work increase, my mother and father will _____.

12. As I do my life's work whom do I fear and what do I believe they can do to me? I fear _____ because they can, will, or might possibly _____.

13. What do I need to know in order for me to be fearless and committed to my work 100 percent? I need to know that _____
_____.

14. What will it cost me if I do not do my life's work and fulfill my mission? It will cost me _____.

15. What is your commitment to yourself? My commitment to myself is
_____.

16. Not having large sums of money and wealth protects me from
_____.

17. My number-one regret about money is _____.

18. (Write your own.)

Some of my students were stunned, as they had no idea of the beliefs and fears that were lurking beneath the surface of their conscious minds. Each reprogrammed his or her receptive subconscious mind with the affirmations, concepts, beliefs, and "Success Mantras" that supported their new ideals and values. This takes some time, but they had tools, and they were resolute.

With this strategy, whatever it was that each desired to be, do, or have, they first looked to see their subconscious operating principle having to do with that subject. If it were counterproductive, they would take it out using logic based on "principle"—remember that that means infinite and limitless supply—and create the belief they desired to accept.

Furthermore, each felt free to accept the idea that he or she was already rich, beautiful, intelligent, and successful. Someone would invariably ask, "Isn't it lying when we recite these success mantras such as 'I am already successful' when we really are not?"

Responding, I would reply, "The subconscious mind cannot tell the difference between something you have actually done and something you are pretending you have done. You are not lying, just accepting the ideal of what is possible and the fundamental truth about you. Say you want to lose weight. It does not work to keep thinking of your body as overweight. Thinking of your body as slender is a much better idea.

Believing yourself to have a slender body will cause you to behave as a slender person. You will eat as a slender person eats and you will move and exercise as a slender person. Study a few slender people and use them as mentors. Act as they do and you, too, will have a slender body. This ends the mystery of how to get where you want to be: be there first.

See Yourself As You Desire to Be, and You Will Be

Everyone is seeking love and happiness, and love is even more important than happiness. Love and happiness do not originate outside a person. Happiness and love are who we are. "Don't expect others to make you feel beautiful. Feel beautiful and radiate your beauty," I coached. "Know you are already a beautiful person and work to see the beauty in others, and others will see you as beautiful" was the lesson.

Beauty Is Within

Lucy was an older woman who had been chosen for a part in one of the college plays in which I had the leading role. Lucy was physically unattractive—so much so that at first I stayed away from her. Within a few nights of rehearsal, however, she had drawn every actor and actress, including me, to her side because of her magnetic, loving, and fabulous personality. She was the life and soul of our theater group and was never alone, not even for minute. Happily married to a very handsome, caring man, she had a life full of love because love and acceptance were what she was giving to everyone. I had never been in the presence of someone who was so accepting of others. Luck had given me one of the most important lessons of my life. I would think of her and this lesson many times to remind me that how I felt about myself was more important than whether or not I had a perfect, beautiful body. Real beauty is of the soul, and when we allow our beauty to shine, everyone sees us as beautiful.

So many of my students over the years loved this story, as many felt insecure about their physical appearance. I loved helping people to feel beautiful from within.

One More Big Question

There was one more question. It was a question that I had found to be the most valuable of all. This question helps us find our way to the root of the weed that has been choking off our self-expression and subsequent prosperity and fulfillment.

This question came to me when I was getting ready to commit to a major project. I felt there to be something inside my consciousness that was causing me to fear success and also failure. During prayer I asked, "What is holding me back and preventing me from using my talents and doing my work at the level I know to be possible?" This question came to me in a flash.

Question: What accumulated injuries do you have that make you shy away from people, avoid your life's work, withhold your goods and services, hide out, and keep you playing small, if at all?

My Answer

Closing my eyes, I concentrated on the question and asked my subconscious to reveal the answer to me. The following thoughts came rushing forward with intense emotion. I wrote the answers in my notebook.

Answer: People being angry, yelling at me, and blaming me for their problems. People criticizing, verbally and emotionally attacking me, being abusive and talking, ridiculing, and laughing at me behind my back were the first thoughts that came rushing out. It was as if I had opened up the gate of a dam and all these feelings came rushing out.

What a realization! I had been holding myself back from doing my work at my optimal level because I feared that others would cause me distress and pain. Now I knew my enemy, and it was I. Rejection, ridicule, or criticism from others has no power to cause us pain unless we give these people the power to hurt us. Unrealistic expectations and lack of knowledge of human nature set us up to be hurt. We are expecting others to do what we want and make us feel good, but things do not always turn out as we would like or expect.

Our work is to understand human nature and not allow ourselves to be controlled by the minds, words, and actions of others. There are two levels of human nature: the higher and the lower. Our higher nature and godlike qualities must be developed if we are to express them, and this takes both awareness and work. Ideally everyone would be expressing his or her god-

like qualities of love, compassion, forgiveness, honesty, kindness, and tolerance, but generally speaking this is not the case. If someone is unkind or
thoughtless, it has nothing to do with us. It is he or she who is lacking the
awareness of his or her higher nature. When an uncomfortable situation
arises, we have the opportunity to act from our higher nature rather than
to allow our lower nature to drag us down.

> "And when they see evil doing they make
> commandments and instruction, and sweet
> and loud singing, and all songs of praise."
> —*Gnostic scripture*

Hiding out and withholding our talents and gifts cannot prevent pain; it
only increases our dissatisfaction and sorrow because we know we have
something important to do and give and we aren't. Our work is to elevate
our minds and be enthusiastic and not fall victim to the fears and negativity of others.

Reprogramming Your Subconscious with "Mind-Talk"

Engaging in "mind-talk," I said, "Of course people ridicule, get angry, and
are rude, as that is the nature of those who are ignorant. So what! You cannot stop people from doing what they choose to do. Give up the idea that
you can get pleasure and avoid pain by gaining the approval of others.
Terry, go forth and do your life's work and leave others to do what they do.
Your real happiness lies, not in trying to avoid rejection, ridicule, and criticism, but in doing your work and living your vision." Once the subconscious mind is prepared and many of the weeds are gone, it is the perfect
time to accept the new ideas. Talking to the mind is a great way to change
your attitude by making your mind your friend and partner rather than an
enemy.

Jean's Husband Got a Great Job

As soon as I was prepared and ready for success, Jean, one of my students, asked if I could teach a night class so that more men, especially her
husband, Tom, could attend. Using the techniques I was teaching, he at-

tracted his perfect right work. He was named president of a major insurance company based in Dallas, Texas.

Tom was so impressed with my classes and what I was teaching that he insisted I come to Dallas and give a three-day seminar for the company executives and managers.

"Goal Setting and Personal Achievement" was the title I chose for my first corporate seminar. I prepared for it night and day for six weeks. This was not the YMCA. I was to be paid $1,500, plus all my expenses. Flying to Dallas I felt like a real businesswoman, and I liked it.

Fortunately my seminar was well received, and it marked the beginning of my corporate seminar business. I had taken a giant leap of faith by accepting this assignment. Preparing extensively for this one seminar catapulted me from YMCA teacher to corporate seminar leader and keynote speaker for Fortune 500 business banquets within just a few months. The work I was doing on my subconscious mind was paying off.

Success mantra: **"It is all right with me if people laugh, ridicule, talk behind my back, criticize, or reject me, for this has nothing to do with me and only to do with them."**

Success Mantras for Reprogramming the Subconscious Mind's Hard Drive

Conducting seminars for corporate America, I continued to teach the same principles I had been learning in church and in my precious books. My students all over the country were learning the value of affirmations and success mantras. It was amazing to me how few people even had a clue as to how their minds worked, let alone how life worked. A big part of my seminars and classes was the affirmation, or what I preferred to call the success mantra. Success mantras are positive statements that we can use to change our mind, belief system, attitudes, and actions and therefore get the results we want. I would invite my students to choose the success mantras most appropriate for them. "Say them out loud with feeling, as often as you can many times throughout the day. Repetition is very important when it comes to reprogramming your mental computer. Write them

down a few times each day, and this will also help you to accept them"
were my instructions.

> "I believe that having large sums of money is good for me."
>
> "The more money and resources I have, the more I can help others."
>
> "Money comes to me quickly and easily from expected and unexpected avenues."
>
> "Money is good."
>
> "Money is now flowing to me in abundant supply and filling up my bank accounts."
>
> "I am a money magnet."
>
> "People love giving me money in exchange for my wonderful and valuable products and services."
>
> "By helping others to be happy, prosperous, and successful I am also contributing to making the world a better place for everyone."
>
> "It is perfectly right for me to have money, fame, and power. I can use these gifts to serve God and others."
>
> "God wants me to use all my talents; that is why He gave them to me."
>
> "My responsibility is to live as I choose."
>
> "What others think and say about me is none of my business."

The Law of Good Fortune

Good things happen to those who are most positive. When I taught the Prosperity Law of Good Fortune, I would ask my students, "Are you ready to become very lucky?" The first thought in most people's minds is getting lucky and winning the lottery. Real good fortune goes beyond winning in gambling. It includes winning in life, and life is not a gamble or a game of chance. However you see life, life will be this way for you.

We have all heard the story of the half-empty and half-full glass. Some see the same glass of water as almost full and others will see is as almost empty. Even though the water is at the same mark, it really matters whether a person sees it as almost full or almost empty. Whether we see ourselves as fortunate and lucky or as unfortunate and cursed makes a huge difference in every way.

Someone would invariably ask, "But if you are really unlucky and bad things just seem to happen to you, wouldn't it be foolish to say you are fortunate?"

We attract and repel according to our state of mind and predominating beliefs and thoughts. Those who say they are always bumping into tables, chairs and things are always bumping into tables, chairs, and things. This is how it all works! If you want to be fortunate you must believe that you are and affirm that you are, and soon the conditions of your life will change to resonate with your new state of mind.

Another Shoe Story

The story goes that a shoe salesman was sent to Africa, as his new territory. The moment he stepped off the plane he became disappointed and dejected, so he called the head office and talked with his supervisor. "I can't stay here, for I will starve. No one is wearing any shoes, so they won't buy any. I am getting right back on the return flight and coming home." Off he flew. On the next flight the following day came another shoe salesperson. The moment she got off the plane, she became elated and extremely enthused. She had to call the home office to share her gratitude with her supervisor. "Thank you so much for sending me to Africa. Hardly anyone is wearing any shoes. I have the potential of selling shoes to every person, and I will become very rich."

Those with the attitude "I am lucky" have a general overall attitude of enthusiastic expectancy. "Just my luck. When my ship comes in, it will sink," say those with a poverty consciousness.

Bad luck follows those with a bad attitude, and good luck follows those who believe that they will succeed. The "Pollyanna approach to life" actually works. It is common knowledge that people who develop and maintain a positive mental attitude and who always look on the bright side are healthier, wealthier, happier, and more satisfied than those who don't.

Winning Prizes

Trying out this "I am fortunate" attitude at a women's luncheon, I visualized myself winning the beautiful and costly oil painting in the raffle. I saw myself knocking on the door of my friend JoAnn's house later that afternoon. When she opened the door I saw the painting sitting there on a bench and I heard her say, "Terry, you won the painting, just as you said you would." When this actually happened, you can imagine my delight. I had been certain it would happen and it did.

Use the following success mantras for good fortune.

"I am fortunate and lucky."
"Good things are happening to me."
"Everywhere I look I see opportunities for me to prosper."
"Everything is working out better than I expected."

Prosperity Action Item # 4

Work at developing and maintaining a positive attitude.

1. Expect that every good and wonderful thing is now flowing into your life.
2. See the blessings and gifts in every situation, and call everything good.
3. Think and speak positive and uplifting thoughts and words.
4. Say your success mantras every day many times. Write out your favorite ones and put them up around the house and office and in the car.
5. Never say, "I can't afford it." Instead say, "I don't choose to buy this at this time."
6. Play inspiriting and motivating audiotapes, CDs, and videos.
7. Talk only about those topics that are uplifting, inspiring, and conducive to prosperity.
8. Speak only with good purpose about others.

The Law of Tithing

GEM
*Giving and receiving make up the two parts
of the most fundamental law of life: reciprocity.*

The Secret to Unlocking the Doors to the Treasure House

Whenever I got the chance, I would tell the story of how I came to find out about this most miraculous law of tithing and how it was working for me as well as for others. Of course I did not teach this law to my corporate clients, but I did to my other students, as they were more spiritually inclined.

My Tithing Story

It all started on a Sunday as I was listening to the sermon. "Give a portion of what God has given you in the form of your time, money, talents, and resources, and God will return the gift to you tenfold or more" were the inspiring words of my minister. Listening to him this special Sunday I thought, "I may as well try this because if it works, this will be wonderful."

Little did I know at the time that this decision to give money, in addition to the service I was already giving to my church, would unlock the doors to the vast treasure house of spiritual and material riches.

All I had to my name that Sunday morning was fifty cents. The rest of my weekly grocery allowance had been spent for food for the family. I could hear my heart pounding and feel the perspiration on my forehead and the palms of my hands, as I opened my purse and took out the two quarters. Yes, I was feeling fear, the fear coming from a poverty consciousness of scarcity, doubt, and lack of faith in God and His laws and promises. I knew that the only way for me to know for sure if this giving stuff really worked was for me to take action and give money rather than withhold because of my unbelief. If I wanted money I would have to give money, for we get back what we give.

Already I had been tithing and giving 10 percent or more of my time and talent to my church and now it was time to also give money, the one thing that I definitely needed more of. Giving 10 percent of my income, which was almost nonexistent, was out of the question for me at the time. I gave what I had. As the basket passed before, me I dropped in my fifty cents and said the prosperity affirmation in unison with the other members of the congregation.

Prosperity affirmation: **"This gift is the outward expression of the law of prosperity and circulation working in my life. I know that whatever I give into God's service is returned to me multiplied tenfold or more. And so it is."**

Increasing Prosperity

You may be wondering if this worked? Yes! From that day of decision my life took a turn for the better. Little by little as I changed my consciousness and practiced the law of tithing and contribution, my prosperity and good fortune steadily increased. (Ten years later I became a television minister teaching millions of people the same principles that had worked to make me prosperous and help me live my dreams.)

> "Great hearts send forth steadily the secret
> forces that draw great events."
> —*Ralph Waldo Emerson*

Ancient Laws of Prosperity

I gave my students some information about the history of tithing: "Tithing has worked to eliminate the money worries of great numbers of people throughout time, making many of them multimillionaires and successful beyond their dreams. Tithing is taught in Judaism, Christianity, and Hinduism. Abraham learned the secret of tithing from the Babylonians, who were among the richest groups of people the world has ever known through their use of the prosperity law of tithing.

"Jacob made a tithing covenant with God, in which he asked for his heart's desires to be made manifest. By keeping his vow of regular giving, he prospered mightily. Everything he asked for he received and more, because he gave something first before he ever asked. God honors us at the level at which we honor our relationship with Him."

Making a Covenant with God

Everything belongs to the Great Spirit and is ours to use in His service, and when we do we flourish, naturally and opulently. This is a secret of prosperity. When people know this for certain they lose all worry and fear and they prosper and obtain the treasure of supreme pleasure.

"**And Jacob vowed a vow, saying, If God will be with me, and will keep me in this way that I go, and will give me bread to eat, and raiment to put on, so that I come again to my father's house in peace, then shall the LORD be my God; and this stone, which I have set for a pillar, shall be God's house; and of all that thou shalt give me I will surely give the tenth unto thee**" (Genesis 28:20–22).

Those who tithe, taking God as their partner in all things, are given the spiritual and material riches of God's kingdom, now and in the future. **"Fear not, little flock; for it is your Father's good pleasure to give you the kingdom"** (Luke 12:32).

Knowing that it is perfectly right for you to prosper and that this is really God's will for you is the first great step on your way to financial, mental, and emotional freedom. God desires that all of us prosper in all ways, and we can when we align ourselves with the existing, eternal principles of prosperity.

Priming the Pump

Giving first is like the principle of priming the pump to get the water to flow. Nanny had an old-fashioned water pump in her kitchen, and I loved getting a glass of water for I had to do some work to get it. If the pump was dry, it wouldn't bring up any water even though the well was full. Some water needed to be in the pump in order for it to work. Priming the pump meant putting some water in it before we could get any water. When we did this, water flowed. But if that little bit of water had not been put in, no water would have come forth. Giving always comes before receiving. The same is true of a carburetor on a car. Even if the gas tank is full, if the carburetor is empty of gas the car won't start until some gas is put in the carburetor.

Our pockets may be empty, but the well is always full. All we need to do is prime the pump by giving into God's service, the very thing we desire to receive.

Love Is the True Gift

Giving is a form of love, and when love is given along with the gift of money, etc., we enter into a special relationship with the Divine and the floodgates of heaven are opened up to us. No one can outgive God. When we give to God with two hands, He can and does give back to us with ten, a hundred, a thousand or more. By tithing we are prospered through our work.

> "But thou shalt remember the Lord thy God for it
> is He that giveth thee power to get wealth."
> —*Deuteronomy 8:18*

I finished up that lesson with "One of the first surprises having to do with the unexpected blessings of tithing happened the first Christmas right after I had started giving money on a regular basis. Because I was very low on cash at the time, as I was going through a divorce it looked as though it would be a grim and lean Christmas. But then, out of the blue, money and gifts came pouring in to me from expected and unexpected avenues. By God's grace I was able to give gifts to my family and friends, and I still had more left over to give to charity. That Christmas proved to be the best one I had ever had, but it was just the first of many."

What I didn't tell my early students was what I couldn't tell them because it hadn't happened yet. As I applied the law of tithing by giving to my spiritual teachers and church, my income rose steadily. Giving over $150,000 one year empowered me to write *How to Have More in a Have-Not World*, which became number one on the *New York Times* Best Sellers list.

More important than any momentary gain, tithing eliminated my fear of not having enough for there always has been enough, and more, to share.

Prosperity Action Item # 5

> Regularly give a portion of your time, talents, money, and resources, 10 percent or more (or whatever you can), to where you are receiving spiritual instruction.
>
> Each time you give, say this prosperity mantra with love:
>
> "This gift is the outward expression of the law of prosperity and circulation working in my life. I know that whatever I give into God's service is returned to me multiplied tenfold or more. And so it is."

The Law of Exchange

Wishful thinking is insufficient for success. Some people dream of being a multimillionaire, leader, star, or highly successful, but lack the necessary faith to carry it through. Undoubtedly, thinking is the seed of all activity, but it must propel us into action, if it is to bear fruit. As a tree comes from a seed, gross things come from the subtle, but positive thinking alone will not lead to the goal of wealth.

You can desire to be wealthy and you will be, if you offer or sell something that others want and need. The lazy hope, wish, and pray, but they refuse to do their part and give their share. Believing that somehow others will simply give them money, etc., literally for nothing, they wait as a snake hoping for a mouse to walk into their open mouths. We are not snakes, but human beings. God has given us intelligence, talents, arms, legs, hands, etc., to use in creating and offering something of value to others in exchange for what we want and need.

Someone said, "The harder I work, the luckier I get." This is true! All kinds of unexpected gifts, opportunities, and riches come to those who are busily engaged in delivering their goods and services. You've heard this said, "The rich get richer and the poor get poorer," and this is why. Once the ball of exchange starts to roll, good fortune increases. It is true that nothing succeeds like success.

> "The intelligent, who have glorious character,
> consider endeavor supreme. Weaklings, who are
> impotent, worship fate."—*Vedas 1.148*

Fate and chance have nothing to do with whether one is rich or poor, but everything to with whether or not one is giving something of value to others. Production and delivery of one's services and products into the hands of one's clients and customers make prosperity certain. There is no mystery about money. If there's no cash coming in, it is because there isn't any product or service going out. Remember that the law of circulation is one of the most basic laws and principles of nature. This law is in operation at all times and in all circumstances.

Mike Wanted to Prosper

Mike looked around to find a product or service that filled a niche that wasn't being occupied. Once he found the service, he got busy finding out all he could about this new service. He got his first job and did his best. Mike took care of his client and then got another client by the referral of the first, and so on.

Mike took motivational seminars on how to succeed in business and followed the instructions. Now he is a multimillionaire. He lives in his dream home with his precious wife, and he loves his work. His newest client is giving him an extra $100,000 a month. One of the special things Mike does is that he also tithes to the spiritual organization where he receives his spiritual knowledge.

Mike never graduated from college or went to business school, but he did follow the system of finding out what others wanted and needed. Next, he offered the solution. He helped his clients get what they wanted at a fair price and he got what he wanted, wealth and satisfaction. All good fortune is based on loving reciprocal relationships.

Sonia Was Given a Mercedes Benz

Sonia was a very loving and giving person. She befriended a gentleman who was going through some difficult times. There was no romance or even hint of romance. Sonia was compassionate as she listened to him confess his problems. She was a psychology student at the time, plus she was taking spiritual psychology classes at her church. One by one she helped find ways to solve each of his problems. Never asking for money or having any thought of payment, she was surprised when one day he gifted her with a new, white Mercedes Benz.

We never know how our good deeds will pay off, or when and how the benefits will come to us, but they will.

Prosperity Action Item # 6

List the products and services that you have to offer that can help others get what why want and need.

1.

2.

3.

4.

5.

What do you have that you can exchange for money?

1.

2.

3.

4.

5.

What have you done that has brought you money in the past?

1.

2.

3.

4.

5.

Help others to get what they want, and you will prosper.

The Law of Love

Doing what you love and loving what you do is one of the most valuable keys to attaining and keeping wealth and happiness.

John Had Been a Loser

John was always complaining about his job, his customers, his coworkers, and his boss. He was the first to criticize others and find fault. He truly believed others were wrong, and he was right. John did as little as possible and felt that others owed him something. He went from job to job and relationship to relationship, and each one would end in the same way. Finally when others couldn't tolerate his negativity and rudeness any longer, even though he was intelligent and had many good qualities, his bosses would fire him and his friends would dump him.

His mother forced him to go to church one Sunday, and the minister talked about the Law of Love. For the first time John listened and realized how foolish he had been. He decided to try out everything the minister suggested. As soon as he could, he got another job, even though he had to perform menial tasks. Given the fact that his employment record was so poor, he couldn't get the work for which he had been trained.

From then on every word out of his mouth was of praise, gratitude, and appreciation. It was challenging for him to change a lifetime of bad habits, but he knew he had to and he really wanted to change. He read at night, listened to the minister's sermons on audiotape, and took classes at the church. He did his work as if he actually loved it, and the more he did his work with love, the more he genuinely loved it. Whatever his boss needed to have done he volunteered to do it. He did his job with enthusiasm and excellence.

In time John was promoted and saved enough to start his own business doing his true life's work. The moral of this story is that there is hope for everyone if he or she is willing to learn to love.

Apply the Golden Rule

Love is the motivating force of life, and love is what everyone is seeking. Remember that everyone wants love, no matter who they are. *Love* is a verb meaning "to serve with care for the purpose of bringing happiness and prosperity to those you serve."

The Golden Rule is golden because its use produces precious relationships and gold in one's bank account. A rule of thumb is try not to cause harm or distress to any living entity. Love is giving and when we give we will receive, especially when we give our best to our family and clients.

People have come to me for counseling so many times with the desire to get money, but most of them were not doing much of anything to actually deliver a product or service with love. Money does not fall out of the sky but comes through an act of reciprocation.

Jesus gave us a most important secret of wealth and happiness when he taught us this lesson: **"Therefore take no thought, saying 'What shall we eat?' or, 'What shall we drink?' Or, 'Wherewithal shall we be clothed?' . . . But, seek ye first the kingdom of God, and His righteousness; and all these things shall be added unto you"** (Matthew 6:31 and 33).

Right here is the secret of wealth. Everyone needs to know and practice this principle of loving reciprocation. When we give of our talents, services, and products with love, we will always prosper, as everyone is seeking to be loved.

We Must Do Something in Order to Get Something

Prosperity Action Item #7

What do you love to do?

1.
2.
3.
4.
5.

Give love and you will flourish.

A. Find something to like about everyone around you and everything you do.
B. Believe you are working for God and therefore your work is important.
C. Do every job with love and excellence in the spirit of devotional service.
   1. Find ways to give happiness to your loved ones and clients.
   2. Try to practice the Golden Rule with every person you know.
   3. Try to avoid causing distress to others, including animals, and you will notice how much more peace and love you experience.

The Law of Communication

If you are going to prosper, you must let others know who you are, what you offer, where they can get your products and services, and also what you need and want. We cannot communicate too much. By the law of averages alone you will succeed if enough people know about what you have to offer, the value in it for them, and where to get it.

We are always communicating something. Even not responding to a phone call or a letter is communicating that you are not interested in communicating. Our clothes communicate a message, as do our printed materials and the language we use. Even our body language is a communication.

Desiring to be a world-class motivational speaker, I needed to make my presentation and communication consistent with my goals and the image I wanted to convey.

> What image do you wish to convey to others?
>
> The image I desire to convey is:

Everything needed to be improved, including my press and promotional materials, speeches, seminars, and my physical appearance. Sloppy doesn't get business, but excellence does.

Presentation is part of the illusion that needs to be created in the minds of one's prospective audience and clients. Given the tendency for people to judge by appearance, few will pay attention and listen to knowledgeable and talented people who dress like paupers. In order to achieve my speaking goals, I needed to change my consciousness, upgrade my skills, reach more people, and become famous. To do this, I needed to look the part.

My problem was that I didn't have the money to dress the way I wanted, so I prayed and asked God to help me to dress for success.

Dress for Success

Success mantra: **"My closet is filling up with beautiful, elegant, and expensive dresses and suits that are free or at prices I can afford."**

Within a week of my prayer, one of my friends shared with me that she knew of a terrific shop that carried preworn high-quality clothing at prices next to nothing. Another friend, who had lost a lot of weight and had no intention of gaining it back, gave me her closet full of costly elegant dresses and suits. With this last gift my closet was full, as I had affirmed. Mind you, I had never told anyone of my success mantra, prayer, or desire.

The general public is not attracted to a simple person. So if you have something to say or offer, you must package yourself to represent the goals and dreams of your audience. Preaching success, prosperity, and "How to get what you want," I had to look the part.

God As My Business Partner

The next thing I needed was to let more people know about my work. Not having the money to invest in advertising I sat down and prayed to God to help get my work known to the general public.

All of a sudden, newspaper and magazine reporters began to write articles on my work and me. People I didn't know were calling me to speak before their groups. L.A. television and radio talk-show producers were inviting me to be a guest on their shows, and would invite me back, again and again. The gift of all this free publicity brought my work to the attention of the people of the greater Los Angeles area, and eventually the world.

No way did I have the money to pay for this kind of publicity and advertising, but it came to me anyway. Powerful things happen when a person aligns her or his conscious and subconscious minds toward the achievement of a divine purpose.

Universal intelligence perfectly orchestrates everything by His inconceivable potency and limitless energies, according to our desires and His perfect plan. Just as we do not know why fire exists or why it works, still we can rub two sticks together or strike a match and fire appears. Electricity has always existed, but it took certain inventors to discover how to harness and use it, but they did not invent electricity. Turn on the television and it works, even though you don't need to know how to make a television, or how it functions. The laws of nature exist eternally and when we work with these laws, what we desire and need comes to us by divine right action.

Prosperity Action Item # 8

1. Pray to God and ask for what you need and want.
2. Think, walk, talk, and behave as the person you desire to be.
3. Have good posture, dress smartly, be clean, and look prosperous and attractive at all times.
4. Package your materials for your market.
5. Use the press to your advantage.
6. Communicate with those you love as well as your clients.

The Law of Appreciation

Above all else, people love to be acknowledged, treated well, and appreciated. Just about everyone wants to feel important and respected. By taking the time and energy to make your clients feel important by giving them great service, you will automatically prosper. When you praise others and treat them well, you raise their self-esteem and confidence. In turn, they like being around you and doing business with you. Whether they will admit it or not, people like to be treated as number one. Find something wonderful in everyone and find ways to make your friends, family members, and clients know you care, and so will they care about you in return. Let them know about their good qualities and what you appreciate in them. Seek out ways to show your appreciation and observe the wonderful results.

Carol Became a Close Friend of Her Hero

Carol had always admired a certain famous dancer who starred in movies. She had seen every movie he had made a least hundred times. Carol, being a movie expert, knew everything about him. Perhaps she knew more about him than he could even remember. Getting up her nerve, she wrote to him on various occasions sharing her appreciation for his work and expressing the desire to meet with him and write an article about his philosophy of dance.

Over time, they become very close friends. All this happened because she was bold enough to communicate and offer her hero her appreciation, and he accepted. It's hard to turn down those who like you and who are persistent in their appreciation and praise.

The Enormously Wealthy Waiter

Watching the television program *Lifestyles of the Rich and Famous,* I was intrigued, as the host interviewed an enormously wealthy European man. "Are you ever afraid that you will lose your great wealth?" asked the host. "No, I never worry about losing all that I have. I am first and foremost a waiter, and I can get all that I have back again by doing the same things I did before. I know how to serve people," replied the man.

He had started as a simple waiter, and he saved the money he earned. When he had enough, he invested in his first restaurant and soon his first hotel. He owned hotels and restaurants all over Europe because he knew how to take care of his customers and his money. God gave him riches in the form of more people to serve and more restaurants and hotels to manage. When we take care of what we have, we do get more to take care of.

> "His lord said unto him, 'Well done, thou good and
> faithful servant; thou hast been faithful over a few
> things, I will make thee ruler over many things;
> enter thou into the joy of thy lord.'"
> —*Matthew 25:21*

Prosperity Action Item # 9

1. Acknowledge those who are giving to you.
2. Thank God and be appreciative for your good fortune and all the wonderful lessons and blessings you are receiving.
3. Write thank-you notes and appreciate others for their kindness and support.
4. Show your appreciation and give something to those who are giving to you or using your services. You'd be surprised at how this will help you prosper.
5. Catch people doing something good and praise them for it.
6. Think of ways to make your clients feel very special.

The Law of Investing

Only the most intelligent and fortunate follow this law. You have heard that "a fool and his money are soon parted," right? The average person wastes her or his riches in the form of time, talent, money, and energy, having no idea that all great accomplishments start out as small endeavors. Extraordinary people are only different from ordinary people because of what they do with their resources. Endow, authorize, and empower yourself through the conscious and deliberate investments you make of whatever time, talents, skills, experience, things, money, energy, and resources you may have, no matter how small. Open an investment account, not a saving account, and put away 10 percent or more of the money that comes to you and refuse to touch it unless you can use this money to bring you more money. Make every penny, moment, relationship, and activity count toward building your spiritual and material estate. Invest 10 percent of your time each day in learning something that will help you to make advancement in your career, family life, and health. Devote some of your time and energy to every area of your life that is most important to you and watch that area blossom and produce blessings and dividends.

There is a law that states that whatever you give your attention, love, and energy to grows. Simply redirect whatever resources you have to what will cause you to prosper spiritually, mentally, and physically, and soon you will find you are a wealthy person in all respects. Money and attention are like fertilizers that help whatever they touch grow.

Those who prosper mightily have a plan to prosper, and this means they have something they are building and helping to grow with their money and time; they are not just living for the pleasure in the moment. I realized that the money I put into my continuing spiritual education was the wisest use of my money and time, for spiritual knowledge also gives us knowledge of what to do to prosper in our worldly activities and projects. No one can ever take from us our spiritual knowledge or the wisdom we have gained. Whatever happens, we can apply this knowledge and thrive. Over the years I would invest thousands and thousands of dollars in my spiritual education through classes, tithing, seminars, books, and audio- and videotapes. All this would prove to give me my highest return on my investment, way beyond my expectations.

Margo's Small Regular Investments Turned into a Good-Sized Fortune

Margo had a job selling yellow-page ads. She had a base salary and made a commission on top of that. Her goals, as a single mother, were to raise her daughter and give her a college education, plus she wanted to be a wealthy woman. She made a plan to buy income property. Margo stuck with the same work, as she was receiving some form of profit sharing and stock advantages. On her average salary she got up her courage and took the proper steps to purchase one piece of income property after another.

She also invested in her spiritual life by taking seminars, reading, and doing some volunteer work where she was receiving her spiritual instruction. Margo is taking an early retirement to travel and do all the things she has always wanted to do, and she can, for she invested wisely.

Savers and Spenders—Which One Are You?

There are two kinds of people: savers and spenders. Savers will never become spenders and spenders will never become savers, but both can become investors. I was a spender so I had to turn myself into an investor, for by indiscriminate giving and spending I was siphoning off my newly acquired prosperity.

Spenders waste what they have, and when they need it most, it's gone. Savers can become hoarders, which is not the proper use of God's money, either. Are you a saver or a spender? Spenders can turn themselves into investors by deciding upon some worthwhile investments—perhaps, for example, a farm or a house at the beach. Because spenders like to have a good time, they need to make investing fun. What woke me up and turned me into an investor was the realization that no one was going to take care of me and if I wanted a secure and wonderful future, I would need to plan for it in my present time. "Aren't we supposed to live in the moment and not think about the future?" asks the spender. You can live in the moment and still build the future you desire. In fact, this is a wise use of the present. If you don't give some of your attention to building the future you want, when the future arrives and it's your present you may wish that you had. Remember, you are not postponing your enjoyment of life; you are merely including prudent investing, as part of your life. Even a little bit invested can grow into a mighty fortune and give you enormous freedom to live as you choose. What are you now—a spender or an investor?

Prosperity Action Item #10

Empower Yourself Through Your Investments

1. Every time you are ready to use money, think: Will this help me to attain my goals? Is this an investment in the present and future I desire to have? Is this the highest use of my money and will this expenditure produce more money?

2. Put away 10 percent of your income in an investment account or use this to buy property or something tangible that you are enthused about and that will help you live your dreams.

3. Decide upon a property such as a farm or a vacation home and start paying for it now. When you are ready to retire, you will have your place and the money you wished you had not wasted you will have invested.

4. Invest in your continuing education. Seek the appropriate classes and seminars that will help enrich you spiritually, mentally, emotionally, physically, and financially.

Investing in Continuing Education

I decided to invest some of my money and time in taking what I considered to be valuable seminars. Late-seventies, pop-psychology, and truth-telling seminars were on the rise and of course I was first in line. Self-improvement was my banner, and I thrived on self-discovery and the regaining of my personal power. Relentless in my pursuit of knowledge and enlightenment, I took a two-weekend seminar in personal responsibility. At that point, my life took a sudden and dramatic turn straight up.

My levels of perception, clarity, and insight took gigantic leaps forward due to their hard-core adherence to the teaching of cause and effect and personal responsibility. We were encouraged to take personal responsibility for everything that had ever happened to us or would happen to us. Their approach was radical but just what I needed to shake me free from my tendency to blame others for whatever was happening or wasn't happening to me. (The problem with blaming other people is that there is no chance for us ever to be liberated from our struggles and problems and achieve our heartfelt desires.)

Results or Reasons

"You either do it or you don't," the trainer would say from the front of the room. "You have reasons or results, but not both" was their philosophy, and I could see the truth in it. This results-oriented training helped me to focus on my work and stop fooling around with all my excuses. If it was to be, it was really up to me! If I was to be an author, a world-class motivational speaker, a successful minister with a church and a worldwide television ministry, I had to do the work, and that was that. It wasn't going to fall out of the air and into my lap.

We Need a Plan of Action

I decided to make a simple business action plan—nothing complicated, for I wouldn't have known how to make a complicated business plan. After some contemplation I came up with a list of things I could do that would help me achieve my career goals. Sometimes we make things too complicated, so we don't do anything. Whatever the goal, you need to have a simple plan of action. Brainstorming, I wrote my twenty-two-point business action plan. Perhaps my list will give you some ideas.

My Twenty-Two-Point Business Action Plan

1. Develop my speaking voice to be melodious, resonant, and easy to listen to.
2. Dress appropriately for my audience.
3. Have printed material be first class and reflect excellence.
4. Speak as often as I could, even for free if need be, just to get experience.
5. Have every group for whom I was speaking advertise and promote my speaking event for their organization.
6. Contact newspapers and magazines to interview me and print articles. Do public relations and advertising.
7. Call TV and radio show producers and request that I be a guest on their shows.
8. Charge a fee, and raise my fee when appropriate.
9. Sell other people's books, given I didn't have any of my own, and sell my audiotapes at each of my classes and events.
10. Ask my students to help me in reaching more people and in getting more clients.

11. Have opportunities at each event for people to sign up for my other upcoming events.

12. Offer opportunities for people to participate as volunteers.

13. Delegate work, so that I can concentrate on what I do best.

14. Add each student's name to a mailing list. Communicate with them on a regular basis.

15. Give luncheons and social events as opportunities for the students to become friends, share their lessons, and assist one another.

16. Increase my knowledge by taking classes and listening to audiotapes of the topmost motivational speakers, psychologists, and scientists and the most inspiring ministers.

17. Constantly improve my material, and be ever fresh in my presentation.

18. Learn from my mistakes, as well as successes.

19. Pray before each presentation that each person in the audience receive exactly what he or she needs to hear, know, and experience from my seminar.

20. Unconditionally love and like every person in my audience, and desire that they flourish.

21. Relate to my audience where they are and help them to advance and make progress.

22. Let go and let God do the work through me, remembering that I am His instrument.

List Ten Things You Can Do Right Away to Achieve Your Goals, Career, or Other Ends.

1.
2.
3.
4.
5.
6.
7.
8.
9.
10.

Commit to Your Plan

The first thing was to commit to doing what was on my action plan. Second, I agreed with myself to consistently keep my commitments once they were made. This was called keeping my agreements and being accountable. Before this I had done only what I felt like doing, when I felt like it. This kind of easygoing behavior pattern would not lead to the level of success I firmly and passionately desired, but keeping my agreements would. I used this agreement-keeping process as a grappling hook to pull me up to where I wanted to be, and it worked magnificently. Most people fail only because they fail to keep their commitments and agreements, but they have a truckload of excuses and reasons why they do.

Keeping appointments on time, and doing what I said I would without fail, increased my self-esteem, confidence, and success, just as it was supposed to. To the degree that I did what I said I would do, I got the results I wanted, plain and simple. By making agreements with others and myself and keeping them no matter what, my ability and success as a speaker skyrocketed. Within a short period of time, I moved out in front into a class of my own. How amazing it all was for I had just needed to take responsibility, stop blaming others, and get going.

On a Roll

Soon I became a trendsetter on the motivational and inspirational lecture circuit. Something profound had happened to me as a speaker. Whatever I had been learning from spiritual and motivational books, I now knew by direct experience and self-evident knowledge. You could say that I was tuned in to cosmic consciousness. I had clarity of inner vision and insights that I had never had before. No longer was I an average, feel-good speaker but someone who could move large numbers of people to stand up and cheer because of what they heard and felt. I had become absolutely certain, self-assured, and, many said, "spellbinding." Something very positive and life transforming had happened to me during that two-weekend seminar on personal responsibility. Because I had been in the same mental and emotional state that most of the people in my audiences were, I knew their thoughts, fears, doubts, heartfelt desires, strengths, and weaknesses. They loved my no-nonsense approach to motivation, and most needed to hear it the way it was: Do it now or forget it.

The Importance of Rituals

By this time I had completed my studies at the seminary, and I was ready to take up my ministerial duties. Saying my ministerial vows in front of my colleagues on graduation day gave me a new and much deeper sense of my obligation to serve others, as their minister. Although I didn't expect anything special to happen that day, it did. Rituals are very important and necessary for us to incorporate spiritual ideals and transcendental experiences into the fabric of our consciousness and our daily lives. Leaving the stage of the church right after I had spoken my vows, I felt infused with the joy of my life's mission. This is what I would be doing for the rest of my life. Yes!

My corporate seminar work was not that satisfying because I felt so limited as to what I could talk about. In the corporate-seminar world there was no room for the subject of Infinite Intelligence, let alone the mention of the word *God*. Besides, speaking to materialistic people gave me a headache, and I couldn't tolerate it any longer. Praying sincerely for a chance to do my real ministry brought about the opportunity to speak at a summer church conference.

Momentum

The conference coordinator was a friend of mine, so he gave me my first opportunity to speak at this summer conference. As an insignificant new minister and seminar leader, I was given a small room that seated about thirty persons. I embraced each of the eager students in a warm circle of love and acceptance and gave them my million-dollar talk. My philosophy was to give my audience, no matter how small or large, my very best speech, which I called my million-dollar talk. People were elated, as they had never heard the spiritual principles of life taught in my direct style of preaching. Everyone in the class was so ecstatically happy and enriched after the session that the next day, because of word of mouth, the room was packed with about sixty-five persons. More people stood outside in the fog for the entire two hours of class just to be able to hear and experience what was going on inside.

The next day a larger place was given us, but already it was too small. Each day we outgrew our accommodations, until the final day of the class when we were moved to the large auditorium that seated twelve hundred people. Never in the history of the church conference had something like this happened. Why had my audience grown so quickly in just five days? My style was blunt, straightforward, no-nonsense, and right to the point. The main premise of my seminar was: "If you want to get to that door over there, you will need to set your goal and get up and walk, run, crawl, or be carried to the door. But if you change your mind, accept your excuses and reasons why you cannot, let someone get you off the track or convince you that you cannot, you never will. The choice is yours. Blaming others doesn't change anything or give you what you want. You either do it and have it or you don't, and that's the bottom line."

Do What Works!

They loved it, for they felt empowered just as I had been empowered when I had heard these same words and instructions from my teachers. The money I had invested in self-help seminars, books, spiritual classes, and audiotapes was paying off because, besides helping me, what I was learning was also helping my students. It was clear to me that there were certain things that worked and if I did these things I would prosper, be happy, succeed in my business, have loving relationships, and be healthy. No one in his or her right mind wants to be poor, miserable, sick, or lonely, but it's amazing how few people see any connection between their atti-tude and actions and their circumstances. How simple it really is: Do good works and you will have a good life. And if you don't, you won't.

Step Five, Control Your Mind and Be Positive

> "We are what we think. All that we are arises
> with our thoughts. With our thoughts we
> make our world."—*Buddha*

Spiritual Courage

Every situation is a test in spiritual courage. We pass when we fearlessly confront the situation from a position of positivity, faith, and strength, and we fail when we don't. Fear has no role to play in a spiritual person's life. I was about to learn that weakness is not meekness, but simply cowardice. Humility isn't about perceiving yourself as no good, but it's knowing that you are connected with a greater Source of Intelligence that you can draw from to help you accomplish your goals.

The meek are the open-minded and teachable and the humble are those who know that everything can be done through the power, love, and intelligence of God working through them. The coward cannot achieve his or her goals, let alone fulfill his or her sacred mission, but the spiritually courageous can and will.

> "The Lord is my light and my salvation; whom shall
> I fear? The Lord is the strength of my life; of whom
> shall I be afraid?" —*Psalm 27:1*

As we pass each test, we are given the spiritual and material treasures and prizes that come with victory. Failing means we must forfeit the treasures and prizes and face the test again at some unknown time and place. Any unwillingness to confront and do the needful in each situation robs us of our precious God-given power, wealth, talents, and enthusiasm. Anyone who desires to obtain the ultimate of what is possible for anyone to attain must be both spiritually intelligent and spiritually courageous. This kind of endowment is given out to us little by little as we prove ourselves by how we handle what is before us.

Up to this point I had worked to avoid what I called "trouble." Trouble for me meant any situation in which there was a chance of someone being angry, critical, judgmental, or ridiculing of me. In other words, I had been giving others the power to control my life and limit my opportunities to fully express my God-given talents, as if he or she were more important, stronger, and more valuable than I was. We make others our authority and then we wait for them to give us permission to be who we are and to do our life's work. Birth gives us the authority, and we need to claim our divine inheritance by using what we have to build our future.

If not corrected, this kind of attitude of avoidance breeds resentment, poverty, dejection, and more fear. Weak people can only hope that by being victims they will somehow be taken care of by others, but instead they are like minnows in a sea of sharks.

Paul Took a Stand

Paul's father had been a screamer. Many times during his childhood Paul had hidden himself in a corner to avoid being the victim of his father's intense rage. Taking to spiritual studies in order to build his confidence and strength, Paul learned that his father's rage had nothing to do with him. The father's rage had everything to do with his father not getting what he wanted.

Paul had been hiding in corners and cowering in fear his entire life. He repeatedly played the role of the victim, which cost him dearly. He unconsciously set up every person to be his victimizer. "Take advantage of me" was his nonverbal communication, which signaled the sharks to come in for the feast.

With encouragement Paul faced one challenge after another with courage, positivity, and enthusiasm. His friends wondered what had happened to him, and his former victimizers accused him of being selfish, cruel, and greedy. They used every trick in the book to make him feel guilty for taking a stand and being strong.

Paul took back his power one step at a time. Now he relishes the opportunity to meet his challenges and face his challengers, head-on. Paul turned his experience into a flourishing career. As a lawyer, he assists victims to become victorious.

Connecting with the Source of All Power

The truth is, everyone draws from the same source of power. We all have access to the same amount of power. Much like the electrical outlets in the house, each outlet offers the same amount of power and each appliance draws what it needs to perform its function. To get the power, you have to make the connection and turn yourself on. This connection is made when one is aware of his or her relationship with God, the unlimited source of power, love, happiness, peace, knowledge, and opulence. The sun is not the original source of power but an emanation from the Unlimited Source of everlasting power. Suns or stars, as we all know, are born, continue for a while, and then disappear, but the Supreme Source is endless and inexhaustible with no beginning or end. We are not made of the substance of the sun but of spirit, which has no beginning or end. As that which is of the earth must always fall back to the earth, we who are spirit must, as a flame always burns toward the sun, be conscious of and mentally pointed toward our Source.

How to Get More Power

God can give to us only to the degree that we allow His love to express through us. Honoring this connection through awareness, love, and giving, we are then immersed in the endless Golden River of ecstatic bliss, infinite intelligence, and opulent supply. Our conscious connection with this golden river allows the Absolute Power to express through us at our topmost capacity and potential like a river rushing to meet the sea. We become as channels and instruments used to express and give God's love and gifts to the world. Spiritually intelligent persons are those who know how to access this unlimited treasure house.

Be Strong

Believing and acting as if we are disconnected, weak, and helpless is the prime way we isolate ourselves from this awesome power source. A phenomenon happens when we meet our challenges and overcome them: we get more power. Instead of life being a confusing struggle it is now an adventure in enlightenment, joy, and love.

Perhaps you have believed that those whom you admire have somehow been handed success, wealth, and fame, when they have actually had to be persistent and determined in their resolve to attain their goals.

There is a basic principle of life called "Increase." Each time we do the needful and meet our challenging situations head-on, our power, wealth, and confidence increase. On the other hand, any duty or important issue we shy away from decreases our power and increases confusion, dread, and discouragement. Instead of cowering in fear, as if this were what it meant to be spiritual, we are to be dauntless and triumphant in our attempts to achieve our commendable spiritual and material goals. We need to hold the vision of ourselves as spiritual warriors charging forward and onward to victory—not to be fanatics, as if our way were the only way, but to follow where our hearts are leading.

In order to accomplish my mission, I too would have to become brave, self-confident, and powerful. Weak isn't meek or humble, for even the most spiritual and humble servants of God have had to muster every bit of their strength to fight for right. Much of the battle is within us, for we must overcome the tendency to be negative, afraid, and lazy. Some misunderstand spirituality to mean that one must live the life of an indolent and unclean beggar dwelling on the steps of a temple, church, synagogue, or mosque.

King David of the Old Testament was a devoutly religious person and the most powerful and wealthy person in that part of the world. Little David became King David because he bravely did what no other man would even attempt to do: he killed the huge giant with a small stone.

PEARL
When you serve a higher purpose, you can accomplish great works.

Sixteenth-Century Spiritual Warriors

Five hundred years ago in India a group of six saintly well-educated and devoted men under the instruction of their highly knowledgeable teacher were told to go to a wild and unpopulated forest and excavate certain partially ruined and hidden holy sites. These sacred temples were covered by thousands of years of dust and forest debris. Traveling hundreds and hundreds of miles of thief-infested and dangerous paths, they finally made it safely to their destination. Under the most challenging circumstances, tigers and poisonous snakes and such, they worked long hours for many years to carry out the instructions of their beloved teacher and friend. Each one lived to an old age.

To this day the Six Goswamis are revered in much of India for their saintly behavior, bravery, and brilliant scholastic abilities. They wrote over two hundred sacred books by hand in order to preserve the ancient and transcendental knowledge of how to attain supreme love and ultimate bliss. *Lazy* was not in their vocabulary, and neither was *fear* or *dejection*.

Spiritual Courage

No one had prepared me for the test that was before me. Little did I know when I prayed to God to give me my life's work that there would be times when I would have to fight for the right to do it. Growing up it was easy, even pleasurable, to fight with my sisters. When it came to something as simple as returning a damaged piece of goods to a store, however, I wouldn't do it out of fear that the clerk would be angry and rude to me. Each of us has our issues, and this was one of mine. Seeking comfort on many occasions, I had shirked my responsibilities just to avoid a possible confrontation.

Once we pray and sincerely desire something, this starts a set of circumstances in motion and we never know what they will be until they appear. But we must be strong and have faith, for then and only then will we be triumphant.

Entering the arena of our life's work we must remember that God has given us a duty to perform because we have asked for the right. Our commitment must be unwavering. No matter what others may say about us or try to do to us, we must continue to advance forward, never stopping, or the alligators that live in the swamp and feed on the weak will try to devour us.

Easter Sunday

Something was about to occur that would forever alter my life. Two events that were about to happen to me marked the beginning of a series of mystical experiences and also tests. This is the way God works, for in one moment as an unannounced bolt of lightning lights up the sky, He changes everything. Over the years, for whatever reason, anything of major importance having to do with my life's work always happened at Easter.

The day was the Saturday before Easter Sunday the year after I graduated from the seminary. As I climbed onto my bed and was about to lie down for a nap, a thought and knowing passed through my head. "Reverend Mark will not be giving the Easter morning sermon; you will. He is extremely ill and in intensive care in the hospital." "No," I thought, "what a terrible notion to have." I put my head down to go to sleep, but that moment the phone rang.

"Reverend Terry, this is Burl (the president of the board of trustees of the church). Reverend Mark is critically ill and in intensive care, so you will need to give tomorrow's Easter service" were his words.

You can imagine that I was shocked to hear the bad news, but I was also awestruck that I had had the premonition. First I went to the hospital to check on Reverend Mark, but no one could see him, as he was in surgery. The group of us who sat together in the waiting room prayed for his recovery. He fully recovered and it was called a miracle, but it would take six months before Reverend Mark could return to his duties at the church.

On Easter Sunday the sanctuary was packed, and the people were very disappointed that Reverend Mark was ill and not there. I prayed beforehand and trusted in God to work through me, the day went magnificently, and everyone was very happy with the sermon.

Each Sunday after that the attendance grew until more people were coming to hear me preach than had been coming to hear Reverend Mark. Naturally, succumbing to the lower aspect of human nature, he felt threatened. As soon as he was well enough and able to return to his church responsibilities, he wanted to eliminate me, the competition.

Facing the Inquisition

To get rid of me, he trumped up some charges that I had given bad advice to one of the members of the congregation. Reverend Mark called me into his office, which was packed with the board members, and proceeded to accuse me of misconduct. His intention was to fire me and stop the process of ordination so that all my years of training would be lost and I would lose both my license and my opportunity to be ordained. In our organization it took two years of service after graduation from the seminary under the guidance of an ordained minister before we would receive our ordination. And now all my dreams and hopes were about to be smashed because of another person's insecurity. All this seemed so unreal, like a bad dream.

Here I had worked for free for six months so that Reverend Mark could continue to get his salary. I was literally shaking in fear, feeling as if I were before the Inquisition, which I was. What came to my mind was something that Ralph Waldo Emerson had written: **"No person and no institution was ever ridden down or walked down by anything but itself."**

Putting My Philosophy to Work

Now was the time to use my positive thinking and not let this man defeat and rob me of all my years of ministerial training and take away my life's work. I sat there praying to God to help me. Silently I repeated a success mantra over and over to myself to control my mind, and keep it steady and positive.

Success mantra: God is my protector and maintainer.
Everything is working out perfectly for my highest good.
There is nothing to worry about, and all is well.

This once-kind minister, who had been my so-called friend and mentor, had turned against me out of fear. It had never entered my mind that I would have to face such a situation, but here it was, so what was I going to do? Perhaps this was happening because I had done this to someone before in another life and this was my karma, or maybe this was simply a test to build my strength and make me face my challenges rather than run away and hide? Whatever, If I wanted to be a minister and do my life's work, I would have to do battle to keep what was mine. As I looked around the small room, I had the sense that not one person in this room was really my friend and there was no one to defend me. In fact, they seemed to be enjoying the show.

Let's Make a Deal

After listening and unsuccessfully defending myself, I finally got up the courage to say, "Well, at least I am not having affairs with two of the married women in the church at the same time." Both of his lovers had been coming to me for counseling, and I knew the whole story—much more than I even cared to know. Under normal circumstances I never would have said anything, but since he was playing dirty so would I. This was a holy war. Spiritual teachings tell us never to willfully cause harm or distress to others, unless they're trying to harm us or take away that which is in our possession.

This stopped him fast in his tracks. He gasped, his face turned white, and he grabbed the cassette tape on which he had been recording every word and yanked it out of the recorder. This tape was to have been used as evidence against me to prove his case. Ripping out every bit of tape he threw it all in the trash. Then we made a deal. I wouldn't speak on Sundays or give classes at the church, but I would teach Sunday school until my internship was over and I could be ordained.

Leaving My Comfort Zone

I learned a valuable lesson about expectations. You can do wonderful things for people, but if something you do makes them unhappy, they may forget all the good and only remember the one thing they believe you did wrong. This is why it's a good idea to do the best you can without expectations about whether or not you are or will be appreciated. God is always grateful, but people are not God. Our good deeds will be returned to us, but these blessings will not always come to us from the same people to whom we gave. God's plan will always be successful, and this was definitely God's plan. Hindsight gives us the ability to look back and realize the perfection of what we believed at the time was a disaster. From this we can understand that each event really does play an important role, as God's plan for our higher good unfolds right on schedule.

We get attached so quickly and then we want things to remain the same as we build our lives around what we believe to be our security, when the only security is our relationship with the Higher Power. This was such a great lesson in detachment, and also trust. God had something better for me and for me to have what I really wanted, I had to let go of what I had and where I had been. No one can stay as they are, for change is the absolute rule of life.

Building Courage and Strength

Another lesson was that it was right for me to protect what was mine. If God takes something away that is one thing, but we have a sacred trust to take care of what God has given us. I was such a people pleaser that I had been afraid to defend myself or take care of my needs out of fear that my accuser would hurt me if I stood up for myself and refused to be exploited. Later I would write my first book, *What You Think of Me is None of My Business*, to help others also to own their power and stop being victims. Progress is made each time we own our power and do the right thing rather than cower in fear.

List three tests of courage that you passed.

1.

2.

3.

Own Your Power

Each test prepares us to meet the next challenge. People think that somehow all their good fortune will descend upon them like pennies falling from heaven. Good fortune comes gradually and builds into an enormous inner and outer fortune as we pass each test and prove ourselves capable of facing our challenges and taking care of what we have been given. This is one of the Laws of Prosperity called stewardship, or appreciation. When we prove ourselves able in the small things, we are given more abundance for our good appreciates and grows. My test was preparing me for the future when there would be other challenges that I would have to overcome on my way to my ultimate destination.

After ordination, I left my first church family, but I kept all the love. Leaving was a blessing in disguise, for it was time for me to move on. Just as a mother bird makes her baby birds fly by gently pushing them out of the nest, God was making me fly. The whole situation gave me so many invaluable lessons, and to this day I am grateful to Reverend Mark for everything he gave to me, including the opportunity to move on to something much better.

Relabel and See Everything As Good

Our attitude will either energize us or rob us of our energy and power. What appears to be bad luck at the time will always prove to be the right thing when we see it in its proper perspective, as a gift from Above. Words are very important. What we label an event has an affect on us, as to how we allow the situation or event to control our attitude, emotions, actions, and future results. A minor discomfort can be built into a major catastrophe simply by the words one uses to describe the event.

People who are stuck in the past lamenting something that happened perhaps years ago are stuck because they have labeled the situation as hurtful or negative. Seeing everything as a gift that is offering you something of value shifts your perception and changes the event. Whatever happens to, around, or through us happens mostly in the mind. Once we label something dreadful we feel dreadful, but if we label it a valuable experience it will be. Simply by changing our perspective and hunting for the treasure, lesson, or pearl of wisdom, what was seen as a dismal failure or disaster becomes a colossal success and godsend. A negative person will say, "You aren't being realistic and viewing things as they are." Who says how things are, anyway? The pessimist says the glass is half empty and the optimist says it's half full and both are right, given their chosen perspectives. But the negative person sees loss and the positive person sees a gain. How we view something will either empower or disempower us, and the choice is ours.

Claim Your Advantages

Whatever the situation, it's much better to look for the advantages, gifts, and benefits gained than to dwell on one's real or imagined losses. Correctly viewed, even a loss or failure can become the motivation and fuel for future gains. Viewing something correctly means first changing the way in which you view it and thereafter think and speak about it.

There are life affirming phrases and life negating phrases. Try changing your language and you will notice a profound difference in the way you feel, how you behave, and subsequently what you achieve.

Life-Negating Phrases	Life-Affirming Phrases
1. That was a horrible experience.	1. That was a challenging event.
2. I was devastated and destroyed.	2. It didn't destroy me; it made me stronger.
3. I will never recover.	3. I will recover.
4. He or she ruined me.	4. Whatever I accomplished once, I will again.
5. I don't have enough time, money, or energy.	5. There is always enough time, money, and energy.
6. Life is not worth living.	6. I am grateful for my every blessing.
7. I can't do it, and I give up.	7. I can do it, and I will give it my all.
8. I'm not good enough.	8. I am good enough and I am able.
9. I can't stand that person.	9. Perhaps I am seeing something in that other person I don't like in myself.
10. What's the use of trying again?	10. I'll keep at it till I get it right.
11. They are prejudiced against me.	11. What they think of me is none of my business.
12. I can't get a job because there aren't any jobs.	12. There's the perfect job for me and I will get it.
13. No one likes me because I am fat.	13. I am a beautiful person.

More Life-Negating Phrases	More Life-Affirming Phrases
1. It can't be done.	1. It can be done.
2. We've already tried it that way, and it didn't work.	2. Sure, let's try it again, and eventually we'll make it work.
3. We can't get the money.	3. There is an abundance of money; we just need to look and find it.
4. You can't get good help.	4. There are always good people who want to work.
5. There's no way to make money in today's world.	5. There is always room for another good idea and great business.
6. The boss won't like your idea.	6. The boss would love a new idea.
7. Life is full of problems.	7. Life is full of adventures.
8. I'm just a loser.	8. God loves me, so I must be good.
9. You're a loser.	9. I believe in you, and you can do it.

Write some of your own.

Life-Negating Phrases	Life-Affirming Phrases
1.	1.
2.	2.
3.	3.
4.	4.
5.	5.
6.	6.
7.	7.
8.	8.
9.	9.
10.	10.
11.	11.
12.	12.

Attitude Is King

Attitude is everything! Actually, it makes a huge difference when we let go of the labels of hurt, loss, pain, and impossible. Calling each challenging event a learning experience or a stepping-stone to something better brings you benefits. It's not a lie to think positively, as it is the truth when seen as such. When you hear yourself using an inappropriate life-negating phrase, say "Cancel" and change to an appropriate life-affirming phrase and notice the difference.

If people could just get the following important concept, they would gladly leave the hurt behind and move forward with positive expectancy.

Some act as if their life purpose is to prove that they have been hurt and cheated. In order to prove the injustice and irreparable damage they must demonstrate their pain and loss by limiting the amount of joy, love, and prosperity they experience. Talking endlessly about their victim story, losses, failures and difficulties they waste their power and spend their precious energy and time in reinforcing the events of yesterday.

This doesn't mean you shouldn't fight back when you are actually victimized. Do what you need to do, but without anger, resentment, or hate.

Recall any situation that you labeled bad or unfortunate.

The situation happened like this:

Now write the blessings that came from this situation.

The blessings are or were as follows:

Relabel, reframe, and redefine the situation.

Instead of calling the situation bad, grim, or unfortunate, I am relabeling it as:
1.
2.
3.

Anger has a negative affect on the body, as well as the mind. Those who harbor anger or who carry resentment for any length of time have defeated themselves.

It takes some work to train the mind and change our words to reflect our highest ideals, but soon the difference will be experienced and you will reap the bountiful rewards. Success breeds success. Remember, you are already a success for you are a precious child of God.

Mick's True Calling

Mick was a wonderful person with a terrific personality, but for some unknown reason he could not keep a job. He had been a child star on television, entertaining millions with his singing, dancing, acting, and drumming. His difficulty came as an adult. Believing he had to give up his entertaining and get a serious job if he was to amount to anything and make some good money, he sought work in the corporate world. During the fourteen years of his marriage he had had about twenty-four jobs.

His wife loved him and felt so frustrated because Mick was always out of work. She was well paid for her work, so they always had more than enough. Mick was not lazy, for he really wanted to work and make a contribution to the lives of others. Mick's wife was a psychologist, and a few times each year she would give lectures on cruise ships in exchange for money and two all-expenses-paid trips. During these cruises Mick was the life of the party. He entertained the people and saw to it that everyone had a fabulous time.

Finally, after years of going from one job to another, it dawned on him that his perfect job was that of a cruise director. On each and every cruise his wife and he had taken, he entertained the guests, but he was doing this as a volunteer and not as an employee of the shipping company. Mick is now enjoying great success because he is doing his life's work and getting paid for it. He was never suited for a corporate position, but then a corporate executive isn't suited for his kind of work.

Having been fired so many times was now seen as a blessing. Instead of calling his lost jobs failures, he relabeled them market research. His dream to make a difference in the lives of others had come true. Everyone who takes a cruise or a trip with Mick has a wonderful time, because he sees to it that they do.

Preparing for My Church

Being fired can discourage and even devastate us unless we choose to rela-bel the experience and find the blessing. I could have said that I was fired from my first job as a minister, but instead I called it a promotion. Imme-diately after my ordination, a friend who was the pastor of a church in Whittier, California, called and asked me to give a weekly middle-of-the-week evening lecture for his congregation. This proved to be very success-ful, and I was also finally getting paid. Every week I had the opportunity to speak to a churchful of eager spiritual seekers.

After a few months of Wednesday Night Specials, I felt a growing need to have my own church. I had a plan that had begun to take form when I was Reverend Mark's assistant minister. He and I had talked about having a television ministry together, and I loved the idea. But as I worked with him, I understood that his idea of *our* having a television ministry meant that I would work behind the scenes and he would be the minister preaching. Right away I started visualizing myself on television preaching the Spiritual Principles of Successful Living to people throughout the world. The seed had been planted, and it was just a matter of time if I did my part.

I believe that each of us can sense and feel when it's time to make ad-vancement toward our topmost goals, and if we listen to that inner guid-ance and take action we will get there. Should we ignore our guidance, we will miss the opportunity. I asked myself, "Am I more committed to living my dream of having my own church and a television ministry or more committed to staying where I am?" Right here is the crux of the whole message. Our desire to attain our goals must be stronger than our fears, doubts, or laziness. However uncomfortable it would be to venture out into unknown territory, I knew it was my time to give it my best shot and make a run for my topmost goals.

Being relatively undisciplined, a free spirit of sorts, I was bothered a lot by the idea of having an office with four walls and office hours. Intuitively, I knew that I needed to be more disciplined if I was going have a big church and a television ministry. Discipline is essential, whatever the goal. Things don't just happen; they come together step by step, and each step must be taken. I call this foundation building. However tall you want your building to be, the foundation will need to be deep and strong enough to support it.

The Price of Success

My dream of having a church and television ministry would remain just a dream unless I took the steps and actually did it. Being the pastor of a church congregation meant that I would have a regular job, which I had never had in my entire life. Here I was, a displaced housewife without any business training who was venturing out into the world of organization, employees, volunteers, board members, and whatever else. Having a full-time job as a minister meant committing every Sunday for the rest of my life. Laziness and unwillingness to commit are two giant obstacles to attaining our topmost goals. Setting the goal is relatively easy, but to get there, there is a price to be paid.

We can get what we want if we are willing to pay the price and everything has a price tag, especially God. Nothing is free, and those who try to get something without giving may accumulate some stuff, but they are never prosperous. I knew that discipline was going to give me freedom to fully express my talents and the chance to live the life of wealth I had always wanted. I had what I believed to be the most wonderful message in the world and I wanted to give it to everyone so that they could be happier, healthier, and wealthier. I made my commitment and agreed to my sacrifices.

I didn't have a clue as to where this church was or when it would happen. All I could do was sincerely pray and ask God to connect me with my perfect church and congregation. Unless God told me that it was my right and perfect church by giving me some kind of recognizable sign, I would stay where I was. Proving God's existence by depending entirely upon Him was my 100 percent commitment. Determined to wait for His sign, no matter how long it took, I even turned down a couple of large churches because they didn't feel right and God had not given me a sign that they were for me.

The Voice of God

From the day I made the decision to wait for the sign until the phone rang was around three to four weeks. Paul, a clergy colleague of mine, was on the other end. "La Jolla needs a minister. Would you like me to tell the board of trustees that you are interested?" was Paul's kind offer. "Do you want the position?" he inquired. "No, it doesn't feel right, but thank you for thinking of me" was my reply. I was waiting for a sign from the Almighty. Because I didn't feel anything, this couldn't possibly be my church.

No sooner had I hung up than the kitchen filled with golden light and I heard a loud voice from within and everywhere around me say, **"That's where you're going!"**

In that moment, in a flash, I knew beyond the shadow of a doubt that the La Jolla church was the church God had selected for me. Besides experiencing a heightened state of consciousness and elation, my body shivered from the glorious symptoms of ecstatic bliss. I was certain at the deepest level of my existence that this was my church. God had told me, just as I had prayed He would.

Say Yes

Immediately I called my minister friend. "Paul, please tell the board that I am interested in being their minister," I sobbed. I had no idea at the time that it would take four months for the board to make up their mind to take a chance on a woman minister.

Silence Is Golden

During this long four-month period I didn't tell anyone about the possibility of my becoming the minister of the La Jolla church nor did I tell anyone of my God-experience and profound realization, except my friend Paul. Silence is very important when it comes to one's desires, goals, and spiritual realizations. We need power to generate our dreams into reality. Sharing something that has not happened is like counting the chickens before they hatch because we really do not know the outcome.

Power accumulates and builds when a person remains silent, keeping his or her own council. Telling others about something before it happens will rob us of the precious energy we need to produce our intended results. Scattering it inappropriately is like taking all your money out of the bank and throwing it in the street just so others will be attracted to you and think you are rich and important. This is called the work of the false ego. The false ego seeks glorification, and thus it causes the person to make foolish decisions.

Telling others of your plans can also evoke envy. Envious people may try to rain on your parade by filling you with fear and doubt. Waiting until you have achieved your goal before you spread the good news is wise; spending the money before the check has cleared the bank is never a good idea.

An Example of What Doesn't Work

Dilbert was a multitalented person, but rarely, if ever, did he accomplish his goals. He had great dreams of fame and fortune, but he also had a couple of bad habits that were robbing him of his fortune. One, he told his friends and strangers everything, keeping nothing to himself, and two, he was closed to any kind of expert advice that would help him prosper and succeed. Being a know-it-all and a blabbermouth are not qualities that are conducive to greatness. Greatness requires enormous energy, which must be generated from within the person and not wasted in idle and useless conversation meant only to impress others.

> "A fool uttereth all his mind: but a wise man
> keepeth it in till afterwards." —*Proverbs 29:11*

Dilbert wanted to be recognized as an all-knowing expert who was highly successful. He really did have singing, writing, acting, and speaking talent that was extraordinary, but his desperate need for recognition and appreciation was far greater than his desire to actually complete his projects, help others, and achieve his goals. All his power was lost in the telling to others every little thing he did, thought, or planned to do. People did not respect him, and generally he was considered to be a fool, simply because he did not do what he said he would. He had fabulous ideas, but after using these ideas to draw some attention to himself, he would drop them.

There was no possible way for him to live his dreams and accomplish his truly marvelous theatrical works. Nothing was left, for he had already spent his supply of energy in fruitless bragging. It takes mental, emotional, and physical energy to transform dreams into concrete forms.

He never changed because he thought of himself as an expert, and perfect in all ways. Dilbert's way of perceiving was to see his failures as always someone else's fault, especially his father's, who he said never loved him. A person may be justified in his or her blaming, for it's true that others have done some horrendous things. *But,* we will either get the cheesy satisfaction of justification or the riches that only come when we attain our cherished goals. We cannot get both.

> "As long as a man stands in his own way, everything
> seems to be in his way." —*Anonymous*

Taking Inventory of Any Excuses

Are you blaming others? Are you giving excuses? What is this costing you? Who, if anyone, are you blaming?

1.
2.
3.

What are your most used excuses?

1.
2.
3.

What does it cost you to blame others and give excuses rather than to take responsibility?

It costs me

1.
2.
3.

I now accept responsibility for my life.

An Example of What Does Work: How Jan Attracted Opulence

Jan, on the other hand, had been dealt some difficult blows, but instead of blaming she set out to get what she really wanted. Jan had been living in poverty since her husband had left her for another woman. She was crushed by his rejection and overwhelmed with all the unpaid bills he had also left behind. Every day was a heavy burden, and there didn't seem to be any hope of her ever prospering and having a good life.

Listening to the radio one morning, she heard the end of an interview that caught her interest: "Anyone can attract wealth and have a fabulous life simply by changing his or her consciousness. You can find out how by reading my book" were the author's final words.

Jan had a very strong feeling that she would find her answers in this book. Taking twenty-five dollars, which was all she had until she received a check from her mother, she drove to the bookstore and purchased a copy of the book.

Reading every word, she decided to try what the author suggested. Jan became absorbed in speaking and writing affirmations and success mantras. Affirmations were taped up on every wall of the apartment. She even audiotaped the most positive and life-affirming parts of the book so she could listen to the information over and over. Besides listening to the information all day, she played the recordings while she slept at night to reprogram her subconscious mind. Repetition is a very important tool for learning anything. Psychologists have found that it can take six times or more for a person to hear or see something before she or he actually hears it or sees it and it registers. Every morning as soon as she awakened and every night right before she went to sleep, she read spiritual material and prayed for God's guidance and love.

Success mantra: **"I am a wealthy person. I think and feel opulence. I live in constant expectancy of my ever-increasing good. Thank you, God."**

Jan changed every single aspect of her life. She cleaned out her closet, car, and house and got rid of everything that was mediocre, which meant she had very little left, but what she had left was quality. Taking a little time each day, she forgave her former husband and anyone toward whom she held any resentment. This was part of the cleaning out of the old and useless. Jan had read that she needed to make a vacuum and space for the new.

She found a clothing store that sold preowned designer clothes, and even though she didn't have much money, she got the owner to agree to a trade. In exchange for helping out at the store, she was given a few elegant and classic-style suits and dresses with shoes and accessories to match. Jan was great with hair and makeup and she used all this, as would an actress preparing to go onstage and play a role.

Dressed magnificently and looking very beautiful, she visited automobile agencies and sat in the most expensive cars just to get the feeling. After this, she would visit the most expensive clothing and furniture stores and walk around with the thoughts and feelings that all of it belonged to her. On weekends she'd look in the newspapers and find open houses and visit the ones in the most expensive parts of town and act as if she was an interested buyer. Walking around in each house, she would pretend it was hers and imagine herself living there. Everything she was doing was making a powerful impact on her subconscious and conscious minds.

Finally, Jan visited the most upscale hotels and pretended that she was a guest. She'd get a cup of tea, as that was all she could afford, and sit for a while enjoying the luxury environment and envisioning herself as enormously wealthy woman.

At the same time she enrolled in a real estate training school and absorbed herself in the studies, because she was determined to prosper and have a good life. Anyone or anything that was negative and degrading was out of her life. Of course, her old so-called friends who had been exploiting her, as had her former husband, were angry. Jan realized that not one of these people would take her place in the coffin when she died nor would they pay her bills or take care of her in any way. She and she alone was responsible for her life.

Soon she was meeting people who were the kinds of people with whom she had always wanted to associate. These people would have never associated with her before, but now they appreciated her friendship, as she was so very positive, lovely, and empowering.

As the story goes, all her efforts paid off, handsomely. Jan obtained the life she had previously only dreamed of having, because she changed her mind, attitude, thoughts, words, environment, associations, work, and behavior to reflect her highest ideals and topmost desires. Jan used the power she had to increase her power and position in life.

The Prospering Power of Positive Thinking

Visiting Mammoth Mountain, California, on a ski trip I had the privilege of meeting Jill Kinmont, an Olympic contender. Weeks before the 1960 Winter Olympics, she fell while skiing and wound up in a wheelchair paralyzed for life, never to ski again. "Jill, how do you maintain such a positive attitude?" was my question. "What's the alternative?" was her enthusiastic reply.

Positive thinking is not just a fad; it is a truth and way of life that works. None of us has accomplished anything of value unless we believed in ourselves, maintained a positive mental attitude, and worked to get what we wanted. Although God had given me a sign and told me this was to be my church, somehow the months of waiting with barely a word from the church board of trustees made me nervous. The lower, negative mind is so clever that it can even make us doubt the word of God.

I wanted this church, and I had to work to control my mind and keep it positive or I would have tossed the opportunity away out of pride and fear. I was used to getting my way and not having to wait, and this was a lesson in faith, positive thinking, and patience. On a couple of occasions I almost picked up the phone and called the board president to say that I was no longer interested, just so I wouldn't feel the stress. But this was not the solution or the proper thing to do. Throwing away something of value is foolish. Those who act rashly without careful consideration of the consequences of their actions, or who lash out at others, are rarely happy. Reading my spiritual books was a better way for me to ease my stress. Sacred knowledge gives us the real and lasting solutions to every problem of humankind.

How to End Stress

Every sacred book and scripture I read on this subject pointed to the same solutions. Basically they concurred that distress is part of our lives until we completely surrender to the will of the Supreme Lord.

Total surrender to God is not as easy as it sounds, or everyone would be in bliss, and they are not. Until we totally and completely trust and have faith in a Higher Power to love, protect, and maintain us, we shall be afraid and anxious, no matter how much wealth, beauty, strength, or power we possess.

Believing that surrendering to a Higher Power means that we will be relieved of all our worldly goods, who in his or her right mind would want to? On the contrary, surrender means letting go of what we don't need anyway: Who needs or wants fear, anger, poverty, resentment, worry, stress, or unhappiness? Why not trust the one who created the entire universe and keeps it running in perfect right order? Who else is a better and more trusted partner?

To the degree that we are overly attached to things turning out exactly as we think they should, we will feel stressed. Outlining is a name for this problem. Praying and asking for what you desire and then telling God how to do His job is counterproductive.

Make Your Mind a Lake of Tranquillity

There are two solutions that will work to bring the mind under control and give you peace and pleasure. One offers more pleasure. Meditation on the silence by making the mind an empty void is the first, and surrender to the will of God is the second. Because we have a mind, it has a function. If it had no function but to remain void and inactive, God would never have created it. Our mind is to be used to contemplate the divine, the beautiful, sacred, opulent, and infinite; and when we do, we are peaceful, blissful and inspired. Imagination, which is part of the mind, is our earthly link with the purely spiritual world of eternal life, limitless ideas, and effulgent splendor.

The saying "The idle mind is the devil's playground" is very true. The mind can play the role of a devil or an angel, and the choice is ours. Nature abhors a vacuum. When the mind is empty it will naturally fill up with something. Our job is to focus the mind and fill it with what we want, or else we will be tormented by a mind that fills itself up with garbage.

When we fill our minds with positive ideas and higher spiritual truths and images, life-negating thoughts and images cannot take over for there is no room and they are not welcome. Nothing else will satisfy us but that which is holy and divine, for we are made of spirit and spirit is our home.

Peace already exists within the soul. All one need do to eliminate any disturbance is to imagine your mind to be a calm lake reflecting celestial beauty and opulence. Close your eyes for a few moments and see your worries and concerns as waves in a turbulent sea. Take each wave and flatten it out to be smooth. Make your inner lake calm and peaceful. Refuse to allow anything to disturb your Lake of Tranquillity.

Worry Is Useless

Worry does not make things happen, nor is worry a substitute for one's not doing everything in her or his power to see to it that there is a favorable outcome. Worry agitates the mind, causes turbulence, and can actually make one ill.

Success mantra: **"There is nothing for me to worry about ever again."**

People can literally absorb themselves in worry and miss out on an entire lifetime. Worry is a habit, and to break the worry habit one needs to realize its useless and destructive nature. Don't engage in anything that will not in some way be of benefit and help you prosper. If you start to worry say the success mantra, let the worry go, and get busy finding a solution to your challenge. There is nothing to worry about when you are doing the best you can, for that is all you can do.

There are two parts to any activity or goal: our part and God's part. Once we have done everything in our power to make things turn out as we desire, we must let go and let God. People stress over every little thing only because they lack faith or they haven't done all they can do, and we need to have and do both.

Without faith in a Higher Power, it is impossible for us not to worry because our powers are extremely small in comparison to The Limitless. But with Infinite Intelligence as our willing and able partner, we can accomplish great things. Absolute faith casts out all fear.

"Thou wilt keep him in perfect peace, whose mind
is stayed on thee, because he trusteth in thee."
—*Isaiah 26:3*

Knowing beyond the shadow of a doubt that, whatever the outcome, Infinite Intelligence will help us to attain our highest goals and objectives, we are then able to remain positive and enthusiastic. With this kind of a positive attitude we can be certain that even failures are necessary steps on the way to eventual success.

From this perspective, everything that happens serves a vital function and is a piece of the puzzle. No one can fail by assuming this viewpoint, for even a failure will lead to the next win. Sometimes the lesson is what not to do, or to get out while you can.

My goal was to be the full-time minister of the perfect right church for me. Because God fulfills our desires I knew this would happen, but I had no way of knowing which church or when. Divine Intelligence knows infinitely more than we do. Not trusting in the Divine can be likened to hiring a genius and then giving him or her the job of sweeping the floors.

PEARL

Don't worry about things that are not under your control!

I couldn't let myself fall into fear and separation from God, for this church was too important to me. Remaining enthused even though I didn't hear anything back for weeks at time was a huge challenge. Positive thinking doesn't come naturally; it must be worked on.

During my waiting period I studied my spiritual books, said my affirmations constantly, attended lectures, and absorbed myself in Truth. Waiting was my time to learn more about the mind and the power of positive thinking.

Positive or Negative Is a Matter of Choice

We have two minds: one is the higher spiritual mind, and the other is the lower material mind; one is real, and the other is false or illusory. Some people serve the lower mind believing that it is better to acknowledge that you feel miserable and depressed rather than to cover negative feelings with a positive attitude. These realists call misery truth and positivity a denial of the truth, but both positive and negative attitudes are simply matters of choice.

You decide which attitude is going to help you get what you want. Can a positive attitude help you to attain your goals or do you prefer to be depressed, resentful, and pessimistic? To be victorious, as every athlete knows, you must lift your spirits and propel yourself to the highest level of certainty and enthusiasm that you can possibly attain. Pumping ourselves up with the most inspiring ideas, visions, and thoughts possible is actually the right thing to do.

How you choose to look at life affects you. Using your mind to reflect God and the higher realms of love, creativity, beauty, peace, and opulence will place you in that mental reality. Soon your outer world will reflect your inner state of beauty, love, and opulence, for that which is within will manifest all around you by the universal law of corespondents. The outer, including the body, is consciousness manifesting into form. What we see around us corresponds to that which is an idea or concept within.

Cosmic Consciousness

This is the true spiritual, and even mystical, power of positive thinking. A heavenly state of mind will produce a heavenly outer world. We naturally gravitate to and attract to us that which is the material outer manifestation of our inner state of mind, imagination, and emotions. Thinking positively doesn't mean that things will always turn out exactly as you had in mind. Positive thinkers know that whatever happens is a blessing. Positive thinkers are certain that they will succeed in their endeavors. They don't plan to bail out just in case there are some problems because they are committed to reach the goal. Why bother even to start if you don't believe you will get there?

Elevated divine thought is the invisible food that propels us to enter the zone of cosmic consciousness and enables us to tap into the vast and opulent resources of Infinite Intelligence. Lower thoughts, feelings, and words, no matter how justified, depress us and consume us with a dark cloud of ignorance and hopelessness. Dejection is a thief that deprives us of our intelligence, creativity, genius, and success.

Nobody can get any good ideas when they are down in the dumps. Just to get a good idea, one has to mentally hang out in the exalted ethereal realms where the best ideas live. Knowledge does not lower itself to where we are; it is we who must elevate our minds to receive the topmost knowledge.

Have Faith

> "Whether you think you can or think you can't,
> you are right."—*Henry Ford*

Affirmative thinking means to believe and have faith that everything will work out fine and you will attain your goals. Why bother even to strive for your goals if you are going to be negative and defeat yourself? Half-hearted attempts are already a failure. You won't even need an enemy if you are negative, for you are your own worst enemy.

By the law of averages alone if you remain positive and do not allow yourself to even contemplate failure or loss, you will eventually win. Above this, by creating and maintaining a positive mental attitude you have already won. Most people do things for the feeling they will get, but if you already have the feeling of success no one or nothing can take this from you.

The fear of being 100 percent positive is that if it doesn't work out we will look like fools. Just in case it doesn't work out we may decide to be negative and drag our feet beforehand, just so that in case it doesn't work out we won't be disappointed. Keeping a steady mind is an art and an art that must be learned and practiced for us to attain anything of value, be it spiritual or material.

God does not want us to be dejected but to be enthusiastic and do our life's work with enthusiasm. The real battle of Armageddon is the one that is going on between the true self and the false, and the true must win. We must take charge and honor the dictates and desires of our higher, true self, and when we do we shall be victorious in everything we do.

Terry and Mimi

My friend Mimi and I decided to take a three-day backpacking trip in the Rocky Mountains high above Jackson Hole, Wyoming. Never before had either of us done such a thing, but we were determined and enthused about the adventure. Carrying about forty pounds of essentials, including our tent, food, and sleeping bags in our backpacks, we began the trek. This got to be old very fast, as the weight of the packs was extremely uncomfortable. We'd rest and then get up and get back on the trail. Views were breathtaking, and the wildflowers and wildlife were sublime. At one point near the end of the second day around four in the afternoon, we were at a turning point. Should we go back down or try to climb to the summit and across the glacier before it turned dark?

Oh how we wanted to go back down, take these heavy, painful back-packs off, and sink into a hot bath, but if we did we would not achieve what we had set out to accomplish. "No one will fault us if we go down. After all, we came this far," we said to each other. Should we or shouldn't we? We went back and forth, and it was getting later by the moment as night was fast approaching. Finally, right before we were ready to give up and go down the mountain together, we shouted, "Yes, let's go! We said we would, and we will."

Our victory was sweet and well worth it because we did not let our minds talk us out of doing what we really wanted to do and what we had committed to do. Mimi and I talked our minds into climbing the last four miles to the top. We stood there on top of the mountain thrilled that we had overcome our doubts. To this day that event serves as one of the high-lights of my life, for I did not take the easy way out.

> "Good fortune eludes a person bewildered by
> doubts, which dampen the spirit of adventure.
> Abandoning all doubt, one must act to achieve his
> end."—*Hitopadesa, book on Vedic philosophy*

Some More "Mind-Talk"

Mind-talk is a process in which you talk to the mind, as you would coun-sel someone in need of good, practical spiritual advice. We all love to give others advice. Mind-talk is a wonderful way for you to give *you* great ad-vice. Who knows better what is right for you than you? It's all right to talk out loud to your mind, for your mind has been talking to you for years. Now it is your turn to take charge. We must refuse to let the mind talk us out of our good.

Whenever I caught myself thinking or speaking in a negative, critical, or discouraging manner about anyone or anything, I would stop the rambling of my mind by saying "Cancel" and then I would speak the most encouraging and positive words I could think of at the time. If my mind thought, "Terry, you won't get the church, because they don't want you," I'd say, "Cancel," and then I'd talk to my mind, as if it were a person. Using mind-talk I would declare, "God has told you the church is yours. Relax and have faith. You know that everything is working perfectly and God is the controller. There is nothing to worry about. You are now and always will be in your right place. God is in charge, and every good and wonderful thing and experience is coming your way. The best thing for you to do is to read, study, and work on your projects. Everything is working according to God's time. Go about your business and do the needful in each moment. Have faith, for all is well."

The Science of the Mind

Every person, without exception, has the challenge of controlling his or her mind, and all minds operate in the same way. The mind is a mirror that reflects back to the self the objects and subjects of one's attention. Ideally our minds are meant to reflect the higher spiritual world of pure love, opulence, and bliss.

The mind can only have one thought at a time and one master. We can choose to be partners with the Supreme Being and Infinite Intelligence or partners with the belief in limitation and fear.

Training the mind to focus on what we desire to manifest is most important. Given that whatever we think about will become our next reality and experience, a wise person carefully plans to attain his or her ideal reality through the proper use of his or her creative faculties, especially the mind and intelligence. We are supposed to use everything we have to our advantage.

Learn to Concentrate

Because it is true that an uncontrolled mind will dart here and there like a mad monkey leaping from tree to tree and dragging us behind, we need to make the mind behave by constantly bringing it back to focus on the godly rather than the god-awful.

The mind works very quickly and has the ability to move from one thought to another faster than the speed of light. Concentration is a necessary ingredient in the formula for attaining success. Imagination is part of the mind and in a fraction of a moment you can be anywhere, anytime, and with anyone just by thinking, feeling, and visioning. The mind is wonderful or God would not have given us one, but it is a tool and must be treated as a tool and not allowed to ruin a life. When people were more godlike and spiritually inclined it was easier, but now one must intentionally create a spiritual environment or community in which to flourish.

Happiness and distress, Heaven and Hell, originate in the mind, so you can understand that there is great power in the mind. An uncontrolled mind is actually more dangerous than a loaded gun in the hands of a small child. A controlled mind will give you peace, pleasure, prosperity, and love.

> "No man can serve two masters; for either he will
> hate the one, and love the other; or else he will hold
> to the one, and despise the other. Ye cannot serve
> God and mammon." —*Matthew 6:24*

Dejection Robs Us of Our Power

If we allow our thoughts to fall from Grace or from the higher realms of Truth and God-consciousness we descend into the lower states of strife, poverty, and dejection. Dejection is the prevailing collective frame of mind of the world. The cause of this dejection is our attachment to the body, possessions, and a fabricated image of ourselves that we cling to and defend. If we see ourselves as martyrs, we must suffer, but if we let go of this fabricated image and remember who we are, perfect children of God, the distress and dejection will also leave.

Clinging to past hurts, memorable events, wins, or losses only increases our dejection, and dejection kills our energy, bodily strength, and creative power. Dejection makes it impossible for one to make spiritual or material progress.

An out-of-control mind can torment someone and convince her or him to take her or his own life, whereas a controlled mind will assist someone to reach her or his highest aims, even beyond this world. Jesus taught us to "know the truth and the truth will set you free." Free means that we can become liberated from dejection, distress, and even the wheel of birth and death.

Getting Rid of Dejection

How do we let go of dejection? Instead of identifying with complicated and puffed-up images of a heroic or a victimized self, we can let out the hot air and return to simply being a human being. If we really desire ultimate bliss and great success rather than taking shelter in people, places, and things, we can take shelter in a Higher Power.

Taking shelter means that we do our best to get the results we want, but we are surrendered to the will of a Higher Power. Refuse to fall into the pit of despair as you affirm the truth that all is well, and you will mentally and emotionally rise to the top. There is no need to ride a roller coaster being up one moment when things look good and down the next when things don't look so good. It's all good because it's All-God! Let go and enjoy the ride, trusting that you will have whatever you need, and you will.

For any of us to reach the ultimate of what is possible, we must work to prepare ourselves to be at that level. A highly elevated, extraordinary, or saintly soul is able to see the Divine reflected in his or her clear, calm, and

---

Observation Exercise

Take a little time and observe the workings of the mind, yours and others'.

✓ Notice how people live, think, and speak and what they do. Notice the cause-and-effect relationships between what they think, speak, and do and what comes to them.

✓ Notice their cleanliness, the language they use, the ways they communicate, and how they treat their clients, strangers, and family members. Notice their conversations.

✓ Notice the cause-and-effect relationship between what you (they) think, say, and do and how you (they) feel.

✓ Notice the differences in people's lives and observe why they are different.

✓ Observe the workings of your mind.

✓ Observe the relationship between your thoughts and what you do and accomplish.

purely spiritual mind. Because he or she has made his or her mind a suitable place to behold the image of Truth, Truth has appeared.

Like attracts like, and this is true on all levels. Just as you don't hang out with derelicts, drug addicts, and grossly negative people, neither do the Heavenly Angels or the most exalted beings. A God-realized soul may pass our way and stick out a helping hand, but unless we grab for the hand and are willing to do our part in being elevated to that same level, she or he will move on to the next agreeable person.

Please write the three main things you discovered from your research.

1.

2.

3.

What is your conclusion?

My conclusion is:

PEARL

*Mental absorption in one's ideals is the
key to success, whatever the goal.*

No one can entertain godly and ungodly thoughts in the same instant: it's either one or the other. Our invisible thoughts actually have weight. Fear-based depressing thoughts are heavy and weigh us down, forcing us into the distressful realms of ignorance, distress, and restriction. Positive thoughts and thoughts of love, spirit, and goodness elevate our consciousness because they are light, inspiring, exhilarating, and expansive.

Emotions are generated by our thoughts. Thoughts of love and God's unlimited goodness will naturally make us feel good. Heavy emotions of anger, guilt, shame, envy, pride, rage, doubt, and fear take us deeper into the abyss of adversity and poverty. Wallowing in self-pity and lamenting the past cause us to feel dejected, tired, and hopeless when all we need to remember is to keep the mind elevated and not let it fall, no matter what. The key to mind control is to make positive thinking a habit having nothing to do with anything in the outside world, but everything to do with attaining and keeping an inner heavenly state of being.

Focus Your Mind on Your Goals

A God-centered life will give us the greatest amount of pleasure, peace, and prosperity possible, because God is the highest of all possible thoughts. At any moment we can enjoy a heavenly state of mind by thinking heavenly, elevated thoughts.

Some Heavenly Thoughts to Think About

✓ Everywhere I go I see beauty.
✓ I see God in the heart of every living entity.
✓ I send my love to everyone I meet.
✓ I know that God loves me even more than I can possibly know.
✓ I am happy and positive that everything is working out according to God's Divine and perfect plan for my highest good.
✓ My heart is beating with the pulsation of peace, serenity, and joy.
✓ I prosper in everything I do.
✓ There is a silent Presence flowing through me and filling me with bliss.
✓ God is bringing into my experience every good and wonderful thing.
✓ I love life, and I am now entered into the joy of living.
✓ Divine love within me is reaching out and embracing the world.
✓ Every moment I am fresh, new, and restored to full vitality.
✓ Good flows through me to all and all good is thus returned to me multiplied many times over.

"And be not conformed to this world: but be ye
transformed by the renewing of your mind, that ye
may prove what is that good, and acceptable, and
perfect, will of God." —*Romans 12:2*

Lifting our minds to the divine, perfect, and True, we are transformed because instead of allowing people, places, things, and conditions to control our thinking, feeling, and behaving we are in charge and can make choices in our best interest. This is what it means to be a human being who is inner-directed and not a computer or that which is controlled by its programming. Human beings have the power of free will and choice, whereas computers can only act on the dictates of their programming and the directions of others.

Consider the Source

One of my old friends called, and I just happened to tell her that I was a minister and was getting ready to take on a church full-time. "Who do you think you are?" was her hostile response. I was crushed. How could she be so cruel and judgmental of me when we had been such good friends? Later on I remembered that she too had wanted to be a minister, in fact she was the one who had first invited me to hear Reverend Mark. Perhaps Lynn was envious, and because I had wanted her approval and appreciation, which she did not give me, I had allowed her to hurt me for a while. Instead of acting from inner peace and confidence, I reacted to her thoughts and words because I had given her the power to determine my thoughts, feelings, and actions. We can't please everyone, for no matter what we do someone will most likely not be happy with us. Years later I would come to realize that if I worked to do my best to please God, that was enough. If others were also pleased, that was nice; but if not, so what.

Envious people usually want to make us feel bad, but if they do it is our fault for allowing it. Your being, doing, and having what you desire, as long as you have no intent to harm another, never take from another. In fact, it's a blessing when you do. When you raise your consciousness and quality of living, you are lifting and improving the quality of life on earth. Others can do the same things you are, if they want to. Those with a poverty consciousness will only see you as someone who is enjoying the life they would like to be living, but are not. One who has a prosperity consciousness will be happy for you and your good fortune.

> "Don't mind criticism. If it is untrue, disregard it; if
> unfair, keep from irritation; if it is ignorant, smile; if
> it is justified, it is not criticism. Learn from it."
> —*Anonymous*

Don't Let the Stimulus-Response Machines
Get You Down

"Great spirits have always encountered violent
opposition from mediocre minds."—*Albert Einstein*

Once we really know that the thoughts of others are just their thoughts and have nothing much, if anything, to do with us at all, we are able to put our attention on living as we choose and doing our life's work. Most people don't know who they are, let alone who you are.

"If I care to listen to every criticism, let alone act on
them, then this shop may as well be closed for all
other businesses. I have learned to do my best, and
if the end result is good then I do not care for any
criticism, but if the end result is not good, then
even the praise of ten angels would not make the
difference."—*Abraham Lincoln*

People only perceive through the filter of their own beliefs and fears, unless they are God realized. God-realized people will always love you, for they are self-satisfied and they see clearly. They know you are God's beloved child and that there is an ample supply of whatever is wanted and needed for everyone.

The unrealized are envious for they perceive through a filter of poverty, lack, and limitation and view others, often even family members, as a threat to their present or future enjoyment.

"These six are always miserable: an envious person,
one who detests others, a dissatisfied person, one
who is irascible (quick-tempered), one who is
always doubtful, and one who depends on
others."—*Hitopadesa, book on Vedic philosophy*

Rising above Negative People

> "Keep away from people who try to belittle your
> ambitions. Small people always do that, but the
> really great make you feel that you, too, can
> become great."—*Mark Twain*

Negative people can also drain us of our power. "Psychic sappers," as I call them, suck our energy by their words, emotions, thoughts, attitude, and actions. Because consciousness is contagious we must keep our minds steady, especially around negative and envious people who are full of doubt, criticism, ridicule, judgment, and fear. You cannot expect someone who is consumed by fear to empower you to greatness.

People can only give us what they have and if they don't have it, they cannot give it. Believing you have something others want, they may try to take it from you. No one can take who you are, and what comes to you is what is coming through your consciousness by the law of attraction. If someone has something you want, instead of being envious say, "That's for me!" You can have it, too, if you do what is required.

Manny's Magnetism

Manny was a minister who was adored by the members of his very large congregation. People gravitated to him because was a rare soul who was not self-centered, but God- and other-person centered. He saw the good in everyone, and people blossomed in his presence. Wherever he went he was the center of attention, not because he worked at being the center but because he was very positive and encouraging to everyone he met. This did not make everyone happy, as many were envious of Manny's magnetism and popularity. Besides those who flocked to him, there were also the critics. Other ministers with smaller congregations found fault in his message and his popularity.

Manny met a woman and fell in love, but she was not content with his being the center of other people's attention. Over time this caused a great deal of trouble to their marriage, for she was dejected and depressed a good part of the time. In her attempt to be the center of Manny's attention she used her suffering, as a way to make him pamper her.

Manny worked to draw the attention of the congregation away from him and directly to her, thinking that if she had more attention from others she would be happier. He praised her continuously to his congregation and did everything he could, but it didn't work. No one was really interested in her, simply because she was not interested in them. Manny also withdrew his love and attention from the congregation and hid his light so that she would be content. Nothing worked to end her dejection. After a while he could see and understand that there was nothing he could do for her, and if she wanted to change this would have to be because of her efforts.

In time Manny went back to his old self, as this was his nature. He loved his wife and he decided to allow her to go through whatever she had to go through. Unable to tolerate the pain of her own envy and jealousy, she sought some counseling. Soon she discovered that the source of her problem was that she was a taker and self-centered rather than God- or even other-person centered.

She had been trying to take what belonged to her husband when all along she could have been happy and the center of attention, if she had only given to others the very things that she wanted: love, praise, and attention. After some time she developed a genuine concern and love for people and worked side by side with Manny to serve their growing church family.

Give from Your Fullness

Desiring to be the object of someone else's exclusive attention will cause anyone to suffer needlessly, because his or her mindset is one of poverty, or not enough. No matter what someone with a poverty consciousness gets, it's still never enough. Right here is the root cause of sibling rivalry. Often brothers and sisters are envious of one another fearing that the other is getting more of the parents' love, stuff, and attention. Someone with a poverty consciousness will think, "They are getting more, so I will have less"; whereas a prosperity-minded person thinks: "I feel so blessed to be able to love and give love to all those around me. Seeing others happy makes me happy. The more love I give, the more love I have to give."

The poverty thought behind envy, jealousy, and criticism is "There isn't enough love and happiness," when there truly is an overabundance and we need to know it. Every time we feel as if someone can take our love or happiness, it is important for us to remember that there is always more than enough because it comes from within. Giving love is the only way to feel love, and this is the secret. If you happen to feel as if you do not have enough of whatever, close your eyes, breathe slowly and deeply, and affirm the following success mantra a few times until you accept it, and then you should feel wonderful.

> Success mantra: **"I always have enough love, time, money, and energy to accomplish all my goals. My cup of every good and wonderful thing and experience is overflowing."**

Giving at church was the most satisfying part of my life because the people were reciprocal. When I gave they gave something in return, and vice versa. Each of us knew that the gifts we were giving or receiving were actually coming from God and we were just the avenues, so no one took the credit or even expected a return.

There was really only one place where I wanted to be, and that was any-place where people were actively engaged in a spiritual quest to find the Absolute Truth. Sincere spiritual seekers attempt to change and perfect themselves by becoming more godlike in consciousness and behavior, thus everyone is working to improve themselves and not just socialize, gossip, or talk about the world news.

There wasn't much jealousy among the members of my new church family in Whittier, and each was genuinely happy for the benefits the others were receiving. We were a team with the same goals: God and a heavenly existence. Church was a place where we, as spiritual seekers, could come and find like-minded and kindhearted people with whom we could share our realizations, challenges, and questions. We felt safe to be ourselves and to talk about God, our favorite subject. What I loved the most was that we could pray and people were healed and lives were restored to sanity, harmony, and prosperity.

To have a church of my own to guide was a thrilling idea. I longed to have the opportunity to find out what was possible for a group of spiritually committed people to achieve. I was ready to begin what I called the Divine Experiment and make a place for spiritual seekers of all faiths and paths to congregate, share, and explore our individual and collective possibilities. Church should be a safe and forgiving haven for anyone to learn and apply sacred teachings. This, I promised myself, was how my church was going to be. By now I was like a racehorse ready to burst out through the starting gate, as soon as I heard the bell.

The Call Finally Came

The call came and the board president said, "Reverend Terry, we have selected you to be our new minister. Would you please come to our board meeting and discuss the details? We would like you to start your work here in two weeks. Is this possible?" "Yes, I am very happy to accept your offer," I responded with joy. Hanging up the phone, I proceeded to dance around the kitchen as I shouted, "Thank you, God." Yes, it had happened just as the voice of God had told me it would. I was the new minister of the La Jolla Church. If we would just control our minds, keep focused on our goals, and think positively there would be nothing to worry about ever again. I thought to myself, "You know, this positive thinking stuff really works!"

Chapter Eight

Step Six, Upgrade on a Regular Basis

> "To aim at excellence, our reputation, and
> friends, and all must be ventured; to aim at
> the average we run no risk and provide little
> service."—*Oliver Goldsmith*

Compromise Is Fine When It Gets You What You Want

Packing my car and my old friend Ozzie's truck with all my belongings, I thought about the results of my negotiations with the board of trustees. Twelve hundred dollars a month, as my starting salary, was quite a bit less than what it cost me to pay my bills. The promise was that in six months there would be a salary review and, *if* it were feasible, I would get a raise. Because the church was so far in the hole financially, they said this was all they could afford to offer me. Never having negotiated before, I didn't know that I was supposed to negotiate or even how to negotiate. The art of negotiation was never taught in the seminary and I was naïve enough to believe that others were looking out for my best interests, especially because I was a woman and a minister. At this point I believed it wasn't spiritual for the minister to show too much concern about money, so I happily accepted their offer.

The church was a couple of months away from closing its doors due to lack of funds and poor attendance. Who cared that I was their last choice as minister and the only one who would accept the offer of $1,200 and no benefits? Starting at the bottom is a good place, for the only way to go is up and there is no way to fail, as any improvement is seen as wonderful. Also when you believe in yourself and your mission, you can afford to take a chance on something that doesn't look that appealing to others. I believed that I had something wonderful to offer others in the form of the Spiritual Principles of Successful Living.

Money Is a Symbol of Wealth, but True Wealth Is an Attitude: Dennis Took a Dirty Job

Dennis was down to his last few dollars. He had moved to Phoenix believing that he could easily find a job and make good money. There wasn't a job to be found anywhere, and now he was desperate. Looking in the classified ads he saw an ad for a dirty, greasy job, which didn't require the applicants to have any experience. Most people don't like dirty, greasy jobs, which meant there was a job opening for him and he grabbed it.

Cleaning out vents in the kitchens of restaurants became his new profession, and he did his work with excellence. At this same time, because he was at a low point in his young life, he started attending a church on a regular basis and learning and applying the spiritual principles of successful living. In a couple of years, he became the top person in the company. Later he went on to open his own company, and today he is a multimillionaire with a thriving and growing company.

Dennis is a tithing member of his church for he has proven over and over that as he gratefully gives a portion of his wealth back into God's service, he continues to prosper mightily in his business.

PEARL
Extraordinary people have a unique ability to see potential wealth in ordinary tasks.

Many Rivers of Income

Had this church been prospering, they would have hired someone else with more experience and a track record of success—but they weren't, so they hired "lucky" me. As for whatever more money I needed to pay my bills, I still had my corporate seminar and keynote speaking business. Having many avenues of revenue kept me independent and I liked the feeling, freedom, and power it gave me to be self-determined. Depending entirely upon one avenue of income sets a person up to be controlled and exploited by the one paying. Financial independence gives us the means to pursue our spiritual life, whereas financial dependence gives others the power to control our time, life, and activities. Working for others is fine, but it's wise to remember that others are not our source of supply; God is. Have as many rivers and avenues of prosperity, money, and opportunities flowing into you as you possibly can, for if one stream dries up there are many others still flowing. We must get right about money or else we struggle and do without, not because there is any scarcity of money, but because we are entertaining poverty beliefs that cause us to behave in ways that prevent us from prospering, as we should.

List your current rivers of revenue.
1.
2.
3.
4.
5.

List your possible rivers of revenue.
1.
2.
3.
4.
5.

Getting Right about Money

I had two self-defeating beliefs at the time. One was "It's crass and unspiritual to speak about money or to even ask for money in exchange for my services, time, or products." Wanting to look good, I'd act as if I didn't need the money to pay my bills, as if I were independently rich. The truth was,

I was embarrassed and uncomfortable when it came to the issue of money. Money is a part of life, but it's not the reason for life or the motivation behind what we do. It isn't the money that is important but what we can get and accomplish with the money that's the object. Money is our most used means of commerce and exchange. People can get very strange when it comes to money, especially when spiritual work is involved.

Recently we bought a color laser printer through the Internet. The first printer was faulty, so we sent it back at our expense and we agreed to take another. It, too, was defective. In our attempt to get our money back we had to deal with the owner of the Internet business, who accused us of being unspiritual because we wanted our money back. To get our money we had to depend upon American Express, and because we had all the necessary documentation, we did get it. To this man, spiritual people would accept defective products and not say anything at all.

When spiritual people ask for money or attempt to negotiate in their own behalf, exploiters accuse them of being not really interested in serving God and interested only in the money. Not wanting others to accuse me of being money hungry, I'd overcompensate by not paying any attention to the money or giving away what I had even if I could not afford to, just to prove I was spiritual and loving.

The Worlds of Spirit and Matter

There are two worlds, the invisible spiritual world and the visible material world. Both worlds have distinct qualities and both need to be recognized and respected. Knowing that you are a spiritual being does not mean you should jump off a ten-story building to prove you are spiritual, because you will destroy your body and you need it. We have both spiritual needs and material needs and, in order to succeed spiritually, we need to succeed materially. That means that there is work for each of us to do, and to do our work it is best to be healthy, intelligent, and prosperous. It's very difficult, and almost impossible, for someone to think about God, let alone help others, if he or she does not have shelter, food, and clothing and the knowledge and wherewithal to survive in the days to come. The key is to remember that you have God-given talents and abilities and when you make a product or a service out of them and offer them to others in exchange for money or whatever you need, you will prosper. There are seven basic reasons why a person is not using his or her God-given talents and therefore not prospering:

- lack of faith in his or her talents and in him- or herself
- laziness
- fear of failure or success
- not knowing how or where to start
- negative attitude
- poverty consciousness
- not producing and delivering his or her products and collecting the money, etc.

Spirituality and Good Business

If the spiritually motivated do not understand and appreciate the principles of business and reciprocation, all their good ideas for helping others most likely will not come to fruition, because of a lack of funds. Business is based on exchange, and so is every good relationship. Depending on others to take care of our needs and forfeiting our responsibility to take care of our needs set us up to be cheated. No one can cheat you if you do not desire to cheat anyone or be cheated yourself. Spiritual people need to make it perfectly all right to have money and to receive money in exchange for their goods and services, because spiritually based people have the most wonderful ideas that will help everyone.

You can have a fabulous product that will help everyone, but if you are unwilling to prosper you will subconsciously block people from purchasing what you offer. Because of an unwillingness to prosper you won't do what you need to do for people to find out about and buy your products and services. As more people pay you in exchange for your wonderful products and services, you can continue to afford to produce and deliver your products and services and help more people.

Success mantra: **"The more I allow others to compensate me for my goods and services, the more money I have to achieve my mission and accomplish my life's work."**

The Wealthy Appreciate Money

Since those early years, I have been close to many lavishly wealthy people who are also very spiritual. They charge, barter, and exchange for the services they provide, and yet they also give generously to where they receive their spiritual knowledge and to their favorite charities. Superwealthy people have no problem with money. They respect it and are not embarrassed about asking for and receiving it. Prosperous people are certain that they must receive in return for what they give. This is why they are rich.

Children of wealthy parents learn about money at an early age, but my precious parents were lower middle class and no one in my family ever talked about money except to complain that there was never enough. Because of the mystery, embarrassment, and fear around money so many really good, talented, and honest people struggle to pay the rent. In contrast some of the most corrupt people actually have good attitudes toward money as they appreciate it and are not hypocritical about it. But what they do never turns out well for anyone involved, because they are misusing the spiritual laws of life.

Money is the ultimate goal of the materialist, but for the spiritualist money is merely a means to attain their altruistic goals. Besides wanting to look spiritual and unconcerned about money I also wanted to appear wealthy, as if I didn't need money. But everyone needs money for what the money will give us in the form of food, etc. We are not taught the basics about money in school, and yet money is something almost everyone touches every day of their lives. I had to educate myself, so I made many mistakes around money until I learned to appreciate it and to take responsibility for having the funds I needed to fulfill my mission and do my life's work.

The other self-defeating belief I had was "If I ask for what I want or negotiate in my favor, they will be angry with me and most likely eject me." I did not like being vulnerable to the anger of others or to their possible criticism and rejection, so I would take whatever they gave me or I'd give away what I had. Right here was the core of my poverty belief: fear of anger, ridicule, rejection, and criticism. Fearing confrontation, I would give up and not take care of my needs and then feel resentful and cheated. We cannot control another's actions, but we can take responsibility for making sure we are fair to ourselves and to others.

The truth is, people will want what you have to offer if what you have to offer is something they perceive as being beneficial to them. This is the name of the exchange game: I give you what you want, and you give me what I want. Loving reciprocation is the topmost level in a relationship, for each is empowering the other to be happy and reach her or his goals. Genuine reciprocators are the exception rather than the rule, so we need to make sure that we set ourselves up to get what is fair and just in return for what we are giving or most likely it won't happen. If you take care of yourself and me, and I take care of myself and you, things will work out magnificently.

Success mantra: "It is perfectly right for me to ask for and get what I need and desire for my services and products."

Dumping False Ego Images

Being strong and assertive about money went against my deepest perceptions of myself as a nice person and a good girl. I had an image of myself that did not support my well-being. In fact, this "false ego image" was creating all kinds of problems for me. If I wanted to take care of myself and get what I wanted and needed, I would have to give up the image of myself as the long-suffering, sacrificing, and exploited heroine of my movie. False ego images cause us to sabotage ourselves. Instead of working to get what we really desire, need, and deserve, we are more interested in proving that our false ego image is true. Most everyone is a slave to his or her false ego images unless they have dumped them. My false ego image was "generous, kind, and unselfish girl who is taken advantage of by cheaters."

Obviously this kind of self-image made me a mark for cheaters. Our false ego image is easy to spot because we repeatedly prove it to be true in our personal and business life. Each time the theme is played out, we get to verify that we are the long-suffering perfect hero of our movie and others are the nasty villains. Our false ego images are complicated weavings upon which we can stitch an entire life of misery, poverty, and disappointment if we don't see these hidden saboteurs and get rid of them. Once we are willing to look and see if our false ego images are working against us and against the achievement of our topmost goals and dreams, we can unravel the tapestry and set a "True Ego Image" and pattern in motion. Some say, "Get rid of ego altogether," but we need to have an ego, as this is our personality and persona. You are a person of value and worth, and you need to know it. My true ego image would come to be: "I am a beloved child of God and a responsible person. I can and do take care of myself very well under any and all circumstances."

It's Okay to Judge

Hindsight helps us to recognize our past patterns and false ego images, and change them if we don't want to continue to repeat our mistakes. When we think "If only I knew then what I know now, I would do things differently," we need to realize that we have an ongoing life; therefore, we can apply our past lessons to our current situations and do things differently. Besides our own experience, we also need sacred knowledge to help us in making our decisions. Because of our tendency to judge people and situations through a filter of our hopes, dreams, and fantasies, we tend to view people and situations as we want them to be rather than as they are. This makes us prone to repeating the same relationship and even business mistakes. It wasn't until I read in the scriptures that people do not change their nature, except in rare cases, that I was able to make wonderful relationship choices in both my personal and business lives.

Discernment means judgment. We need to observe someone or a situation for a while before we get too close so that we can make the proper judgment as to whether or not this person or opportunity is a blessing or a curse. Once you sign up for the relationship, it's like getting on an airplane and not being able to get off until the plane lands, so be sure you want to go on the ride. They say love is blind, but I say that true love can only come when one's eyes are wide open.

Discrimination is the key to doing things differently. If we want to achieve our heartfelt goals, we need to have the proper knowledge with which to make our moment-to-moment choices, because each choice of action will produce a result and cause a reaction, good or bad, to come back on us. Gathering the proper knowledge of what works to get what we want and what we should avoid is the right use of intelligence and our power of discrimination. Once we understand the power of "Righteous Discrimination" we will choose to think, be, do, and have only that which is for our highest good fortune and benefit and forget the rest. Why do anything else?

Righteous Discrimination

Righteous discrimination means to make the right decisions given our goals. During moments of decision, fate is written. Every action brings a result, and if we want the right results and to determine what is right for us, we must do only those things that will automatically and naturally give us the outcome we desire. Those who make mistakes may want to blame fate—or their parents, teachers, or spouses—for their misfortunes. To disown responsibility symptomizes pettiness of heart. Instead of blaming fate or time, we should take full responsibility for our condition and work to solve our problems by gaining and applying knowledge.

Do you want to have loving, honest, and mutually supportive relationships? Of course everyone wants to be loved, as this is the goal of life, but love can never come from someone who is a cheater. Unfortunately, many of us tend to choose our most intimate and important partners in the heat of physical attraction or from ignorance, which means having our eyes closed to the way they really are. Changing our conditioned nature is quite possible, though challenging. We can become any kind of person we desire if our desire to change is strong enough and we work at it. Two people with the same spiritual and material goals who agree to do so can help each other eliminate self-defeating behavior and develop new habits of thinking, behaving, and relating. True love will blossom when both choose to help each other to achieve their common goals, but this must be a mutual choice for it to work.

When choosing both intimate and business partners, we want to opt for loving, straightforward reciprocators. The cheated believe they are going to change the cheaters and make them loving reciprocators, but this dream can be compared to someone who is going to change a hungry crocodile into a tiny pet turtle in a bowl. Cheaters, the cheated, and reciprocators are the three kinds of people. Obviously the cheaters and the cheated wind up together because they feed on each other's false ego images. One sees her- or himself as a shark and the other as a minnow.

Our work is not to change others so that we get a fair deal, but to learn to apply the art and science of righteous discrimination by carefully selecting our mates, partners, and friends. So many of the spiritual people I've met had little if any ability to discriminate in their best interests, because they didn't want to judge others. We have to judge people, not criticize them, but use our eyes and ears to gain knowledge of what kind of people we are dealing with or if we even want to deal with them. Wanting to see only the good in others can set a person up to be victimized, even harmed, by someone who sees you only the way a shark sees a minnow. God gave us intelligence so that we can take care of ourselves by making the right decisions, especially when it comes to our associations.

> "No one is another's friend or enemy. Friends or
> enemies are created by conduct."—*Ancient proverb*

What, if anything, has been your false ego image?

My false ego image is:

What is your new true ego image?

My true ego image is:

Sometimes It's Best Not to Compromise

In accepting a position as the minister of this tiny church of fewer than fifty people, I needed to be strong and assertive, as well as sharpen my powers of discernment. Even though the congregation was small, I still needed to be positive and assertive. Spiritual doesn't mean feeble, ineffectual, or wishy-washy. Those who are will never have the opportunity to do their good works, as they will most likely be run over and run right out of town before they get the chance. People work to compromise you, but if they do and you are the leader, you have lost your opportunity to really help people.

The church board thought they had purchased me, as a hired hand rather than a partner, for $1,200 a month. Right away I knew I had to have the correct attitude of independence and take control, as well as I could. During the board meeting they asked me a few personal questions. "Where are you going to live?" inquired Tom, the vice president of the board. "Well, Tom, I want a house within a block of the ocean with a view, preferably in the Shores" was my reply. "You can't afford to live in the Shores, and you are not going to find anything that fits your description," he retorted, as if he were the absolute authority on what was possible. "Tom, I am teaching positive thinking, and with God all things are possible. Why would I limit myself by thinking it is impossible for me to get what I desire? I know that if I have the desire, then it is possible and will happen" was my comeback.

Sure enough, I found the house and it was exactly what I wanted. The ocean view was out the bathroom window, but I had my view. Actually, in my prayer I had never stated how large a view I wanted, so I got just a view. We have to be specific when we ask for what we want and feel certain that it's possible for us to attain it. Don't let others tell you what you can or cannot be, do, and have. Be strong and feel certain that it is possible for you to live your dreams, just as you have imagined.

Chris Got His Dream House at the Lowest Price

While taking one of my classes called Mastery in Manifestation, Chris decided to affirm that he would get the beautiful and spacious condo he coveted, in the exact location he wanted, with a fabulous view and all for a price that was much lower than the going rate. Before the class he never would have thought or believed it possible. Using his success mantras and also doing the necessary legwork of actively seeking the condo, he was led to the perfect place. Everything was exactly as he had stated in his prayer. At the time he closed the deal, other condos like his in the same building were selling for 23 percent more than what he had paid.

> Success mantra: **"I know and accept that the right home I desire, in the right neighborhood I desire, and at the right price I can afford is made known to me and is mine."**

How to Be Better, Do Better, and a Have Better Life

In preparation for my move to La Jolla, my most major move, so far, I had cleaned out an entire house, office, garage, and life and dumped everything that was not at the level where I now opted to be. When you want to get the treasures, you will need to get rid of a lot of trash. We can't move forward and attain our ultimate goal or dream if we are dragging dead weight, engaging in self-defeating activities, or attached to people, places, things, and activities at the lower and now-undesirable level. You need to know it is perfectly natural to desire to improve your condition—in fact, this is what we are supposed to do. Naturally everyone wants to be better, do better, and have a better life. The role of our intelligence, in combination with the vast and limitless resources of Infinite Intelligence, is to help us to attain our goals, solve our problems, and get us to the ultimate and most prized of all riches, found only at the very top of the mountain. Follow your bliss and your intelligence and they will take you to your desired destination, but never follow your mind. The mind, or false ego, acts as a spoiled child and when it does not get its way it cries, wails, throws a temper tantrum, and causes us to fall into a heap on the floor as we wallow in lamentation and self-pity. If we want to be better, do better, and have a better life, we must keep our minds focused on our goals and the attainment of our life's mission.

Saints

Saints are saintly because they follow their bliss and never their minds. Saints are those who seek and find the topmost treasures of human existence. Saints are ordinary people who sought and found the secrets of life. Saints have developed the ability to be in a continual state of bliss while performing their missions and lives' work.

Someone who is able to transcend the ups and downs of this world, scale any mountain to achieve his or her topmost goals, while remaining as calm and peaceful within as a crystal-clear mountain lake is called a saint. They know exactly what to do that works and what not to do that doesn't work, and they do what works to give them the results they want and they avoid what doesn't.

Sin means wrongdoing or to miss the mark. The mark is the goal and objective. A sinner is someone who keeps on doing the same thing that has been causing suffering while expecting to get a favorable result. Missing the mark and wrong actions result in distress, poverty, illness, and failure.

A person who eats the wrong food can get sick; someone who doesn't work, most likely, will become poor; someone who gambles may lose all her or his money and fall deeply in debt; someone who is an alcoholic or drug addict can ruin both his or her health and life; a person who thinks negative and fear-based thoughts will be miserable. This is called cause and effect or "as you sow, so shall you reap."

Hitting the mark at the center of the target brings treasures, riches, rewards, and prizes. Eating healthy food and exercising keep us strong; those who work with the right attitude will prosper; those who are positive and have faith in God will be peaceful; those who are loyal, supportive, and faithful in marriage will be happy; those who serve God with pure love will be blissful, etc.

Saints exist in business, sports, humanhood, marriage, parenting, art, education, health, finance, and spiritual matters. Sainthood is not awarded to the fainthearted or to the lazy, weak, or cowardly, but to the visionaries and warriors who never allow themselves to be defeated. If they do fall, they get back up and try again and again until they succeed. Candidates for sainthood continuously upgrade, as they keep on keeping on, allowing no one or no thing to stop them no matter who or what it is. Fearlessly and tirelessly they endeavor to fulfill their sacred mission and reach their ultimate goal and objective. You may not want to be a saint, but most likely you would like to improve some area of your life, and if so, you will need to improve by upgrading.

The Sixth Step on the Sacred Treasure Map

Upgrading on a Regular Basis is the sixth step on the Sacred Treasure Map to the Spiritual and Material Riches of Life. Upgrading is the process of releasing something you consider inferior and replacing it with something you consider superior. All things have a season and when that time is over, it's right to move on to the next more desirable situation just as winter moves into spring. Upgrading is a simple name for positive, deliberate, and favorable change. You let go of one thing for another and in this way you climb from where you are to where you want to be. When you upgrade, you need to know the goal and objective and you let go of anything and everything that is not at that level and bring in and add everything that is.

A New Way of Setting Goals

I have a special technique that works really well when it comes to setting and achieving your spiritual and material goals, but it is unusual. Instead of just setting a goal and then planning how you are going to get there, my way is to decide what you would like to have happened and what you would like to have achieved. Notice the use of "have happened" instead of "will happen"? Rather than starting from here and going to there, you start from there, the goal having already been achieved, and you look back and figure out what you would have needed to do to have achieved your goals.

What would you like to have happened? Not just "happen," mind you, but "have happened," past tense. I strongly suggest that you do this exercise, and as we move along and you do each of the subsequent exercises, you will understand the reasoning behind this unique and extremely powerful method. More important, simply by doing the writing exercises, what you desire to have happened will automatically start happening. Opportunities will come to you that before seemed out of the question, and even impossible. Some who have done the exercises get what they want without doing anything except writing out the exercises; that's how powerful they are.

What would you like to have happened?

Spiritually:

Relationships:

Career:

Health:

Investments:

Home and lifestyle:

The Miraculous Science of the Be, Do, Have Model

I work with and teach the "Be, Do, Have Model." From this model, we can mold our lives as we choose.

1. Decide what you want to have happened and what you want to have achieved.
2. Be an actor and take on the consciousness, beliefs, body language, knowledge, and attitude of one who has already attained what you would like to have happened and attained.
3. Do what someone who has achieved what you want to have achieved does.

The question I ask my clients and students is "Having to do with your ultimate and topmost goal, what would you like to have happened?" Challenging them even further I say, "Go even further to the end of your life in this body and look back to what you wish you had accomplished, attained, and achieved." I mix the past and present tense on purpose. I know this is not proper English, but it is proper having to do with the science of manifestation and miracles.

Writing these exercises will help us work miracles, for they challenge the mind and intelligence by presenting us with the opportunity to go beyond the mere setting of a goal to the point where we have already

> Having to do with your ultimate and topmost goal, what would you like to have happened?
>
> What I would like to have happened is that:

achieved it, past tense. Once we have attained the goal in our mind, we can look back to where we are now and ascertain exactly what it is that we needed to have done to have attained the goal. Take those steps now and bring everything you can up to the new standard, and you will be there.

After my students and clients answer the first couple of questions, I ask them the following question, "Who would you have had to become in order

> Looking to the end of your life in this body and then looking back, what would you have liked to have accomplished, attained, or achieved?
>
> I would like to have:

for you to have attained your ultimate goal?" Furthering my instruction, I say, "Being has to do with attitude, consciousness, self-image, and state of mind. Before you can reach your goal, you must have the attitude and consciousness of someone who has attained whatever it is that you would like to have attained. Once you get clear about what you would like to have happened, you would do well to take a little time to contemplate what it would have taken for you to have accomplished and achieved it. If you don't know, then do your market research and ask those who have already accomplished and achieved your same or similar goals how they did it. This is the value of seeking knowledge from those who have already climbed the mountain you wish to climb. They can tell you what to do and what not to do."

> Who would you have had to become in order for you to have attained your ultimate goal(s)?
>
> I would have to have become:
> 1.
> 2.
> 3.
> 4.
> 5.
> 6.

Nothing happens by accident. Consciousness has two parts: knowledge and action. Once we acquire the proper knowledge, we need to act on it and do the saintly or right thing. Between being and having is doing. Doing is the mechanism that turns an idea into a form, but it is the mental and emotional acceptance of the goal as having been achieved that makes it all possible. A Higher Power comes into play that brings forth the right people, situations, events, and knowledge needed for the goal to be accomplished in this three-dimensional plane that has already been accomplished on the mental and causal plane. "What would you have done in order for you to have attained your goal(s)?"

> "Just as a potter can make anything he desires from
> a lump of clay, one can create good and bad results
> according to his activities."
> —*Hitopadesa, book on Vedic philosphy*

What would you have done in order for you to have
attained your ultimate goal?

1.
2.
3.
4.
5.
6.

Own Your Ranch and Dream House

Perhaps you would like to have purchased a ranch in Wyoming. Create in your mind and imagination the concept and image of your having already attained it. Use your intelligence to help you figure out what you would have needed to have done to have purchased it. Then make a plan of action and follow it. If there is an error in your plan, correct it and continue with your plan until you actually own your ranch. Wishful thinking will not do it, but when you have already attained it in your mind, accepted it in your heart, and are doing what you can to make it happen, the power of Infinite Intelligence joins with you to manifest your dream into reality. As you work to attain your ranch, the right people, situations, and circumstances come to you, as if by magic. But it is not magic at all; it is the way things are supposed to work when one is in tune with Spirit and the universe.

Another example: If you are a writer and you desire to have had a best-selling book, get rid of all your habits and attitudes that are not at the level of one who is a best-selling author. Keep whatever you know, do, or have that is favorable to your having a best-selling book and then find out what else is needed and add that. You see, it is not just about writing the book; it is about the book already being a best-seller. Writing is part of the process, but not the goal. Your goal is for the book to have been a best-seller for which you have already received large sums of money. The only way you can get from here to there is by being there first in your mind and behavior and then upgrading, step-by-step, until you have actually achieved it.

How to Reach the Top

You've got to climb if you want to make it to the top. Social climbers are not well thought of but if you want to get to the heights of anything, especially spiritual life, you will have to make advancement. Advancement purely and simply is the process of exchanging a less desirable situation for a more desirable one, a lower state of mind for a higher one, mundane knowledge for absolute truth, a degrading relationship for an enriching one, an inferior teacher for a superior one, etc. No one believes it cruel to sacrifice a diseased part of the body to save the body. Why is it not just as important to release someone or something that is keeping us in a condition of mediocrity, abuse, poverty, or ignorance? I like to illustrate the upgrading philosophy with the story of "The Little Jeweled Box."

The Little Jeweled Box

Once there was a man named Soli whose best friend was a king. The king presented Soli with a precious jeweled box that had been handmade by the finest jeweler in the kingdom. This precious little box was exquisitely carved and inlaid with costly and precious jewels. Taking the box home and placing it in a prominent place, Soli noticed how shabby his home appeared in comparison. The little jeweled box became the standard and model for the quality he wanted to have achieved throughout his home. Soli set to work clearing out everything that was mediocre, which left very little. Next he cleaned his home from top to bottom until everything sparkled. After fixing everything that was broken, he proceeded to paint and decorate until the living room was almost as beautiful as the box. This made the rest of his house look shabby. Soon he had redecorated his entire home until every room almost matched the quality of the little jeweled box. Soli was not a rich man so he could not afford to make his home as exquisitely magnificent as the box, but he did his very best with what he had.

Walking outside, he noticed that the outside of the house looked shabby in comparison to the inside, so he set to work fixing and painting the outside of the house. His newly repaired and beautified house made his yard look shabby. Soli got to work in his yard. First he cleaned up his yard, pulled the weeds, cultivated the soil, and planted a colorful and bountiful garden. The outside was now just as beautiful as the inside. But his newly opulent house and yard made the entire neighborhood look shabby.

What did the neighbors do? Some were envious and steaming with jealousy and criticism, and others got to work and made their homes and yards as beautiful as his. Yes, soon most of the whole neighborhood was lovely, and so were most of the people. The moral of the story is: Once you set a standard of excellence, beauty, and quality by your own example it uplifts all others to also rise to that level. This is how we change the world, one person and one home, yard, and neighborhood at a time.

> "Always do your best. What you plant now, you will
> harvest later."—*Og Mandino, author*

The Ritual of Upgrading

A sculptor was looking at a large piece of marble when a bystander said, "What are you going to make?" "The figure of a beautiful woman," was the reply. "How are you going to do that?" asked the bystander. "By chipping away what is not needed," concluded the artist.

There are Nine Steps in the Ritual of Upgrading

1. Know what you would like to have happened.
2. Clean out everything that does not meet the standard of what you would like to have happened and achieved.
3. Choose your associations at the level of what you would like to have happened and achieved in partnership.

4. Develop the habits you would have needed to have had for you to have achieved your goal.

5. Upgrade your personal presentation including voice, posture, clothing, and grooming to the level of what you would like to have happened and achieved.

6. Have the beliefs, thoughts, attitudes, and knowledge of someone who has achieved your same goal.

7. Develop and offer your products, talents, and services at the quality level of what you would like to have happened and achieved.

8. Design and make your living space and lifestyle as you would like to have achieved.

9. Communicate about you and your products and services in the manner that would guarantee that you achieved your goal.

PEARL

Clean out everything that does not meet the standard of what you would like to have happened and achieved.

You have set your goals as to what you would like to have happened. You have created the consciousness of one who has attained the goal, and now you need to clean out the trash of the old life to make space for the treasures of the new. One of the first things I say to my new students is "Please take some time this week or the next and clean out your closets, cars, office, garage, and house. If you want something better than what you have, you will need to make a space for it. Letting go of something you no longer want or need puts your trash back into circulation so it can become someone else's treasure. Very soon, as you will see, because nature does not tolerate a vacuum, that empty space will be filled with something that is exactly what you need and desire."

I give this assignment because it works, every time. Cleaning out stuff that doesn't fit our ideals and standards is an empowering and valuable exercise. Physically giving away in charity to some worthy person or cause, or selling or trading stuff that reminds us of unhappy experiences or things we don't need and cannot use helps us to let go of energy-draining mental and emotional attachments. Miserliness is a form of poverty, which produces a hard heart. Our nature is to share and to give love. Giving things away with love for the purpose of helping others in need helps us to soften our hearts and gives us a sample of the joy that comes with giving. Have a big garage sale and invest the money in your new moneymaking project. Circulate what you no longer need, as this action of giving opens you to the mode of receiving.

> "These four beneficial combinations are very rare:
> charity accompanied by sweet words; knowledge
> without pride; valor without forbearance; and
> wealth with a charitable disposition."
> —*Eastern wisdom*

Associations

We rise or fall mainly because of our associations. Ninety percent of the results we achieve come to us because of our associations. Books, music, movies, television, friends, family, coworkers, etc., are all considered associations. The ideal is to associate with people, teachers, books, etc., that are at the level you would like to have attained. We become like those with whom we associate. Because there is only so much time in a day, if our time is spent with people who are not the kind of people whom we admire and desire to emulate, we are sabotaging our efforts and defeating ourselves. Once you set your ultimate goal, seek out those who have already attained the same goal or that which is similar. Surround yourself with that which is at the same level as what you desire to have attained and happened, and you will have arrived.

The Failure Factor of False Loyalty

Being overly attached to people, places, and things, as well as to circumstances remaining the same causes us to suffer needlessly, clouds our better judgment, and makes us slaves to the objects of our attachments. This happens because we identify with the person, place, thing, or situation as the source of our respect, love, prosperity, fame, and security. Actually God is our Source and supply and when we can go with the flow, so to speak, we are able to allow people and things to change around us and we can adapt and progress.

The Old Well

Once there was an old well that had been furnishing this one family with an abundance of sweet water for ten or more generations. The family members were very proud of this well, for it had the reputation for having the purest water around. Travelers would go out of their way just to pass by the old well and get a drink of the legendary sweet water. Gradually over time the water had become polluted because of poor sanitation and industrial toxic waste. Family members were getting sick, and some had even died from drinking the water. Many of the neighbors advised the family to stop drinking the water, but the remaining family members were too proud to listen. After all, this old well was famous and they had a family tradition to carry on. Soon after this, not one member of the family was still alive. All that was left was an old polluted well.

> One should abandon a family member for the sake
> of the family, the family for the village, the village
> for the district—but one should abandon the
> whole world to save one's own self."
> —*Hitopadesa, book on Vedic philosophy*

Releasing people, places, things, and conditions can be compared to dancing. Choosing a partner, place, or situation, we may dance for a while because there is value in the relationship. Watch ballroom dancing or professional couples ice-skating and you will see the beauty and harmony that can be attained when people of like minds and hearts work together for a common goal. Should one or the other choose not to practice or progress, what will happen? Either they will both quit or one will quit and the other will go on, or perhaps they will both find other partners. For relationships to thrive, those involved must have the same goals and, spiritually speaking, the same God.

Would you condemn someone who leaves a relationship, city, material possession, or job situation because he or she desires to progress toward his or her ultimate goal, or would you say, "This is understandable"? Would you criticize someone who lost one hundred pounds and call her or him disloyal to the fat, or would you congratulate her or him for upgrading? Some will call this ruthless when it's just a matter of choice to move up the ladder to a superior position. Relationships change when the persons involved either never had the same goals so when the lust wears off they have nothing in common, or at some point they change and one goes in one direction and the other in another. Those relationships and dances that continue are those in which the people change together. Upgrading on a regular basis is not about dumping people, as you climb over them to reach your goal, and then again it is, if your goals are important enough to you.

Everyone is using others to get what they want, as this is human nature. Some abuse others to get what they want, while others engage in loving reciprocal relationships. God brings people into our lives because they can help us and we can help them, but when and if that time is over, people will naturally discontinue the dance and choose other partners. Everyone has a right to change, and the ideal is for couples and families to change together, each helping the other to make spiritual and material advancement.

PEARL
Making good choices in relationships has to do with how well we use our ability to discriminate.

"Friendship between the prey and the predator is the cause of distress. Just see the great difference between the predator and the prey. The predator momentarily enjoys the flesh, while the other loses his life."—*Hitopedesa*

PEARL
Choose your associations at the level of what you would like to have happened and achieved in partnership.

A wise teacher told me, "Choose associations of people, places, and things based on your goals, ideals, and standards, and then you will surely attain your destination."

Look at the value of associating with those who can help you to attain your goals, aspirations, and dreams. Because we become like those with whom we associate, it only makes sense to choose our associations wisely. Here are some suggestions to help you decide what suits you and your ultimate desires.

A. Associate with people who are the most famous, intelligent, spiritual, expert, and wealthy and get a sense of how they believe, think, and behave.
B. Associate with those who have reached the top of the ladder of success in your fields of interest, ask them for advice, learn from them, and work with and model yourself after them.
C. Associate with those who can give you credibility because others judge us by those with whom we associate. Your reputation is valuable, and it should be protected and enhanced whenever you have the opportunity.
D. Associate with people who can buy your products or services.
E. Associate with the most wonderful, loving, happy, honest, and saintly people as possible.
F. Associate with the people who have the habits and qualities that best represent the habits and qualities you desire to obtain and demonstrate.

PEARL
*Develop the habits you would have needed
for you to have achieved your goal.*

Gene Chose a New Life

Gene had been a marijuana smoker for over eighteen years. Whenever he felt dejected, stressful, bored, or anxious, he would smoke to alleviate his suffering. During these years he lost his will to do his life's work, seeking shelter from his distress in marijuana. Gene believed that smoking with friends and getting high was the best part of his life, because he could laugh, relax, and forget his problems, as if they did not exist.

While smoking all kinds of great ideas would pour forth from his imagination, but when the effect of the smoke was gone, so would his will or desire to carry out his elaborate visions and revelations. During these eighteen years he fell further and further into lethargy, laziness, and poverty, but when he smoked he didn't care. Gene's real life had become a pipe dream.

Gene was very talented and had wonderful gifts to offer, but he was unwilling to do his life's work out of fear of failure, criticism, hard work, and success. The truth was, he was impotent, as his fears of both success and failure kept him in the purgatory of nowhere land. He hadn't always been that way, but after some setbacks in his career and personal life and because of the vicious criticism and attacks he had received because he was so extraordinarily successful, he just wanted to escape from it all. His solution for eliminating pain and getting pleasure was to drop out and avoid any possible situations that could produce the slightest bit of stress or anxiety. Smoking always put him in another reality, free from care.

Upgrading One Step at a Time

Watching his life ebb away he knew something was wrong, but he felt powerless in the face of his addiction and, besides, he was attached to the feeling. Praying with sincerity, he begged God to help him get rid of his bad habit and also give him the strength to resume his life's work with enthusiasm.

Gene did his part by upgrading everything he could. He stopped associating with his pot-smoking so-called, friends. When they called, he either didn't answer the phone or he gave an excuse for why he couldn't see them. Some were actually cruel, as they accused him of abandoning his friends who had been there for him, as if the right thing to do was to continue being a drug addict. Misery loves company, as the saying goes.

Why should someone remain in an undesirable situation just to please others who want to stay as they are and not better their existence? Cleaning out everything that had anything to do with marijuana, he made his home and life drug-free. Methodically he replaced his pot-smoking relationships and activities with positive and life-affirming relationships and activities. By attending spiritual gatherings and classes as often as he could, Gene met new friends and started growing in spiritual understanding and knowledge. An inferiority complex, laziness, and fear of abandonment had been at the core of his problem.

Within time thanks to God and Gene's efforts his desire to smoke completely disappeared, whereas before he prayed and asked God to help him, no matter what he did he could not stop. With the help of a spiritual teacher he learned that he must tolerate distress when it comes, for it will pass. Gene used success mantras to help him to think higher thoughts and to elevate his mind and keep it steady. If he became bored, he understood that it was he who was boring. Immediately he'd jump into his work or do something worthwhile that was inspiring and interesting to him. Methodically he replaced each negative habit with a positive one.

Now he had a goal, which he had not had for many years. Gene realized that anyone who wants to achieve his or her goals must win the battle of positive over negative that is going on within. Instead of seeking the easy way out through intoxication, he faced his fears, rolled up his sleeves, and got back to work. If people criticized him, so what? And if they appreciated him, so what? He was doing the best he could.

Soon he loved the hard work, for it was proving to be satisfying and very profitable. Money started rolling in and filling up his wallet and bank accounts. Gene's goal was to build a retreat center to help other recovering addicts to also become victorious in their battles to conquer fear and weakness by becoming courageous and strong. Instead of running away and avoiding his challenges, he met them head-on because he saw himself as a spiritual warrior on a mission to serve God by helping others to help themselves.

Gene didn't always win the outer battles, but every time he tried and gave his all he became a bigger winner within himself, whatever the outcome. Turning his life and the final results of his endeavors over to God, as he knew God to be, he lost most of his anxiety. As Gene continues to upgrade his inner and outer worlds, his dreams are coming true and he is finally manifesting his great ideas into reality, one step at a time.

PEARL

Upgrade your personal presentation including voice, posture, clothing, and grooming to be at the level of what you would like to have happened and achieved.

The heroine of *My Fair Lady (Pygmalion)* is a perfect example of a person who, shall we say, lived in the gutter and then became the queen of the ball by transforming her voice, manners, dress, hair, posture, etc. We can learn, and because we can learn we can become anyone or anything we desire.

Aristotle Onassis, the Greek shipping tycoon who married Jackie Kennedy, was not always a rich and powerful man. In his early poverty days, in order to impress others, he would make sure that he had a year-round tan. To accomplish this he always carried a reflector with him, and when he had a few minutes, he would sit outside and get some sun. His reasoning was that the rich always have tans because they have time to vacation at expensive resorts, and he wanted others, especially his clients, to perceive him as being rich. It worked!

I could not stand to hear my high-pitched, harsh voice on audiotape. Given the fact that all my talks and seminars were recorded and people were purchasing them, I felt responsible to see to it that they were of the best quality. I took voice lessons and worked to make my voice pleasing and easy to listen to. In a while the problem was solved, and tens of thousands of people have since listened to my lessons and messages on tape.

The body does not lie, as it is communicating to others what we really think and believe no matter what we say. This is why it is very important to learn to make your body say what you want to say and express to others. Good posture expresses health, vitality, and enthusiasm, whereas slumped shoulders and a hanging head express hopelessness and lack of confidence. Simply by changing your posture and body language to reflect how you want to feel and think will also change what you really think, feel, and believe. Walk with confidence, and you are confident.

Describe your voice, posture, clothing, and grooming at the level of what you would like to have happened and achieved.

Voice:

Posture:

Clothing:

Hair and grooming:

PEARL

Have the beliefs, thoughts, attitude, and knowledge of someone who has achieved your same goal.

What would you have needed to have known, believed, and thought in order for you to have achieved your goal?

Known:

Believed:

Thought:

GEM

Develop and offer your products, talents, and services at the quality level of what you would like to have happened and achieved.

The supersuccessful constantly endeavor to achieve higher levels of excellence. Do some market research and study the quality of the most excellent products and services that are similar to yours. Apply this knowledge and upgrade your products and services to be at the optimal level of excellence that you can afford.

Why do hundreds of thousands of people travel to India and tolerate the most difficult traveling conditions just to see the Taj Mahal? Why do people spend great sums of money just to travel from all over the world to Paris to stand in line to view the *Mona Lisa* painting or to Florence to see the sculpture of David? Why do people save all year for a two-week vacation in the wilderness?

Perfection, or the closest that we can get to perfection, causes people to resonate at a higher frequency. God's creation is perfect, and it is the integrity in nature that calms one's nerves and brings peace to the soul.

When we attempt to do our best and reach perfection through our work and creations, we are exalted and lifted above this mundane world to the noble and majestic. Work done at this level of love and commitment inspires and enthralls.

"It is the quality of our work which will please God
and not the quantity."—*Mahatma Gandhi*

Describe your products, talents, and services as they would be at the level of what you would like to have happened and achieved.

Products:

Talents:

Services:

"If a man is called to be a street sweeper, he should
sweep streets even as Michelangelo painted, or
Beethoven composed music, or Shakespeare wrote
poetry. Then they will say, here lived a great street
sweeper who did his job well."
—*Martin Luther King Jr.*

PEARL
*Design and create your living space and lifestyle to be
as you would like to have achieved.*

Using my upgrading process, as soon as I caught the flavor of a higher taste or a glimpse of what others had that I also wanted, at the first opportunity I would abandon the lower by choosing the higher. Once I got the sweet taste of being a vegetarian and eating foods in the mode of goodness (besides my health improving a thousand percent), I became happier and got better results faster, because nothing dense was holding me down. The moment when I noticed a rarer state of being, a state of bliss, a general feeling of well-being, I would include whatever was giving that to me, and drop whatever detracted from that.

Instead of staying at a Motel Six, in Los Angeles, I would choose to stay at the Bel-Air Hotel in Beverly Hills. The quality and elegance of the hotel's rooms and gardens and the excellent service would so inspire me that everything I had set out to accomplish on my trip I did, and at a much higher level of excellence and productivity. The difference in price was an investment that paid off. Surround yourself with excellence.

PEARL

Communicate about you and your products and services in a manner that guarantees that you achieve your goal.

How would you and your products and services have needed to be perceived by others in order for you to have achieved your goal?

My clients and customers would have needed to perceive me as:

My clients and customers would have needed to perceive my product and services as:

Success mantra: **"It is perfectly right for me to be surrounded by excellence and beauty."**

I had completed the cleaning-out phase of the ritual of upgrading, and now I was ready to bring in the life I desired to have. The life I wanted to have was that of a minister of a large church congregation, a television minister, and someone who makes a difference in the lives of many. Saying good-bye to old friends, a few I would see again and most I would never see again, I put my Volvo, the first car I had bought all by myself, in gear, backed out of the driveway, turned around, and headed south.

The First Sunday

Arriving in La Jolla that night, a few days before my first Sunday service, gave me time to move everything into my house and set up my office in the church's small office building. There was also plenty of time to take a few peaceful walks on the beach, and contemplate the opportunity before me. Taking my notepad to the beach, I would spend a little time each day writing down my plans for the church and my new life.

The sun rose on my first Sunday, as the new minister of the La Jolla Church of Religious Science. Wearing a rose-colored two-piece dress with a white gardenia pinned on my velvet vest and carrying my freshly typed sermon in a folder, I drove to the La Jolla Women's Club on Prospect Street and confidently walked into the building. One of the board members ushered me backstage to a spot where I could sit and pray before the service.

After a while the sound of the old organ started up, and the room was filled with familiar old church tunes. Peeking out through a broken seam in the faded golden velvet curtains, I almost fell out onto the stage when to my amazement I saw the room packed with people. Many had to stand, as there were no more chairs. Twenty-five people had attended the week before my first Sunday, and today there were over two hundred and fifty.

Enthused about the life-transforming message I had to give, I made my last-minute preparations. Mentally I went down my checklist to make sure that my mind was focused and I was clear about the results I intended to produce.

My Checklist for Giving a Valuable and Memorable Speech

1. Know my subject and be prepared.
2. Feel whatever I am feeling and experience the feelings with acceptance, even if it is nervousness. Trying not to be nervous would only make me more nervous.
3. Visualize everyone being happy and receiving value. Envision the congregation giving me a standing ovation.
4. Pray and turn it over to God through the Holy Spirit, Jesus, and the Angelic Realm, trusting that whatever happens will be God's will.
5. Concentrate on the message, main points, and the sum and substance of what I intend to communicate and *give* to my audience.

6. Remember I am talking to only one person. Don't see a crowd, but a gathering of individuals.

7. Think "I love you" in my mind and project it out to every person. Unconditionally accept everyone exactly as they are, without criticism or judgment.

8. Be clear about how I want the people to respond and the action I would like each of them to take.

Making My First Entrance

"Terry make a great entrance and a great exit, for people forget what goes on in between" was the advice my college drama teacher had given me many years before. He added, "The audience only remembers your first entrance and your last exit, so be certain and deliberate in both. In between your entrance and exit take charge, and own the stage and hold the audience in your heart. Love them and give them your full attention. Always leave them wanting more."

PEARL
"No one does anything alone, for every successful endeavor involves the contributions of many."

As the organist played the call to worship, I found the center of the curtains, opened them deliberately and with style, and made my first grand entrance. Smiling radiantly, I walked to center stage and right up to the podium. Glancing out over the packed house, making eye contact, and projecting "I love you" to everyone, I boomed out with cheery enthusiasm, "Good morning." "Good morning," they replied in unison.

My first sermon as the minister of the La Jolla church was received with a standing ovation and thundering applause. They liked what they heard, and my job was set; now it was time to get to work and build the church of my dreams.

Because I had walked into an all-but-defunct church, it was up to me to clean house, dump everything that had been killing the church, and upgrade just about everything to a high standard of excellence. Everything that first Sunday went pretty well given it was the first day, except for the music.

I Had to Take a Stand

Hell hath no fury like that of a church organist or singer dumped. She did not let go gracefully, for she had been playing the organ in this church for years. As far as she was concerned this was her church, and I was the one who was going to leave and she was going to see to it. If she had stayed, the congregation would have dwindled back down to its former twenty-five members who had been tolerating her playing for years. Before I came, half the people slept and snored during the entire service. Having spent a few years doing my research about what worked and what didn't work in church, I knew that the music needed to be inspiring, uplifting, motivating, invigorating, and current.

Right away I knew I had to be firm by taking the reins of the church, or I would have been defeated before I had a chance to make my contribution and build my ideal ministry. If you have big dreams, you will have to think and act big by taking a firm stand for your ideals and values and then back them up with strong and well-thought-out decisions. Lives, companies, and fortunes are destroyed or built one decision at a time.

You Are in Charge of Your Life

Whether people like it or not you are in charge of your life, and whether or not the board of the church liked it I saw myself as the one in charge of the church. Someone has to take 100 percent responsibility, and that person had to be me. There are always those who can tell you how they would do things differently if they were you, but they are not you. This is your life! No matter what others think or tell you, your decisions are 100 percent up to you. You will be the one who will either reap the rewards for your decisions or have to pay for your mistakes. Be aware: Others will not pay for your mistakes even if they gave you the advice to do the thing that turned out to be a mistake. Opinions are cheap and everyone has one, but if you take others' advice, be prepared for your life to become as theirs. These board members had compromised the previous minister into failure, but they were not going to get me. I had nothing to lose and everything to gain; but if I had been totally dependent upon the church for my livelihood, I might have been a coward and compromised every decision.

Criticism Must Be Overcome at Every Point of Decision

Each decision you make requires strength to back it up. As a leader you must make decisions in favor of the greater good of all. Do not think that every decision you make will be appreciated and accepted by everyone, even when those decisions actually improve conditions. Criticism from the board for my firing of the organist was my first hurdle to jump. They felt that she should stay because she had been there all those years. Sentimentality is the killer of excellence, happiness, wealth, and progress.

I was getting my first taste of politics, and somehow I knew to hold the reins tight, stand my ground, and be firm in my decision so that all those involved knew that there wasn't even the slightest possibility that she would stay. If you allow politics, everyone's opinion, and all the problems and challenges that will appear to stop you, you won't get anywhere and you will be consumed by fear, poverty, and weakness. As Truman Capote said in response to the question of how he handled criticism, "The wagon trains keep rolling and the dogs keep on barking." Eleanor Roosevelt's favorite aunt had given her similar advice on the eve of Eleanor's becoming first lady of the United States of America: "Tell others what you think and believe, Eleanor, because you will be criticized whatever you do, so you may as well be who you are."

Dogs Will Bark

Critics, as I came to realize, are like barking dogs running after the wheels of a moving car. Not all critics are dogs, for some have good advice, but then they are not critics but friends, advisors, and consultants. Constructive criticism is helpful, whereas malicious criticism is self-defeating.

Right away I had to get used to the idea that the minister, boss, leader, or teacher is the one who gets the greatest amount of criticism, and this is the way it is. When things go well others take the credit, and when there is trouble they blame you, the leader. Envy is in the heart of most people until they see it for what it is—an ugly, burning, and debilitating feeling— and get rid of it.

Envy comes from the belief that others are getting more of the riches and treasures of life than we are. The solution to this problem is to realize that God is the unlimited and rich source of our supply, and the love and bliss we desire comes from within us. Regardless of what anyone else has or does not have, we can have as much love and happiness as we want. Instead of staying awake at night fretting over those who were criticizing me, I decided it best to consider the source and let it go. Some people only know how to criticize because they do not know any better, so why would I let a barking dog bother me or stop my forward motion? Dogs will be dogs, you know.

> "A good man out of the good treasure of his heart
> bringeth forth that which is good; and an evil man
> out of the evil treasure of his heart bringeth forth
> that which is evil: for of the abundance of the heart
> his mouth speaketh." —*Luke 6:45*

The Church of "What's Happening Now"

With new music and the congregation spreading the good news of the church, the attendance at the Sunday service jumped from two hundred and fifty to almost eight hundred a week in five months. We were the Yuppies of the late seventies and eighties, and we liked it. Everyone wanted the good life that before had belonged only to the so-called beautiful people, power brokers, and elite. Soon I would be called the "High Priestess of Yuppiedom," but that was fine as it's perfectly right for someone to desire and work to improve the condition of her or his life and strive for the topmost of what is available. Everyone would do well to seek to improve him- or herself and continue to stretch and reach for his or her ultimate goals, for this is what brings forth the greatness from within.

We were the place to meet and greet the most alive and beautiful people in San Diego, including the police chief, the future governor of California, and the stars and the best-selling authors of tomorrow, including Anthony Robbins, Marianne Williamson, Mark Victor Hansen, Louise Hay, Neale Donald Walsh, and Spencer Johnson. Whereas before I had been a fan of certain celebrities, now some of my heroes were coming to church to sit in my audience and listen to me. Each Sunday morning it was a surprise to see who was sitting in the congregation waiting to hear my message. One morning it would be the Pointer Sisters sitting in the church, another Sunday it was Greg Louganis, the Olympic diver, then Reverend Ike, the prosperity minister, Barry Goldwater, Jr., and even Harriet Nelson of Ozzie and Harriet fame. Of course extraordinary people need inspiration and constant encouragement to rise above the criticism of the petty and envious. Celebrities and public figures need to be coached and fed with spiritual knowledge, as well as motivated to accomplish even greater results in their life's work. Those who accomplish the most are those who work to develop and keep the right attitudes, and those who need it most never show up even to hear the lesson.

Another Lesson in Negotiations

Six months passed, and I was ready for my first salary review. My promise had been kept, as the church was prospering in every way and what had been dead had been more than resurrected. The church was flying. Now it was time for the church board to raise my salary, as they had promised.

Feeling a little anxious, I drove to the church offices for the board meeting and my six-month salary review. The church was prospering mightily, and now instead of being in the red the church was in the black and money was filling up the bank accounts. Naturally I thought the board would be so happy with me that they would give me a nice raise, and even a pat on the back, but instead, Tom, who was now board president, scowled right at me and said, "What makes you think you should have a raise?" I was dumbfounded! How could he be saying this to me in such a mean tone of voice, as if I were a bad little girl asking for a raise in my allowance that I didn't deserve? This was negotiation strategy, only I didn't know anything about negotiation, remember? This wasn't fair, for I had no experience at this negotiation stuff and besides I had been good and done my job, so where were my acknowledgment and reward? I was learning that ignorance is no excuse when it comes to the laws of land, God, and negotiation.

Save Yourself First

During the meeting not one board member smiled or came to my assistance, and these were the same people who would stand up and applaud after my sermon. Tom had the upper hand and used his surprise hostile tactics to weaken me, and make me defensive and powerless. Finally we compromised and I was given a six hundred-dollar-a-month raise, plus some benefits. They agreed that my next salary review would be in four months instead of six. Still, my salary was not at the level of other ministers who had only a couple of hundred people at their Sunday services. Obviously, I had a poverty belief that was preventing me from prospering at the level I desired. This incident was simply a reflection of my inner state of mind, and I vowed to change it. Actually Tom had done me a favor, for he taught me a valuable lesson: Take care of yourself, for others are not your caretakers; you are.

Tom saw me not as a minister or friend who had been working side-by-side with him and the board for the same goals, but as someone on an opposing team he needed to defeat. I did not like this, as it was wrong and not in harmony with the spiritual principles I was teaching. We needed to put these wonderful principles I was teaching to work in the church, and this was my job. "Ministers, presidents of companies, and leaders all face these same challenges, and I have to find a solution" was my resolve. We had wonderful things to accomplish and this board power-struggle game was beginning to wear thin, as it was taking too much time away from our real work: teaching spiritual principles to as many people as possible. My dream was a team that worked together in harmony for the greater good of all concerned. Was this possible?

PEARL
*You may not get what you're worth unless
you negotiate for it.*

Something happened that night: a profound awareness, a kind of "welcome to the real world" kind of realization. I thought, "Terry you are on your own here, and these people are not your friends; even though you pray for them, teach them, listen to their problems, and help them through their difficult times, they are not on your side. Actually these people are your adversaries and working against you and your goals for the church. Never let these people know what you are doing or where you are going because if you do, they will use everything in their power to defeat and stop you." Yes, it was time to build a winning team of my people,

people who were with me who wanted to accomplish the same goals. I desired to be a member of a cooperative team of committed players striving to attain a mission and purpose greater than any one of us could accomplish alone. Tom didn't stay too long after this because once we declare what we want to bring into our lives, as I did when I realized we needed to do some serious team building, anything unlike that automatically leaves.

> "As straws twisted into a rope can bind even a mad
> elephant, so the unity of the weak can accomplish
> great tasks."—*Hindu proverb*

You Gotta Have a Winning Team

I didn't need yes or no people, but people who would work with me by using their knowledge and talents to help the team reach our common goals. One horse can pull two tons, but two horses together can pull twenty-two tons. Team, as an acronym, is Together Each Achieves More. Clearly it was my job as the minister and captain of the ship to teach the principles of win/win business to the board, volunteers, and staff, if I wanted our boat to reach its destination without the team members sinking it. Our enemies are not from the outside, they are from the inside. All that is needed to sink the ship is one person drilling a hole in the bottom of the boat. Therefore, it was up to me, as the captain, to see to it that we had good team members in the first place and that everyone was rowing together in the same direction for the greater good of the individual team members, as well as the congregation. After this if anyone tried to sink our ship, he or she had to leave our boat and find another.

My Experiment

My plan was to inspire and motivate the volunteers, staff, board, and congregation to strive for and attain the highest level of excellence in everything they did in the church and in their personal and business lives. Something miraculous occurs in a space in which people, as a love offering to God and others, are 100 percent committed to getting the job done with excellence. Miracles happen in the space of commitment and excellence and this is what I wanted, a church of miracles.

"Give, and it shall be given unto you; good measure,
pressed down, and shaken together, and running
over, shall men give into your bosom. For with the
same measure that ye mete withal it shall be
measured to you again."
—*Luke 6:38*

Getting People to Give Is the Greatest Challenge

Too often people do the bare minimum with the attitude of who cares, it doesn't matter anyway and we can't do any better than we are, so why even try. This kind of attitude robs people of their divinity, life force, and creativity and bogs them down in struggle and strife. The attitude of possibilities, miracles, and excellence brings forth genius, greatness, and godliness. When people are challenged to bring forth the best that is within them, some accept the gantlet, rise to the occasion, and attain honor and fame for their accomplishments. But, there are those who resent the challenge because they don't want to grow or strive for anything higher than where they are because they are afraid. Choosing to set a goal beyond that which we have achieved before or believe we can accomplish opens the door for the Great Spirit to join forces with us in producing results out of the ordinary. Once we witness this supernatural process in action, our faith in God will increase and accomplishing what others call impossible becomes our norm.

My experiment was to find out what would happen if a group of people came together and agreed to create opportunities for others to experience their true godlike nature. The idea was that once people could get a taste of the power and intelligence that was flowing through them, they would believe in God, fulfill their mission, and attain the spiritual and material riches of life.

On a Mission

I was on a mission of God, and I was determined to reach the ultimate goal of human life, even though at the time I did not know what it was. What I did know was that I got my life out of serving God through His church, and I wanted to provide that same opportunity for others. Why not give God and others our best, even if it's just to find out what will happen when we do? There is absolutely nothing to lose and everything to gain. Since we know what life is like where we are, why not climb a little higher up the mountain and relish the pristine?

I decided long ago that it is much better to strive for what seems to be the impossible and fall short than strive only for the possible and attain it. Those who desire to reach their goals must release anything of a lower quality, or they will remain as they are or fall into a lower state of mind and condition. Upgrading is the only way to get from where you are to where you want to be.

Doing Our Best

We cleaned the facility where we held our Sunday service as if we were cleaning God's house, because we were. The staff and volunteers did their jobs as if each was on a mission of God, and they were. The choir members practiced and sang on Sunday, as if they were singing for God, and they were. The greeters and ushers cared for every person who came to the Sunday service as if each was a precious child of God, because she or he was.

Anyone who graduated from our volunteer training program would also come to excel in his or her own career. They came to know the importance of keeping their word, being personally responsible for getting the job done, keeping their time and other agreements, empowering others, being straightforward, supporting the team in winning, clarity of intention, and serving God and others with excellence. We were hot and happening. When our staff of volunteers moved on and found work elsewhere, they were immediately raised to managerial positions because of their superior skills and attitude.

Finally our team was coming together, and the church was on a roll. People were hanging out the windows on Sunday morning, classes were full, and now it was time to upgrade and move to a larger space. Our new location could seat 750 people per service, which meant 1,500 a Sunday. Soon both services were filled to standing room only.

The Ongoing Ego Trip

We had a new board president, and he and his wife loved the church. As the money increased and the status of the church was elevated in the community, the new board president decided that he and his wife were in charge and I was a hired employee. They didn't like my independence and believed that they should control and direct the church instead of me. These two were not standing up in front giving the sermon each week and no one was coming to see them, but somehow they missed this very important bit of information. "Reverend Terry is too powerful and we, the board members, are in charge of the church," they told some of the other board members, who agreed.

Yet Another Lesson in Negotiations

My next salary review came, and this time I was going to receive $4,500 per month plus part of the money that came from the classes and tape sales, and that was that. This did not go over well with our lawyer board president and his wife. Their plan was for the church to rent a house for me, not in La Jolla where I was living, but in another location of their choice. The church would buy me a car, but it would belong to the church and I would have use of it. Because of these benefits my salary would be kept at a minimum, and this would eliminate any way for me to gain any assets or financial independence.

Mr. K., as I shall call him, had a plan to fire me and he was gaining support from a few who had also decided that I was out of control—meaning *their* control. When he called me to come right away over to his office, I had a feeling something was up.

When I got there, he let me know I was on my way out and that they had already been searching for another minister. I thought being a minister meant everyone would love me and work with me to help others, but this is not the case. I had to take a stand once again, and this time I knew my rights and what I was worth. It's strange that if you know your value, you are called arrogant and aggressive; but if you don't, they may call you nice names but you are out on the street without a job.

"First of all, you cannot fire me unless you have a two-thirds vote of the congregation, and they like me and will not fire me," was my strong response. His jaw dropped to the floor, and I continued: "The second thing is that if you fire me I will take my students and congregation and move somewhere else, and you will be left with the empty legal shell and nothing else. Do you understand?" "Mr. K., perhaps you haven't noticed, but under my leadership this church has grown from less than zero to where it is today. This is my church and I am staying, and you and your wife are leaving. I am sorry that it has come to this, and you are welcome if you ever want to come to church to learn about spiritual life." Then I closed by saying, "You will be a board president for only one more moment, but I will be a minister for my entire life and this is where I am staying." That was the end of it and I left his office, and he resigned.

There's an Abundance of People

Who came and went never really mattered to me because I had learned a long time ago that it was not my business what others did, as that was between God and them. I taught the principles to whoever came to church, and whether they remained or went somewhere else was God's business and not mine. I choose not to be attached to anyone out of sentiment and the belief in scarcity. Attachment causes people to suffer endlessly over what other people do or do not do, as if people were inanimate objects and toys meant to give us pleasure. No one owns another person and what another does or does not do is his or her business, as long as they don't attempt to harm, cheat, or hurt someone else.

Besides, God was my source of supply and my congregation was the whole world. Watching the comings and goings of a few people, as if I were a hawk with its eye on its prey, was not my style. Wanting something from people makes you a slave, and if you are a slave of the people whom you are trying to help then you will try to take advantage of them and they of you. My philosophy was to deliver the message and encourage people to think for themselves and do what they believed was right for them.

Spreading my positive spiritual message to as many people as possible was more important than getting caught up in people's petty likes and dislikes or whether or not someone came to church. Of course, if they needed help, that was another issue and the church was there to give support if anyone wanted it. My philosophy was "Love the one you're with."

> **PEARL**
> *Releasing people, habits, activities, and things that were once valuable, but now only serve as dead weights, roadblocks, or as sources of trouble, is a necessary part of every successful person's life.*

When in Doubt, Clean House

By releasing the old board members so they could gravitate to someplace more suitable for them, I was making way for new ones to come and take their place. The new board gave me my much-deserved raise, and I didn't have to fight, cry, and plead out of sentimentality, for they just looked at the numbers, and could see this was appropriate.

> **GEM**
> *Just as a boat leaving one shore has people waving good-bye to the passengers, there are those waiting on the next shore, waving hello.*

Write Your Book

With the completion of my first published book, *What You Think of Me Is None of My Business*, I set out on my first book tour. This first of many book and public relations tours opened the door to a whole new world of celebrity status. Now I was interacting with America over the radio and television, being recognized in public, signing autographs, and meeting and interacting with anyone who was anyone in the entertainment, political, and book arena, just as I had visualized. *What You Think of Me Is None of My Business* became an overnight best-seller. The book assisted many to give up abusive relationships and achieve mental, emotional, and financial freedom by following the principles of successful living.

Communication Is the Key

Advertising and promotion proved to be the engine that powered the ministry and my career, as it has any successful business or product. You've "gotta" let people know who you are, what you have to offer them, where they can get it, and how and why it is important that they receive what you have to offer. I knew this, and I used this knowledge to make the ministry and me front-page news. Jesus said, "Do not hide your light under a bushel but put it on a hill where it can be seen," and this is what I did and what I encouraged others to do also.

The whole country was now learning about us, and I felt this was the right time to start our television ministry. But how was this going to happen, as I knew nothing about what I needed to do to have a successful and thriving television ministry? I knew that God knew and there were others who had accomplished what I wanted to have accomplished, so it was possible. Sitting down one evening, I imagined myself already on television preaching every Sunday morning to millions of viewers. Then I prayed and asked God to guide and direct me and give me the intelligence I needed to have an international television ministry. The dream I had had for years was about to come true. But, if I had not taken the steps and upgraded from one level to the next, this opportunity would not ever have happened.

> "Nothing great will ever be achieved without great
> men, and men are great only if they are determined
> to be so."—*Charles de Gaulle*

Chapter Nine

Step Seven, Keep On Keeping On

> "For a just man falleth seven times, and
> riseth up again." —*Proverbs 24:16*

> "A jug fills drop by drop."—*Buddha*

> "What this power is I cannot say; all I know is
> that it exists and it becomes available only
> when a person is in that state of mind in
> which he or she knows exactly what they
> want and is fully determined not to quit until
> they find it."—*Alexander Graham Bell,*
> *inventor of the telephone*

Success Is Just Around the Corner

Success appears as a great mystery to those who have not attained their topmost goals. Once someone has found the treasure at the top of his or her mountain it's easy to tell others how they can also find the treasures they are seeking, as the map is the same whatever the treasure. This is the value of hindsight, for once you have attained your topmost goals, by applying the same principles and taking the same steps you will be able to attain any new goals you set as well. Knowledge solves mysteries. From this perspective, "Keep On Keeping On" is the perfect seventh step on my Sacred Treasure Map to the Spiritual and Material Riches of Life. Wherever we stop is where we end up. The key is to keep on keeping on until we reach our topmost and ultimate goal and treasure. It is legend how many people give up right before they would have attained the riches they were in quest of.

> "Many of life's failures are people who did not
> realize how close they were to success when they
> gave up."—*Thomas A. Edison*

Giving up are not words in the vocabulary of those who are determined to reach their most precious destination or to accomplish a meaningful act. With persistence and determination, it is possible to achieve and enjoy the ultimate in spiritual and material riches, but without persistence and determination it is impossible. You cannot even walk to the door unless you persist in taking one step after another until you make it. You may have to walk around a table, chair, or some other barrier, but if you keep on keeping on, undaunted by any obstruction, you will make it. You must give up everything that is unfavorable to the accomplishment of your goal and take on whatever is favorable. If you have no mindset other than the goal and never give up, the destination is certain. Part of achieving any goal is being able to tolerate any inconveniences or impediments along the way. Because all acts occur first in the mind as thoughts, unless we change our mind by focusing on the inconvenience or the impediment, our thoughts and desires will take form. Our outer world is a result of those thoughts that we have settled for and accepted as true. The forms our ideas and thoughts have taken surround us in our outer world of people, places, conditions, and things. If we want to know what we desire and believe, all we need do is look around.

> "Nothing in the world can take the place of
> persistence. Talent will not; nothing in the world is
> more common than unsuccessful men with talent.
> Genius will not; unrewarded genius is a proverb.
> Education will not; the world is full of educated
> derelicts. Persistence and determination alone are
> omnipotent . . ."—*Calvin Coolidge,*
> *thirtieth president of the United States*

PEARL
Don't give up on your original good ideas; see them through to completion.

GEM
See only the goal and never the obstacles, and the obstacles will be passed through, as if they did not exist. If you focus on the obstacles, that is all you will ever achieve.

Walking on Fire

Around the time I was seriously contemplating the possibility of starting and building a new television ministry outreach, I took a little time off and went on a retreat in the woods. Going on retreat was a wise decision, especially because of three activities in which I participated: fire walking, wood breaking, and iron bending. When the retreat leader announced that we would have the opportunity to walk over hot burning coals, I thought, "Oh no, I can't do this!" But if I missed the opportunity, I knew I would regret it, so I signed up.

We built three five-foot-high piles of lumber and then we lit them on fire. As the wood burned, our instructor taught us the principles behind walking on fire and the technique to do it safely. She said, "As you stand ready to walk the hot coals, think only of reaching the other side." Never did she say, "Don't think about the burning-hot coals," for of course we would. "The coals are the impediments between you and achieving your goal of getting to the other side. All you need to think about or image is your having made it to the other side. When the feeling, or knowing that it is the time to walk, comes over you, walk quickly to the other side keeping your mind and eyes on the other side: your goal" were her clear instructions. We stood there listening to her and watching the blazing fire consume the huge piles of dry wood. After a while, all that was left were piles of red-hot coals. The instructor and her assistants raked the coals into an eleven-foot-long and three-foot-wide path of fire. We waited until the flames were down before the instructor made the first crossing. She did it so effortlessly that I was impressed. Logic, reasoning, and science tell us that this is impossible to do and not get severely burned or even permanently damaged.

Focus on Your Goal

When it was my turn, I knew it. My sixth sense gave me the signal to walk. I felt absolutely certain that this was the right thing to do, so I stepped out onto the fire and walked to the other side. I did exactly what the instructor told us to do, and it worked. Keeping my mind and eyes focused on the goal, the other side, I did not stop, look down, or allow my mind to think about the burning-hot coals. Instead I thought about the cool ice that was waiting for my feet on the other side. I kept on keeping on and in a few moments, there I was safe on the other side, burn-free and exhilarated. What a great lesson! The secret was to be at the other side, and not on the hot coals. Not everyone made it without burns. Instead of keeping their eyes on the goal, they looked down at the coals or worried and lost their faith.

This same principle works in every area of our lives. See the goal, get the knowledge and instruction, tune into Divine Mind, and when it feels right, go for the goal. Problems, obstacles, barriers, challenges, etc., are on every path and part of every goal, project, and mission, for this is life. The burning, red-hot coals were my obstacles, but they also become my trophies. Almost any person can walk eleven feet, but walking eleven feet on hot, burning coals when our experience tells us that walking on hot coals will severely burn our feet is a definite victory of mind over matter. Walking on the fire is not important on its own: it's what the experience teaches us. The exact same principles can be applied to any situation. Lessons we learn by personal experience we always remember.

> "I am a slow walker, but I never walk backwards."
> —*Abraham Lincoln*

Breaking Wood with the Hand

"Now you will have the opportunity to break a one-inch-by-one-foot piece of wood with the side of your hand," called out our coach. I had seen martial arts people do this, but how was I going to do it? "See your hand through the wood and then raise your hand and swing your hand through the wood to the other side. Keep your mind focused on the goal of your hand having arrived at the destination" were her instructions.

- seeing the end result
- taking action
- following through

These three points worked for everything, not just the fire walk or breaking hard wood by the touch of one's hand. How simple it is, but the challenge is always first the mind. The mind sees a big piece of hard wood that could hurt us, if we hit it hard, and we have to hit through it with all our strength in order to achieve the goal. Again, it's not the breaking of the wood with our hand that is important but the lesson and experience of doing something that looks impossible to do without an ax with a very sharp blade.

True Love Works in the Same Way

We tend to get caught up in the fear that if we give our all we will be hurt, so most people hold back. As in the case of breaking wood, those who held back and didn't follow through to the goal did get hurt, but the ones who kept their minds focused on the goal were successful. This is especially true in our intimate relationships. True love is the goal of life, and without love and intimacy a person suffers and over time becomes hard-hearted. Love requires that we give selflessly of ourselves to the other, but if there is fear that we will be hurt, we will hold something of ourselves in reserve, just in case. Most obstacles are figments of our imagination, but if we believe them and allow them to control our minds, these obstacles will steal our happiness, prosperity, and peace of mind. True love is the unobstructed flow of love toward the object of one's affection.

Keeping the Mind on the Goal and Not the Obstacle

As I watched a few of the participants before me, it was obvious to me that all some could see was hard wood that was impossible to break.

Impossible was the word that loomed large in their minds. "I could hurt myself" was a phrase I could see passing through the minds of many, as they contemplated the danger that awaited them if they chose to accept the challenge.

List any mental or physical obstacles that have been blocking your happiness, prosperity, or peace of mind.

1.

2.

3.

Given the principles you are learning, what you are going to do?
I will:

We Get What We Expect

Each person got exactly the results she or he expected. The obstacle, in this case called "hard wood," stopped many a hand that tried to break it. You can only eliminate your obstacles if you pass through or go around, over, or under them, but never if you give the obstacle the power to control and stop you. "Resist not evil" is an important teaching of the Bible. Fighting our obstacles, or even our critics, only gives the obstacles or critics power to determine our destiny. Keeping our mind, energy, and actions, focused on our goal, we can pass through the obstacles, such as the wood, as if they weren't even there.

Sure enough, those who could see only the obstacle hurt their hands and did not succeed in arriving at the destination on the other side of the wood. Those who passed their hands right through the wood, as if the wood were nonexistent, simply followed the directions. The mind is the challenge. If the mind sees the obstacle as real or impossible to overcome, then the person is defeated. Success in any undertaking—personal or business related—requires that one take charge of his or her mind, apply the principles, and follow through to the goal. Consistently achieving results out of the ordinary means going beyond the mind and beyond what we have been told or previously believed possible.

Success mantra: "The power within me to achieve my goals is greater than any seeming obstacle or barrier. I am successful."

It was my turn. I visualized my hand having already passed through the one-inch-by-one-foot piece of wood. Then I raised my hand and swung through the wood with all my strength. It felt as if I had passed my hand through a cracker. "Amazing!" I thought. "It really worked!"

My singing teacher, the maestro, who is also a mystic philosopher, told me, "Every day there are a thousand instances that could stop me and make me believe in limitation. To each seeming boulder in the road I say, ' 'taint so,' and somehow the problem goes away or it is solved easily and effortlessly."

Mark the Star

Mark's dream was to be a singing, acting, and dancing star in Broadway musicals. For years he desired and worked to attain his cherished goals, but the so-called breaks never came. Mark took acting, dancing, and singing classes and he auditioned whenever there was a part that suited him. It frustrated him no end when his friends were offered leading roles and he was getting only rejection. Mark knew he was just as good and even better than his colleagues, so what was the problem?

What was stopping him? During a counseling session, Mark discovered that he was at cross-purposes with himself. His father had wanted him to work in the family clothing store and had told him that if he didn't, he would fail in any other career. Upon realizing this, he chose to let this unwanted belief and roadblock disappear. His fear and belief had been holding him a prisoner of his own mind. Realization of one's subconscious roadblocks is over 50 percent of the work to be done. Next he programmed in a new positive and life-affirming belief: "It's perfectly right and natural for me to succeed in my life's work." God is the giver of all good things, but no matter how hard we try, if we are not in agreement on both the conscious and subconscious levels of mind as to the good we desire, there is no way we can achieve it. He used the following success mantra to reprogram his subconscious mind.

Mark's success mantra: **"It's perfectly right for me to be a star on the Broadway stage, as this is my right livelihood and my true mission. My work is to use my God-given talents fully and express my true self."**

Mark became the star he had always wanted to be simply because he got out of his own way. Because he was overly attached to what his father thought about him, he was afraid that if he became a Broadway star his father would reject him completely. Fear of rejection by a loved one is often a rock on the road to success, and it must be overcome if one is to go forward and live his or her dream. People who really love you and want the best for you never stand in your way. It's just that sometimes the people we love believe they know better what's right for us than we do, but this is not the truth. If this were so, each of us would be making decisions for another and someone else would be making ours.

Mark thrilled his audiences with his brilliant talent. Soon his father reluctantly came to see him perform. With tears of joy, his father confessed that he had had no idea that Mark had such a great talent. Finally, after years of tension and alienation, Mark got the approval he had been seeking, but only after it no longer mattered whether he got it or not. Because Mark loved his father, he didn't want to make his father wrong, so he kept on failing in his attempts to fulfill his life purpose just to make his father save face and be right. His fear of his father's disappointment and his own belief that he could not succeed unless he followed in his father's footsteps had been derailing his success-bound train. Recognizing an obstacle acts like a piece of dynamite set off under a rock. Mark got back on his track by being true to himself.

PEARL
When you keep on keeping on, problems solve themselves automatically and you pass through easily on the road to your prized and precious destination.

Anyone Can Do the Impossible

There was one more event at my weeklong retreat. This one was just as spectacular as the other two and appeared to be just as impossible to accomplish. The last trick we were to accomplish was to bend in half a six-foot-by-one-half-inch round metal rebar. Two people standing opposite each other, each having an end of the rebar at his or her throat, were to walk toward each other until the metal bar bent in half. A rebar is that long metal bar you see construction workers use to reinforce cement walls. The instructor placed a soft piece of leather at my partner's throat and another at mine to protect this delicate but strong part of the body. We stood six feet apart and faced each other. One end of the metal rebar was placed at his throat and the other at mine. We were told to mentally see the pole bent completely in half and then walk toward each other without stopping until it actually did bend in half. We could *not* use our hands. All we had was the power of our minds and the strength of our bodies as we pushed on the six-foot solid metal bar.

"Don't worry about how it is to be done; see it done, and then walk toward each other," said the instructor. This looked totally impossible. In the end only three couples out of ten were actually able to do it, because the mind is so strong in its belief of "It can't be done!" They say the bumblebee should not fly because its wings are too small for its large body. But the bumblebee doesn't know it can't fly, and it goes on and flies anyway.

PEARL
If you believe you can, you can; and if you believe you can't, you can't.

My partner's and my first attempt to bend the rebar met with defeat. How could two people not using their hands bend this metal bar? I couldn't even do it with my hands, let alone my throat and mind. It felt as if the pole would pierce right through my throat, so I backed up and stopped. Because of the strength of the metal bar, it seemed impossible. Because I had seen our instructor do it, I knew it could be done and I was determined to do it, no matter what. I thought about how extraordinary people are really ordinary people who perform extraordinary tasks. They accomplish what ordinary people call impossible feats because they believe they can and they persist with determination until they do.

> "My greatest point is my persistence. I never give up
> in a match. However down I am, I fight until the
> last ball. My list of matches shows that I have
> turned a great many so-called irretrievable defeats
> into victories."—*Björn Borg, tennis great*

On the third try you can imagine my thrill when the bar bent completely in half. Somehow, through the power of the mind and our relentless endeavor to keep on walking toward each other, it bent. Even though it appeared totally impossible given our past experience and our prior beliefs, my partner and I were successful because we had the desire and followed the directions. We weren't special people, just determined and persistent. Once you have the desire to do something, if you seek the knowledge of how to do it you will do it. Remember steps one, three, and four on the treasure map (1. Desire the Topmost, 3. Seek Knowledge of What Works, 4. Do What Works and Don't Do What Doesn't Work)? Truth is always truth

---

Take a moment and rewrite your topmost or ultimate objective, the end result you would like to have attained.

I would like to have attained:

List the obstacles in the way of your attaining your topmost goals.

1.
2.
3.
4.
5.

> What can you do in each instance to follow through and reach your desired outcome?
>
> I can:
>
> I will:
>
> When:

and it can be applied successfully to any and every situation, even walking on fire, breaking wood, bending metal, or living your most precious dream.

Birthing a Television Ministry

Armed with the broken wood and bent rebar, as souvenirs to remind me of my priceless lessons, I drove home enthused about the opportunity before me: producing an international television ministry. What were my obstacles? My obstacles were: the board of trustees, lack of money, lack of knowledge as to what to do, lack of people to help me, and no television ministry experience on my part. What were my advantages? I had my eternal loving reciprocal relationship with God, as does everyone, a burning desire to have a television ministry, my newest lessons about the power of persistence, and the spiritual principles of successful living. I had been visualizing myself as a television minister with an international ministry since my days as a student with Reverend Gus. My sixth sense told me that I was ready to take the leap, and go for it. "Go for it!" became my slogan.

The time was ripe to make my move to take my ministry to the airwaves and preach the gospel of "Prosperity Is Your Divine Right" and "What You Think of Me Is None of My Business," but how? My simple request was "God, What am I to do now?" Quietly the still small voice within me said, "Call a meeting of interested persons and begin the conversation." Something incredibly powerful and creative happens when like-minded people get together and discuss their common goals and challenges. Within a few minutes of brainstorming for solutions, each person is mentally lifted into the realm of Infinite Intelligence, and splendid ideas and solutions pour forth. Group mind generates a certain sixth-sense power that proves that two or more minds are better than one. What I call Creative Conversation among interested and mutually supportive persons is a perfect way to start any project.

> Who are the interested persons with whom you could engage in a Creative Conversation for the purpose of solving problems, inventions, and moneymaking?
>
> 1.
> 2.
> 3.
> 4.

Don't Ask Permission

Who were my interested persons? Asking the board would have been foolish, for all they would have told me was "No! No! No!" Knowing that if I had even mentioned that I was thinking about going on television, besides saying no, the board would have found a way to stop me before I even got started. Even though the board was doing a little better, as a team, every time we would have a church election and get new board members the same power struggles would blaze anew. Control issues are basic to human

> Are you waiting for permission?
> Who or what have you been waiting for to give you permission to do what you really want to do?
>
> I have been waiting until:
>
> The person who I am allowing to control my decisions is:
>
> My number-one fear about doing what I know is best for me is:

nature, and when someone who hasn't had power before gets a taste of it, there is the likelihood of his or her becoming power mad and trying to lord it over others. This is just the way it is. "Don't ask permission from those who won't give it, and do it anyway" was my philosophy.

Success mantra: **"This is my life to live as I choose. It is the right thing for me to make decisions in my best interest."**

Taking Your Liberties

Jim Marino, a member of the congregation, contacted me and expressed his interest in volunteering to work with me on the project. Although I had no idea about the person who was going to work with me, I knew that God, Who is in the heart of every person, did know. By asking a Higher Power to work with us and bring to us the right people, the right people show up and at the perfect right time. All this happens in some inconceivable way. It's beyond our ability to understand how or why this works, and we don't need to. It just works. "Why" questions about God are useless, as no one can ever know why. The spiritual and material worlds are the way they are because God made them so. Our work is not to question why, for this is impossible and totally unnecessary, but to live true to our nature and in harmony with the system. A perfect system, created by God, exists for our benefit. Anyone who chooses to live by the system will attain his or her topmost desires and goals. Part of the system requires that we ask for what we desire. Try asking God for who and what you want, and notice what happens.

Cosmic Dating System

People use computer-dating systems to find mates, but the cosmic dating system works much better. Infinite Intelligence knows better than any man-made system who is best for you. Decide upon your requirements and then pray and ask for this person and you to meet and have a loving and committed relationship. The right person is then selected from the sum total of all eligible persons in the entire world, and at the right place and time, you and your right mate will meet and be together.

Jim was the perfect right person to partner with in creating a television ministry. He could work a camera, produce, direct, edit, and deliver to the television station a finished twenty-eight-minute show and I could give a sermon, teach, motivate, and inspire. With Jim I had at least one committed team member, and this was enough to start. You and God are a majority anyway, but once you get even one honest and genuine partner who is willing for you to succeed, you have multiplied your possibilities exponentially. With Jim's support, I called a Los Angeles television company and negotiated with them to buy one-half hour of television time every Sunday morning at 7:30 A.M.

The board members were upset with me for bypassing them and signing the six-month contract with Channel Nine Television in Los Angeles, but I knew they would never have agreed. Sometimes we have to be bold and do the thing, because if we wait for others to give us the permission to do the thing we may never start. The deed had been done, for I had signed the binding contract. Making the shows, airing them, fulfilling the requests from the viewers, and generating the money to afford all this were our next challenges. Fire, aim, ready had happened again.

Start and Get Prepared Along the Way

Jumping in prepared or not and getting prepared along the way had always been my style, and still is. Since that time I have read that this has been found to be the most effective way to accomplish great deeds and the favored method used by supersuccessful entrepreneurs. I didn't know this information at the time, but I went ahead anyway just because this is how I did things. (Not that my way is the only way, for there are many paths that lead to the same destination. Others may try to convince you that there is only one way, which is their way, but this is not true.)

Soon the board reluctantly agreed to give the new television ministry the financial support it needed until we could be self-supporting. Neither Jim nor I had any experience in the television ministry; therefore it was vital for us to find an expert consultant. Step three on our treasure map is to seek knowledge. Trial and error would give us about two—perhaps three— months before we'd be finished because of lack of funds. No one can really afford the trial-and-error method to reach their goals, as there is an infinite number of possible errors. Being babes in the television ministry business, we needed to have someone take us by the hand and walk us through the steps that would lead us quickly and safely to our goal of an international television ministry reaching millions. There was work to be done, and wishing and hoping wouldn't do it; we needed an expert navigator.

Prayer and Intelligence Work Together

Spiritual people tend to believe that if they just pray and think positively their project will all come together without doing much if anything to make it happen. If you say anything to the contrary, they accuse you of being faithless and negative. We need to pray *and* use our intelligence—not just one or the other. God gave us our intelligence so that we could be successful in this world and also make spiritual progress. Being spiritual means using everything that we have been given, including our intelligence. Calling on the wisdom and knowledge of expert advisers, whatever the goal or dream, is the right use of intelligence. Our plan was to hire the topmost expert and have him or her give us his or her wealth of knowledge in exchange for money.

Identify and list the topmost experts and examples of success in your chosen area of interest. How can you enlist their help in achieving your goals?

1.
2.
3.
4.
5.

An Answer in a Dream

No one was showing up, and time was running out. One night in a dream I saw myself calling Reverend Robert Schuller and asking for his help. Instantly I woke up, sat up in bed, and called Jim. "Jim, please call Reverend Robert Schuller's television ministry in Orange County and ask to speak to

Reverend Schuller's television consultant. When you get whoever it is on the phone, invite her or him to be our consultant" was my urgent request. Robert Schuller was very successful and had been in the television ministry business for a number of years, so I knew he and his advisors knew what worked. This is called "head-hunting," and it's done all the time. Bill U., the foremost television ministry consultant in the world, became our new consultant.

Bill U. had been a consultant for many of the top television evangelists and their ministries. The Reverends Oral Roberts, Pat Robertson, Jim Bakker, Jerry Falwell, Jimmy Swaggart, Billy Graham, and now Terry Cole-Whittaker, were some of his clients, but I was definitely different from the rest. Number one, I was a woman. At that time, no other woman preacher had her own national program, much less a program that was televised internationally. Second, I was the only minister giving a message people labeled as New Thought, metaphysical, and "New Age." I didn't like labels because labels separate us and cause us to take sides. Camp consciousness causes us to do battle with those we have decided are in the other camp, even though we are praying to the same God who loves all of us. Our ministry was an original and would become the prototype for a whole new generation of prosperity ministries and women preachers.

Yes, You Can

Everything was happening at once. Right around the same time that we were preparing to go on television, my lease was up where I had been living and I had to move. I had just received a good-sized chunk of money from the sale of a house of which I had been a part owner, so I had some money for a minimum down payment; however, I had *no* credit history because, even though I had been a part owner of this property, I had never made any payments. Besides, this was my first full-time job, and I had had this position for only a year. I was not considered a good risk, especially for buying a luxury home in one of the most affluent locations in the world.

What stops people from getting what they want is the thought "I can't." "I can't" is not a valid answer or reason. Most of the time when people say "I can't," they mean "I won't" and "Don't press me, for I won't even try." A closed mind is actually the greatest barrier to enjoying the spiritual and material riches of life, whereas an open mind is the gateway to the opulent and virtually unlimited riches of God's glory-filled kingdom.

The first step to acquiring or achieving anything is mastering the attitude of "I can" and the belief that "there is a way." *Impossible* is not a word in God's vocabulary, and I didn't want it in mine, either. Whenever I had a challenge or I needed anything, all I knew to do was to pray and ask God to help me to get what I needed. No one knows why or how electricity works, but we know how to use it. The same is true of the power of God and Infinite Intelligence. When you turn on the light switch on the wall, you will have light if your house is connected with the power of the electric company; when you call out to a Higher Power and pray for what you want and you have at least as much faith as you do in the electric company, your prayers are answered. Faith is always the coin of spiritual life and miracles. Misplaced faith is the cause of unhappiness, poverty, and even illness.

There's Always a Way

"Lord, I know you know that I need a home and I know you know where my perfect home is and how I can acquire it. I accept that this home is mine now, and I ask this to come to me in a way that is for my greater good. Thank you, God. And so it is, amen." Working with what some call the Force is so much fun, and things work out so beautifully with much less effort and no strife.

The question I asked myself was "If I could live anywhere, where would I want to be living?" My ideal scene was to continue to live in La Jolla Shores, but a little closer to the beach and with an ocean view from every west-facing window. Why not set your sights on your ideal scene? The only thing that can happen if you don't get exactly what you want is a little temporary disappointment until you find that God has something much better in store for you. Those who are spiritually in tune with the Divine

Write your ideal scene having to do with your topmost goal
or a current objective.

My ideal scene is:

don't feel even the slightest bit of disappointment, under any circumstances, for they are surrendered into the will of God and are certain that whatever comes to them is exactly the best for them at the time. This is advanced stuff, but when we learn this we are happy and peaceful because we are certain of the beneficial outcome.

A Dream Home with No Credit

Phyllis, my friend who was also on the board of the church and one of my few dedicated supporters in those days, "happened" to be a real estate agent. I put *happened* in quotes because nothing ever just happens by accident, as there is a cause behind every effect. Once we are in tune with the Infinite, things come together, because a master director has orchestrated the events. "Phyllis," I said, "please take a drive with me and let me show you where I would like to buy a home." Driving down one particular street, I leaned over to Phyllis and said, "This is the street, this is my ideal." I had learned to speak the truth at least to God and myself and not hold back or settle for anything other than what I really wanted. There is no harm in asking for the topmost. Experience had taught me that there was no harm in asking or striving for the best. If you don't get it, then it's no big deal; but if you do, great!

"Set for yourself the highest goals you can think of and then double them" was my usual instruction to my students. Asking them to do this exercise would cause them to use their imagination and mentally reach way beyond what they believed was possible. Achieving easy goals doesn't give one a taste of the Supreme, but impossible goals do. Great goals make us depend upon a higher power and force us to stretch and grow way beyond where we are now. Great challenges make great people, and small challenges make small people.

PEARL

Consistently going beyond the arbitrary limits we have set for ourselves, be they based on past experience or common knowledge, challenges us to constantly produce results beyond and out of the ordinary.

Phyllis never said one negative or limiting word and was completely supportive. There was no resistance or obstacle in either of our minds. Her father had been a minister, and she knew the power of God. "When two or more are gathered in the name of Jesus, ask anything and it shall be done" is a paraphrase of one of the most important scriptures in the Holy Bible. Phyllis was happy for me, had no envy, and was in complete agreement that I get the house that I really wanted and in the exact neighborhood. Reality is created by agreement and that is why it's good to get the alignment of those who are willing for you to have what you desire, if you want to get what you want. You don't need opposition; you need agreement and alignment.

PEARL

Everyone has a motive, even if it's selfless service. Find out their motive and you can engage them in helping you get what you want so that they can also get what they want.

Besides being a spiritually minded person, Phyllis would also be the recipient of a good commission when I bought a house, so she had a vested interest in my getting my ideal home. There is nothing wrong with this, as this is the way it is. Whatever people are doing, they have a motive for doing it. If you can find the motive, you will know what your friends and associates want and then you can help them to get what they want, as they help you get what you want. "I help you and you help me" is just good business. Reciprocation is the foundation of every good relationship, especially with God, and for certain with our mate, family, friends, and even coworkers and clients. If there is no reciprocation, there is no loving relationship or even business deal. After a while if the one giving is not receiving any reciprocation, she or he will find others who will reciprocate.

The Prospering Power of Agreement

Phyllis and I prayed together, agreed, and then I let go by surrendering the whole matter into God's hands, knowing that it would happen. The first thing the next morning the phone rang and it was Phyllis telling me in an excited voice, "Terry, your house just came on the market this morning. Meet me at the coffee shop in the Shores in an hour and we will go and see your new home." The house was on the exact street that I wanted and, sure enough, God had found me the right house in the Shores, with a big ocean view, plus a sauna and every possible luxury I could imagine or need. Somehow, with God's help and Phyllis's capability, I was able to buy this almost-new and beautiful house in the vacation paradise of La Jolla, California, and move in with *no* credit. My ideal scene had become a reality, again proving the power of the Holy Spirit over any limiting conditions or seemingly impossible situation.

The Purpose of Miracles

The higher purpose behind miraculous events is that we recognize that there is a Greater Power and Presence working with us, and for us. Each time we get the answer to our prayers in such a wondrous way, we know it is beyond coincidence or happenstance, especially when these experiences become commonplace. Within time, our faith in God increases because there is no way to explain these miracles as chance. Miracles and extraordinary happenings are ways for the Creator to get our attention and thus increase our interest in God and the Universal Principles of Successful Living. Working with the Spirit is like riding down the river in a boat, going with the flow and enjoying the ride rather than struggling to paddle upstream against the current.

Every impossible situation that proves to be possible and every so-called unexplainable event causes us to question our materialistic belief system and helps us to pay more attention to the supernatural and the superpossible.

A Message from Beyond

Sue was the singer at the Whittier church where I had been an assistant minister. Sue's daughter was at her high school when the opportunity came to climb up on and take a ride on a large tractor. The tractor was full of students all having a great time when Sue's daughter fell off. In a moment, her body was crushed beneath the wheels. The phone call came, and Sue was stunned and devastated.

In another part of town, a woman was vacuuming her carpet when she heard a voice calling out to her. She stopped the vacuum and listened to the voice. No one was around, but someone nevertheless was talking to her. The voice said, "Please tell my mother, Sue Harmon, that I am perfectly fine and not to worry about me. I'm in a good place. Also, please tell her I love her." The woman knew she had to find this Sue, so she called information to find her phone number.

The phone rang, and Sue answered it. "Hello," said the woman on the other end of the line. "Is your name Sue Harmon?" "Yes," replied Sue as well as she could. "You don't know me," continued the stranger, "but do you have a daughter who just passed away?" "Yes," sobbed Sue. "How do you know? No one knows, as I was just told a few minutes ago." The woman told Sue the story, and they both cried in sorrow and in joy. Sue's daughter had found a way to communicate with her mother. Who knows how this was possible or why this stranger was the one selected to carry the message. All this is beyond our understanding and certainly out of our control. When events such as this happen, we are given a clue and a view into a world beyond this world and an experience of a power much greater than our own.

After that, when Sue sang at church she had a special look of knowing and faith in her eyes that had not been there before. Sue had completely lost the fear of death, and she was able to peacefully release her daughter, certain she was perfectly all right and in God's hands.

Miracles Build Faith

Many believe that miracles occur because a Higher Power actually cares whether we get this house or another house, this job rather than that job, or find our right mate. However, it isn't the outer world of form and circumstance that interests the Divine; it's you or I, the eternal person who exists beyond time and space, who is vitally important to the Lord. Everything in this world exists to encourage us to turn to the Higher Power in order that we become blissful, prosperous, and successful human beings, as we make spiritual progress into a more opulent, loving, and glorious tomorrow and next life. Miracles and demonstrations give us a sense of an Unlimited Invisible Power and Intelligence behind everything. This taste of the supernatural causes us to become curious so that we will seek to find answers to the most important questions: Who am I? Is there a God?

Who and where is God? What is the purpose of life? What can I do to have happiness and love? What is the topmost goal of life? What can I do to attain the topmost that is possible for any human being to achieve?

Most people seek God and the answers to these most important questions only when they are suffering, have a financial need, are curious about higher knowledge, or have a burning desire to attain a heartfelt goal. Intelligent people seek help when they are in need, in trouble, and hurting; whereas the less intelligent get used to the misery and poverty and never question their condition or seek to find a better way. Once we ask for answers and assistance from this unseen Power and Presence we call God, help comes and often the help is instant. Don't give up if the help is not instant. A delay never means a turndown or a denial. It's not the right time as yet, but it will happen when it is right. In the meantime we must continue to endeavor for the attainment of the goal.

Be Open and Ready to Receive What You Desire

Too often people neglect to observe and witness the cause-and-effect relationship of the miracle or demonstration that just occurred. Both miracles and demonstrations are for the purpose of awakening us to the reality of a higher law and a higher existence beyond the limitations of the rational mind, human beliefs, and the theories of science. People often pray and ask for what they want, but either because the answer didn't come in the form they expected or it took some time to happen, they forgot that they had even asked. The answer to prayer can actually take years to manifest because it takes that long for the person to be ready to receive it. You see, it's our responsibility to make sure that we are ready to receive that for which we have asked. Other times, in situations such as Sue's, we are given a supernatural gift to comfort us as well as give us knowledge of the world beyond physical appearances. From time to time, if we are on the spiritual path, the veil between the two worlds is lifted and we are given a sneak preview of coming attractions.

It's good to recall our miracles, the unexplained events, and the times we prayed and answers and solutions came. It's the right thing to ask for help and to use our curiosity to seek out the mystical and the supernatural. By paying attention, we are able to observe the cause-and-effect relationship between what we pray and ask for and what comes to us. God

also has a sense of humor. I must have asked in my former life to be born
rich in my next life, for my maiden name was Reich, which means "rich" in
German. Answer to prayer is one of the ways that God speaks to us. God
has given us the kingdom, but it is we who must have faith and be open
enough to receive the blessings and the treasures we are seeking.

> Recall a special time when you wanted something that seemed impossible
> or not probable, and you got it anyway.
>
> I got:
>
> The lesson I learned was:

Do Good, and Good Will Come to You

I must have done something good to attract two such fine people into my
life. Having Jim and Bill as my team members and reciprocating business
partners for the new television ministry was a miracle. They both came to
me as an answer to prayer at a time when I had no idea of where to go or
what to do. Prayer is the request, faith is the power behind the request,
and Infinite Intelligence manifests the prayer by providing the right people
at the right time. I wouldn't have known where to find such people, but
God, Who is in the heart of every person and Who has an inconceivable
way of fulfilling our heartfelt requests at the perfect right time, does know.
By now I was certain of the Unseen Power behind all outer manifestations
and effects, and I was able to work with this principle on a consistent basis, as can anyone who so chooses. Once we ask for what we want, a demand is placed on the law of life. As the unseen forces gather behind us
and for us, conditions are rearranged in order that our request be manifested in our outer world of experience, provided we have accepted it and
have the pious credits to warrant these benefits. If we want to guarantee
for ourselves the best possible future, we need to build up our pious-credit
cosmic account by doing good works. By the law of life good attracts good,
and one good turn deserves another. Simply by doing good we can work
ourselves up the ladder to a better life.

Turning from a Life of Crime

Jerry wanted to be a member of the Mafia because he had a taste for fast money and the exciting life of crime, gambling, and cheating. Jerry met Mike at a card parlor where Jerry was using his crooked dice and cards and was winning big time. Of course, since Mike was also a cheater in gambling he spotted Jerry's tricks. Mike was in his late seventies and had been on the leading edge of crooked gambling for years, as he and friends had found ways to win at slot machines and card and dice games even in Las Vegas. Jerry was excited to meet his new mentor, Mike. Mike, liking Jerry, poured out his knowledge of every possible way to cheat the professional gamblers, as well as the amateurs.

Mike taught Jerry everything he knew, and this combined with all the tricks that Jerry already knew was giving Jerry a great deal of easy money. But along with this Jerry had become a greedy, angry, and hostile young man. One day Mike took Jerry aside as he could see that Jerry had the potential of being a very fine person and extremely successful without crime. "Jerry, what did you do before you took up cheating the public?" inquired Mike. Jerry told him about his unglamorous job, which he really hadn't liked. "Jerry, let me make a deal with you. Go back to this work and do it conscientiously for three years. At that time we can reevaluate your situation as to money, attitude, and general all-around good fortune. And Jerry, I want you to watch this woman preacher, Reverend Terry Cole-Whittaker, who is on television every Sunday morning."

Jerry started watching my television program and then coming to church each Sunday. Within three years he and his best friend Mike reevaluated his life and career, and Jerry was much better off in every way. To this day Jerry cries tears of love when he thinks of his friend Mike, who has since passed on. Jerry is who he is today because of one person who cared enough about a young man to set him straight. Today Jerry continues with his same business, but now it is enormously successful and he uses his entrepreneurial talents not to cheat but to create new businesses for the purpose of helping people. Even his favorite television show is not a crime show, it's *Touched by an Angel*. If you had the good fortune to meet Jerry, you would think him to be one of the most honest and wonderful people you had ever met. He and his wife have dedicated their lives to helping other people to succeed, and they continue to prosper mightily in the process. We can only get back what we have given out, as this is the law of life.

Sitting at the Feet of a True Expert

Something powerful happens when we listen to those who know and have what we want to know and have. With the transference of consciousness, we upgrade to the level of the master or expert simply by hearing the wisdom of those who have made it to the place where we aspire to be. The opposite is also true. Listening to those who are not where we want to be can throw us into a hellish existence. There are two parts to knowledge: what to do and what not to do. Just as electricity can light our home, if wrongly used it can burn down the house. Our hearing can bless or curse us, depending upon that which we choose to hear. When Mike realized his influence over a young man, he decided to use his influence to help create a great human being. Anyone can be influential if he or she chooses to step out from the crowd, take a stand, and work to uplift society. You don't wait for permission to be influential. To be so must be the result of an inner decision to dedicate your life to making a difference in the lives of others.

Who said I could go on television and preach my message to millions, or that I even had the right? I decided that I had the right because I wanted to make a difference. Who gave Martin Luther the right to establish the Protestant movement? He did. Who gave Mahatma Gandhi the right to free India from England's rule? He did. Who gave Abraham Lincoln the right to run for president and do what he did? He did. Who gave Bill Gates the right to build a computer software empire? He did. Countless numbers of people are waiting for someone to say "You can do it, because I am giving you the permission." We have been given the permission, for if we have a dream the fulfillment of that dream also exists, but it can only manifest when we take command of our lives and our destiny.

Because this message had made such a difference in my life, I had a burning passion to share it with the greatest number of people possible. Fame is a necessary ingredient if a person wants to influence great numbers of people, and in fact this is the purpose of fame. If you want to be an agent for positive change and influence large numbers of people, you must have fame. What better way to both gain fame and influence people than television?

Jim and I sat at the feet of Bill, our television ministry guru, and listened to every word he spoke. He was a wealth of knowledge in terms of what worked to build and run a flourishing and growing television ministry and spiritually oriented business. Some people think it crass to call religion a business, but the word *business* means one's occupation. What better way to be occupied, in my opinion, than to be doing the work we love that also is a benefit to others?

> As an agent for positive change, what would you like to offer that will make a difference in people's lives?
>
> I would like to:
>
> What could you do to become more famous than you are and therefore influence greater numbers of people?
>
> I could:

It's Perfectly Right to Make Money Doing Good Works

A woman in one of my classes said, "Reverend Terry, please help me solve my dilemma. I feel guilty about making money by doing spiritual work. Since spiritual work is what I want to be doing and I have bills to pay, what should I do?" "Anita, if you don't make money doing good then you have to make money doing bad, so what is better?" was my question. Continuing, I said, "Do you believe in your product and service? Do your product and service help people? Do you want the greatest number of people to be able to get the benefits from what you offer? Since what you offer is good for people, is it the right thing for people to pay for what you have to offer?" Anita said yes to every question. "Money," I said, "is never the goal of life. Money is wonderful, as it can help us to help others through our products and services, and can help us to provide for our family members' needs, as well as our own." I gave her a success mantra to repeat until she firmly accepted the belief "It's perfectly right to make money doing good works." She realized that if she accepted the belief that is was okay for her to make money using her talents and propensities to serve God and others, she would be able to take care of herself and her family. But if she didn't, she would still need to make enough money to meet her needs by doing work that was not her life's work. In this world everyone must take care of him- or herself, and money is the acceptable means of exchange. "Anita, it's honorable to do an honest day's work. Any work is honorable, if it's done in the spirit of service and contribution to one's higher purpose and mission." Anita went away with a smile on her face, for now she could do her work, accept payment and support herself, and also create her ideal lifestyle by doing her life's work.

Success mantras: "It is perfectly right for me to make money using my talents, skills, and propensities to help others." "It is perfectly right for me to make money doing my life's work."

Being a minister and teaching about God and the spiritual principles of successful living was my life's work. I also had to accept that it was perfectly right for me to prosper by doing my life's work.

> As you prepare to do your life's work, perhaps in a new and expanded way, are you willing to prosper and succeed?
>
> I am:

Nothing Happens Without Commitment

At one of our meetings Bill looked right at me and said, "Terry, are you one hundred percent committed to this television ministry? Do you realize that the only person you can count on is you? That others may come and go? No matter how committed they are at this time, for some reason they may change their minds and it will be you who is left to continue on. This is your ministry and your responsibility, and no one else's. I know this is strong, but it is the truth." I sat there weighing the importance of what he had said, and I knew that what he had said was true. If it was to be, it was up to me to keep on keeping on—no matter what.

Commitment is an inner vow that one makes with oneself and one's

God. Without commitment there is too much that will take our attention away from our goal and defeat us mentally, emotionally, and physically. A promise to accomplish the task must be made in one's heart of hearts. That night I wrote out what I called my "Commitment Medicine" just in case I should fall victim to the contagious diseases of fear, laziness, miserliness, doubt, criticism, or weakness of conviction. I kept it posted in my bedroom, and I read it every morning and evening to keep me strong and unwavering in my dedication and decision to keep on keeping on regardless of outer appearances or mental challenges. Our work is to win the battle of mind over matter, of positive thinking over negative, and of faith over doubt.

Commitment Medicine

(Take as often as needed and be sure to say it with conviction and feeling.)

I know that I have what it takes to achieve my objectives, ideals, and my mission in life. Now I demand of myself total commitment and continuous action toward their attainment. I now promise to dedicate myself, without reservation, to the attainment of my objectives, ideals, and mission.

Because the dominating thoughts in my mind will produce themselves outwardly into physical action and results, I keep my mind positive and focused on my ideals and the image of my vision attained.

There is no turning back or alternative, as the past no longer exists. The only way for me to go is forward, full speed ahead toward the attainment of my objectives. I am confident, strong, and able. I am victorious. Yes, yes, and yes!

The next day I listened as Bill finished up his consultation by reiterating his main points. "Terry," he said, "there are a few most important main points you need to know. You must remember and apply each of them if you are to stay on the air and fulfill your mission." I listened intently, took notes, and after this Jim and I got busy to implement as many points as we could before the taping of our first programs.

Everything Big Starts Out Small

Show time! The big day had arrived. I got up early and drove to the studio. Dressed in a dark blue suit with a light pink silk tailored blouse, I was ready to go before the lights and cameras. The team, members of the congregation who had volunteered to be in the audience, and the crew and I gathered together and prayed: "Lord, please use us to manifest your message and take this program into the homes and hearts of those who can receive and benefit from this teaching. Thank you, God, and so it is. Amen." Whatever challenges I had to face with an oftentimes more than difficult board of trustees, the members of the church more than made up for in love and overwhelming encouragement and support. Without them, none of this could have happened. Right after a big group "Amen," we cheered and shouted, "Let's go!" and the camera started to roll.

Standing before the camera, I now had my chance to deliver the message I had been waiting for years to speak to all the people of the world. Remembering to make a strong entrance, as my college drama coach had instructed, I looked right into the camera and with a big smile on my face said, "Good morning. My name is Reverend Terry Cole-Whittaker, and my topic today is *The Courage to Be Yourself.* Today you will learn how to get the courage you need to live the life perhaps you have only dreamed of living. Call a friend and invite her or him to tune in, and I will be right back with today's important and valuable message." After a few words from our announcer, I came back on and delivered the message.

At the end I invited them to write and ask for their copy of today's message in booklet form and to also send a donation to help keep the ministry on the air. I gave a closing prayer, and my final words were "Please tune in next week and be sure to tell your friends to also tune in. I love you, and see you next week right here on this station at the same time." We called the program **With Love, Rev. Terry.**

Your Thoughts Will Take Form in the Outer World

Next Sunday came and our first program hit the airwaves, but we had neglected to tell the congregation or the newspapers, or make mention of it in our church newsletter. Even though Channel Nine gave us the potential of reaching millions of people throughout the greater Los Angeles area and some three hundred miles beyond, not one soul out there knew we were to be on television. I hadn't even told my mother, who lived three hundred miles away. If no one knew, how was anyone to know to get up and turn on the television at 7:30 A.M. on a Sunday morning?

I soon realized there were a few beliefs hidden in my subconscious mind that were sabotaging both the success of our television program and my personal success. One: I had the belief that it wasn't okay to want to be wealthy, powerful and famous. I felt embarrassed at the prospect of others knowing that I wanted to be wealthy, powerful, and famous, so as to protect myself from possible criticism, I didn't tell anyone about the program. Here I was attempting to hide my innermost dream and live it at the same time. When you get what you want, you cannot pretend that you don't really want it because it's obvious that you do. Two: If too many people listened to me speak and teach my spiritual philosophy so openly on television, then I would be opening myself up to even more criticism—especially from the hostile, fanatical, fundamentalist fringe. Three: If I told too many people and if the show wasn't any good or if we couldn't stay on the air, there would be more people to talk behind my back and laugh at me for failing. I had kept the program a big secret just to avoid criticism, ridicule, rejection, and possible harm. I was definitely at cross-purposes with myself, and something had to change.

The fears of rejection, ridicule, criticism, and harm run deep; and each time we let them go at one level, a deeper level, will still remain until the whole issue is rooted out at the source. The desire for glory, praise, and validation of my existence was at the root. I had still been giving others the power to validate my existence and worth, when in truth I would always exist as an eternal spirit soul with or without anyone's praise, permission, or validation. Yes, everyone would like to be appreciated and important, but these desires when not fulfilled plunge us into dejection. I had to learn to take appreciation and dejection in the same manner by being detached. From now on I would refuse to think about these issues or give credence to them, as I had work to do and a life to live.

Success mantra: **"I am an eternal spirit soul, and no one can harm, invalidate, or negate my existence."**

Success mantra: **"I no longer need to try to avoid the pain of criticism by hiding out or failing in my endeavors."**

Success mantra: **"I exist eternally to give and receive love."**

Are you keeping your products, talents, and services a big secret?
If so, why?

I am:

Because:

What is this costing you? It is costing me:

What will you do about it and when? I will:

Unfulfilled Expectations

There were three of us at the office on Tuesday waiting for the mail. The mail arrived, and there were thirteen letters. Jim and I felt somewhat encouraged that people were watching and that thirteen out of millions got value enough to take the time to write and even send donations. But, deep down inside, I was very disappointed.

I felt dejected because we were not flooded with mail and donations; I made some excuse and turned and went into my office and closed the door. It had cost the church about ten thousand dollars this first week, not including Bill's consulting fees, and we only received about thirty-five dollars in the mail. This was going to take a big miracle and some intense and dedicated work for us to even pay for the expenses, let alone expand into other cities and countries. How would I get the money to continue? We had to do something fast, for at this rate we'd be finished before we even got started. How often I had been at a similar point before, but never to this extent. Having just made a commitment with all my heart and soul to keep on keeping on, now when a huge boulder appeared to be blocking my path, I just wanted to quit and run away and hide. So soon were my faith and commitment challenged. Somehow I thought that thousands of letters and dollars would come pouring in this first day, but they didn't. I took it as a sign that God didn't want me to be doing this. My mind was taking me on a ride away from the truth and the attainment of my life's mission and goals and toward a bottomless pit of depression.

Sitting down at my desk, I looked out at the garden and prayed, "Help me, God. Please, tell me what I am to do next?" In that moment of dejection and hopelessness as I pleaded for help, something came over me. All of a sudden I smelled roses, but there were no roses in the garden or to be seen anywhere. A feeling of great peace came over me, and the energy of my office changed dramatically. Energy ran from the base of my spine up to the top of my head and then out of the top of my head. Knowledge poured through my mind, and I knew I was being infused with cosmic consciousness. I was the essence of love and, having no fear, I felt profound love all of humanity. In the next moment I felt the presence and love of people, very special people, but I couldn't see any person. You could say that angels or at least highly developed emissaries and counselors were visiting me on some kind of mercy mission to help me in my time of need. Answers and guidance came to me, and I knew the truth.

Unseen Counselors

These emissaries were whispering to me, "You have been waiting for an instant victory that you have not earned. Your unrealistic expectations have always made you unhappy because you have believed that things are supposed to be different from the way they are. Things are the way they are because there is a lesson for you. Life on earth is a school of higher knowledge, not just a playground for children. The actions and results belong to both you and the Supreme Being because this is a partnership. Because you have asked to do this work, you have been given the opportunity, and it is up to you to fulfill your part of the bargain. For each step you take toward God, God takes at least ten toward you.

"The Great Spirit works through people even though He could do everything automatically. It's not about God doing everything for us because it is a partnership. Each one develops him- or herself into a great soul through his or her own endeavors to gain knowledge and develop his or her consciousness. Be grateful, dear one, for the opportunity that God has given you to serve. Let go of your fears, and trust that you will have exactly what you need, when you need it and not before. Yes, endeavor as if the results are all up to you, but also let go and let God, knowing that God is the Supreme Controller, and all is well. With a heart full of love and appreciation continue to strive every day to do your best and to reach out to more people with your message and ministry. That is all you can do.

"These thirteen letters are enough. When you have served these thirteen people who have reached out to you for help and guidance, you will be given more. The truth is, if you could have handled more, more would have responded. Never do you serve masses of people but one person at a time.

"The reward for spiritual workers is not only the attainment of inner and outer riches but also more and greater opportunities to work to inspire, teach, and uplift humankind. Once a person does a good job with what he or she has been given, he or she is then given more abundance to use to continue the work. My child, it is not about quitting and having nothing to do ever again, as the real bliss is in the giving. Your work now is to find out the mistakes you have made and correct them. Continue to move toward your goals with persistence and determination. Once you have completed this, you will move on to the next opportunity. God's opulent kingdom is limitless. The good works we do and the advancement we make in this world give us admission into a far more wonderful experience.

"Don't worry, you will succeed as will anyone who does not give up. Now it is time for you to do the work that is required to bring you the success, fame, prosperity, and power you desire. Be happy, for all is well" were the last words I heard and then the whispers disappeared. This most wonderful feeling of absolute and perfect peace and love would stay with me for the rest of the day and night, and I would remember the experience forever.

Time for Victory and Never Defeat

I turned around, and Jim was at the door staring at me. "What happened in here?" was his question. "Oh, I was just thinking about what we should do next," was my reply. "Jim," I said, "we got on the air, and I guess you could say this was a trick of spirit. If I had had any idea that the tons of mail and money that I expected would not have come to us this first week, I think I might have said, 'Forget it.' But if I had said 'forget it' at this point in my life, my life would have been over. Something vital and alive in me would have died. I just didn't realize what keeping on keeping on no matter how great and impossible the challenges or how dismal things may appear really meant. Anyone can say 'I am committed' and 'You can count me.' But the true test of fire comes when we see what looks like an enormous obstacle that can kill our dream, defeat us, and rob us of our destiny and still, undaunted, we persist.

"This is it, Jim. This is our test. It's now or never. There is no turning back and no alternative, for the past no longer exists, and the only way for us to go is forward full speed ahead toward our objective of an international television ministry. We made our first goal: we're on the air. Now we've got to stay on the air and get more stations. We need to serve our viewers starting with those thirteen people, generate the money to pay our bills, and expand. Right now we need to let as many people as we possibly can know about our program and the message we are offering. Our work is to pass over or through our challenges, as if they did not even exist and reach our goals. Jim, how about if we meet this afternoon, strategize, and make a plan?" "Absolutely!" was Jim's positive response.

You Have to Ask for Money

Walking out of my office, I was a new person and everything was different, for I had had a change of heart and experienced a transformation of my basic belief system. No longer was it about how many letters, how many people, or how much money but about serving those who had responded and making the effort to continuously reach out to more. Enthused and ready to continue doing my life's work, I couldn't wait to call Bill and tell him about what had happened in my office and about my revelations.

Bill responded with "This is good, and now I have something to add that you may not want to hear, but I encourage you to listen. Terry," counseled Bill, "here is the secret of secrets having to do with the work of a minister. It is only when people give some of their money or whatever is most dear to them, which is usually their money, that they will start to soften their hearts and begin the process of awakening from their deep sleep of ignorance, scarcity, and fear. In this sleep people believe they are the owners of all that is around them or associated with them, but in truth they are not. God is the possessor of everything, and everything comes from God for God is all there is or ever will be. Those who honor this eternal relationship become the most fortunate of all, for they will always have enough and more.

"Regularly giving a portion of our time, talents, and money to our teachers or spiritual organizations from which we are receiving our spiritual knowledge is the only way we can ever make real and lasting connection with our Source. All who desire to receive the optimum benefits from the knowledge they are receiving must give in return for what they are receiving, as this is the law of life. Remember that you are where you are because you practice the law of tithing and contribution. If you do not instruct people on the law or ask them to give, you cheat the people. Only those who honor the law of giving and receiving are able to prosper and love at the maximum level that is possible. When they give and the results happen, their faith will increase and fear subsides. This is the hidden purpose behind tithing. The money that comes to the ministry is a measure of the value that people are receiving. Your work is to challenge people to mentally and emotionally connect with the Unlimited Source of Supply through the act of giving back into God's work.

"I know this is a challenge for you because you want people to like you, but the envious will never like you. Love the people and teach them what your teachers have taught you. Let them prosper through the law of tenfold return. As you ask for money and, as a result, prosper, the critics will come, for envy is the disease of humankind. You must allow the words of the critics to roll off your back as you continue on teaching. Your responsibility is to teach the principles. What the people do with the teaching is their business and not yours. Remember your book title, *What They Think of Me Is None of My Business*?" Bill was absolutely right and I knew it, but I also knew that some of my weaknesses were very strong and I would have to work to become victorious over them.

Correct Our Mistakes Along the Way

Making mistakes, finding the errors, getting the proper knowledge, putting in the corrections, and continuing on toward the goal seemed to have become a way of life for me. And I learned that this is what life is all about. No one is born the perfect self-realized person they're meant to be. Many times during each day we may want to give up because things look tough or because we have made mistakes and then feel worthless. Our work is to get back up, forgive ourselves, dust ourselves off, and continue until we do make it. At that point there will be the next goal, for life is an ongoing opportunity to love and to grow in knowledge, peace, and love. Facing and moving through our challenges strengthen our good qualities and destroy our weaknesses and flaws. Each time we say "No" to a fear and "Yes" to doing that which will make us strong, we make advancement toward our goals and the treasures we are seeking. This is the only way we can achieve our goals, for God can only do for us what God does through us. If we desire love, we must give love; and if we desire to be happy, we must work to bring happiness to others.

You've Gotta Tell People Who, What, Where, When, Why, and How

Jim and I decided that our first task was to let the greatest number of people possible know about the television program and our message. To do this, we needed a top-of-the-line press agent. Seeking to work with the best, off we went again to Reverend Robert Schuller's organization, and this time we hired Chicki K., his press agent. Getting the word out there in the shortest possible time was most important.

Chicki and I met at the Polo Lounge of the Beverly Hills Hotel, the world-famous spot for Hollywood power meetings. Chicki was a fashion plate in her size-three designer dresses and so perky, positive, and tremendously supportive. Having lunch with her, I thought, "There really are positive and extremely supportive people in the world who want to help me to succeed." You might say, "Of course she was supportive because you were paying her a big salary." But there are plenty of people who will accept a big salary who are not supportive. It was also her personality and character. Just as Bill and Jim were highly supportive, so was Chicki. Working with top professionals was so different from working with those who thought they had to control me. My critics on the board almost had me convinced that I shouldn't have dreamed such a big dream. Those who live from fear are afraid that others will enjoy and have more than they have. Instead of helping others to get what they want, they work to pull others down to their level or below. Finally I had worked myself free from the quagmire of mediocrity and fear-ridden people. It really was true that the air is better at the top.

Soon Chicki had me in every paper, magazine, gossip column, and newspaper in Los Angeles, San Diego, and some of the other major cities in the nation. She set up interviews for me on the most popular radio and television shows. Chicki had a formula that she had used with Robert Schuller and other notables, and she was using the same formula for me; it was working, magnificently. Our television viewers, donations, and church attendance were all on the upswing and increasing. This is the power of the press and public relations, for a great deal of one's success in business is a matter of numbers.

Simply by the law of averages, the greater the number of persons who know about you, the more people there will be who are naturally attracted to and interested in what you have to offer. I started thinking that my potential congregation was made up of all the people in the world. Our work was to communicate with as many people as we could, and those who were interested would then accept what we had to offer. Regardless of what type of products or service you deal in, your work is to offer them, and those who are interested will respond.

The Challenges of Growth

By following the steps of My Sacred Treasure Map and by God's grace, the ministry grew and grew. During this period of dynamic and unprecedented growth that the press was calling extraordinary, we were in a constant state of breakdown and breakthrough. In other words, we were constantly reorganizing and upgrading to new levels to accommodate the achievement of old goals and the setting of new ones. Just when things seemed to be perfect, in the very next moment a challenge to come or an opportunity to expand would present itself and things would be in chaos again. But we never stopped just to deal with a problem, as the problem was seen as part of the solution and part of the opportunity given to us by God in order for us to make advancement and reach our objectives. Before we can receive the blessings at the next level, we must let go of something at this level.

Getting Fired Can Be Wonderful

Bernice came up to me in church one Sunday morning and said, "Reverend Terry, I just lost my job. At first I was disappointed and wondered, 'Where had I gone wrong? I thought they were happy with me.' Then I remembered that I had been praying to get a better job. At this one I was paid far less than I was worth and the working conditions were not supportive of my maintaining a positive attitude, nor could I make any advancement. Here's the good news. Right after this realization I went out to lunch and by 'chance' I struck up a conversation with the person at the table next to mine. Reverend Terry, you know how God works in mysterious ways. Anyway, this person was starting up a new business, and she needed a partner who had my qualifications. Now I am making more money than ever before, and there is virtually no limit to the amount of money I can make and the benefits I can receive. Being part owner of a rapidly growing business gives me the power to encourage others to maintain a positive mental attitude. What I believed was my life falling apart was Spirit reorganizing things so I could get my perfect life's work. Now I understand how God never takes something away without replacing it with something that is better for us."

PEARL

Breakdown of the old structure or organism always precedes reorganization and breakthrough into a new order.

Science has found a principle that supports the theory that falling apart is falling together. It's called the Theory of Dissipative Structures. When a living organism stays vulnerable and open to outside influences and new challenges, it will remain in a constant state of reorganization: breaking down the previous form, reorganizing and breaking through into the next form. When confronted by challenges, instead of hiding and protecting itself in fear, it welcomes the opportunity to grow and become something new and unexplored. The organism welcomes the new influence and reorganizes itself to include it. The outcome is a new entity that is stronger and more complex in its capabilities than the former. New people would join the staff while others who couldn't keep up the pace or were not qualified would leave, and everything in the ministry was in a constant state of growth. There is always a price to pay for every gain. Bill was right, for many decisions that only I could make were extremely painful, and for the most part I had to keep my own counsel.

As Good As It Gets

Soon I couldn't go anywhere without being recognized. People were wonderful as they came up to me to share their miracles and their appreciation for the weekly telecast. Speaking to packed houses from coast to coast, appearing on national and international television programs, and working from sunup to sundown on class materials, articles, and fund-raising occupied my time. I had created a new organization, and my new board of trustees was a solid team behind me.

My entire focus was on my work. As I had no time to drive myself, I was driven everywhere in my dark blue limousine. Every minute was used to prepare a talk, write a book, plan a class, design a seminar, work with the staff, and dictate notes to my four secretaries. Letters were pouring in, and almost all of them contained wonderful stories and testimonials of how the program had changed lives for the better. Every Sunday morning across America people would gather together and watch our program, have brunch, and share what they had learned from the message.

Writing a Best-Selling Book

Late one night I got a call from my brother-in-law, who was working as a guard in a Louisiana prison. His voice was sorrowful and he sounded so very dejected. "What's the matter, Bob?" I asked. He described the horrible circumstances under which he was working and complained that this job was killing him. "Bob," I questioned, "why don't you get another job and quit that one?" "I can't. There aren't any jobs" was his hopeless reply. He wasn't in any mood to hear my positive-thinking remarks, so I just listened and said, "I understand."

After hanging up, I thought, "He could get any job he wanted, if only he knew he could. He could become whatever he wanted to be and have the ideal work that perfectly suited his personality and talents." This realization inspired me to write a book and put in it everything that I knew worked. Using the same process I used for my first book, I sat down and prayed to receive the guidance I needed. Visualizing myself autographing copies of my new book in bookstores, I got the feeling of having achieved my goal. This time I did something different, which was, I saw the book on the *New York Times* Best-Sellers list.

Making It

How to Have More in a Have-Not World, hit the number-one position on the *New York Times* Best-Sellers list. With this new book came another book tour, and this time it was easy to get on the top talk shows, and be interviewed in every important newspaper in America. Larry King, Charlie Rose, Joe Franklin, Michael Jackson, Tom Snyder, *Good Morning America*, and so many other famous TV and radio shows and hosts whom I had listened to and watched were now interviewing me. My new public relations person was Lee S., the most important press agent in Hollywood, whose clients included Barbra Streisand, Liz Taylor, and Frank Sinatra.

The Love Boat Captain and Me

Enter Gavin McCloud, the handsome captain on the hit television show of the eighties *The Love Boat* and the highest-paid entertainer on television at the time. He said he watched the program every Sunday, as did most of the entertainment world of Hollywood and New York. Gavin became one of our celebrity supporters, and through his support we attracted media attention that made the ministry and me well known throughout the world.

At one of the last Hollywood events I attended with Gavin, no sooner had we climbed out of the car when it seemed as if a hundred photographers were taking pictures with flashes going off in our faces. I was stunned at the prospect of even more fame, for by now my face with Gavin's was on the cover of the *Star,* the *Globe,* and the *Enquirer* and in the pages of *Time, Newsweek,* and *People* magazines.

By now everything I had ever wanted to have happened had happened, and I had attained much more than I had ever dreamed of having. After six years on television our program was aired throughout America and in Guam, Puerto Rico, Mexico, and Canada. Every dream and goal I had ever desired to achieve, even the ones that seemed so far beyond possibility for the little girl who ran with the deer in the valleys of the Sierra Nevada Mountains, I had achieved with God's help and the help of many wonderful people. Every treasure I had hoped to find and possess I had found or had come to me, as I followed each of the seven steps on my treasure map. After all this and having come all this way, I had the strangest feeling that something wonderful was waiting for me to find it. I was sure of it. Perhaps there was another hidden treasure to be found, but where?

You see, I had been on a spiritual quest since childhood. Whenever I'd get to the top of one mountain, if what I was seeking wasn't there, I would resume my search. I would leave no stone unturned, for I was relentless in my pursuit and hunt. No one or nothing was more important to me than finding the spiritual secrets of life. People would accuse me of leaving friends behind, which was true. If I found my friendships were wasting my time and not leading me on to make progress in my search, I had to go on—for the quest was everything to me.

Divine discontent was growing as I began to wonder if there was something more to be found. I was at the top of my mountain, and yet I was feeling an ever-growing hunger inside of me that was not being fed. Questioning my goals, values, and ideals, I began to spend more time alone in prayer and meditation. Most people are, as Ralph Waldo Emerson said, "Living lives of quiet desperation," because they know that something is missing but they don't know what it is or where to find it, and they're afraid to go in search of it. Fear of losing what we have causes us to hang on to even that which is making us miserable and dissatisfied. I could feel that it was time to move on, but what about this huge organization, all the people, and everything I had built. What was I to do?

The Quest for the Topmost of Treasures

Great sages and mystics teach about secret treasures that when found offer one the fulfillment of every wish, mystic abilities, and entrance into the tabernacles of the most high. Jesus in his parables taught about the kingdom of Heaven, but what did that mean? It was time to take the first step on my treasure map once again, only this time I was searching for an unknown treasure and goal. All I knew was that that if there was something more precious than what I had found so far I had to have it, and, besides, the one thing that I had failed to achieve was a truly-made-in-heaven kind of marriage. I still desired the topmost that was possible for any human being to attain, but what is the topmost and where would I find it and how would I attain it?

Chapter Ten

Finding the Topmost Treasures

> "The desire accomplished is sweet to the soul."—*Proverbs 13:19*

> "If a man constantly aspires, is he not elevated?"—*Henry David Thoreau*

The Voice of Spirit

You're not doing this anymore" were the words that I heard loud and clear. The theater we used for our Sunday service was packed, and I was the only person who heard this audible voice. Immediately I recognized the voice to be the same as the voice that had told me, so many years before, as I was standing in my kitchen, that I was going to La Jolla to be the minister of this little, almost defunct church. The voice was accompanied, just as it was before, by all the symptoms of direct revelation, including: bliss, tears of love, an electrical charge through the body taking the form of goose bumps, absolute knowing, and the "peace that passes all understanding." No one can completely understand the inconceivable workings of Divine intervention, nor can anyone plan for it or make it happen.

As I sat there in my chair and heard that familiar voice, I knew it was the voice of Spirit. In that instant of direct revelation I was certain, beyond the shadow of a doubt, that my time as a television preacher and minister of a church was complete. Reverend David, the assistant minister, finished his opening remarks and then he announced that we'd be videotaping next

Have you ever had an experience of Divine intervention? If so, give a
brief description of the event or events.

1.

2.

3.

month's television programs during next Sunday's service. With enthusiasm he said, "Please welcome Reverend Terry Cole-Whittaker." I got up
from my chair and walked to the podium. Standing there for a few moments, as I looked into the eyes of the members of the congregation, images of my past eight years, as their minister, passed through my mind.
"Good morning. It's wonderful to see your beautiful faces and to be in
your loving presence," I proclaimed. Continuing on, I said, "Today I have a
special announcement to make. I didn't come here to make this announcement, but while I was waiting to give my morning lesson, Spirit revealed to me what I am about to tell you. Two weeks from today, Easter
Sunday, will be my last Sunday, as the minister of this church. We will not
videotape next week, as the television ministry will also be discontinued
within two weeks. My work at this level is complete, and it's time for me
to continue on my spiritual quest. The ministers, whom I have trained and
ordained, will take over and set up their own ministries in order to serve
your spiritual needs. Even though I have no idea as to where I am going or
even that for which I am searching, I only know I must move on. There
will be a period of transition and reorganization, especially for the staff,
but change is the nature of life.

The Challenge and Science of Change

"Just know that I love you, and as you must continue to grow in knowledge
and understanding, so must I. My spiritual life is most important to me,
and being a student and disciple is my true path. Because of the unusual
circumstances this morning, I have decided to speak on the subject of
change.

"My topic is 'The Challenge and Science of Positive Change.' Psychologists tell us that change is the most disturbing part of a person's life. Even though people pray for a better life, they are afraid to let go of where they are and what they have in order to make room for something better. Listed at the top of the most distressful kinds of change are the death or loss of a loved one, being fired from a job, illness, moving, divorce, and loss of things. So we associate change with loss. There are two ways to perceive change: spiritually or materially. Viewing change from the spiritual perspective we welcome change, for we know that something more advantageous is coming to us. Those with a materialistic point of view perceive change as an enemy that can rob them of what they hold near and dear. The spiritually intelligent have developed a prosperity consciousness; therefore, change to them means new opportunities to prosper, grow, and thrive. To one who views life from a frame of reference of poverty and scarcity, it appears as if there is never enough of anything, and the best part of his or her life happened somewhere in the past.

"The key here is to identify ourselves with that which is eternal, limitless, and opulent so that when change comes, we don't fear it. In fact, it is something we have planned for, striving as we always are to improve our present situation. The temporary will and must change, but you remain as a constant. Change happens around you but not to you, for you are not a thing, but a living being. God-centered people are never afraid of change because they understand both the laws of the universe and the laws of Spirit. Change is actually the friend of the spiritually intelligent, for they view the inevitability of change and ride the wave from one adventure to the next. The spiritually intelligent know that the outer world of change is simply the reflection of their inner world of consciousness. Understanding this and the inevitability of change, we can make the correct changes in thought, feeling, imagination, and action that will naturally give us the inner and outer results that we desire.

> "We must become the change we want to see."
> —*Mahatma Gandhi*

Success mantra: **"I welcome the changes in my life, knowing that each change offers me the opportunity to improve the quality of my life and bring me even greater prosperity and good fortune."**

Time Really Does Stand Still

"Time is a constant. It never moves or changes, for it is eternally now. Change happens to things, as the world turns, but never to the indestructible soul. If change upsets us, it's only because we are suffering from an identity crisis. Instead of identifying with the living God, as our true Source, Soul, and Substance, we are identifying with impermanent and impersonal inert matter. When we look in the mirror, it's obvious that our bodies are not the same as the ones we had when we were children or even the ones we had a moment before. Perhaps you believe that, as the body changes, your chances for happiness, love, fun, and security are dwindling. But happiness, love, peace, joy, and pleasure are qualities of the soul and not the body.

"Change is the law of nature. The cycle of change has three parts: beginning, middle and end. Everything, including our bodies, has a starting point and from here it grows and continues for a while, produces some products, and then it begins to dwindle, break down, and finally come to an end. But the end of one form is the beginning of the next. The soil of the earth is made of the fallen and disintegrated forms of countless humans, animals, insects, plants, trees, etc., and the womb that gives birth to each new generation of life forms.

Freedom from the Fear of Death

"We are the exceptions to the rule of change. As eternal living entities we were never born nor shall we ever die, but the bodies in which we travel are subject to the laws of nature. Time and the whole creative process set the stage for boundless variety and the opportunity for us to fulfill our desires and create our dreams into living reality. From the moment we first conceive of an idea, the idea starts to take on shape and form until it manifests in the outer world, continues for a while, and then falls away, just as a leaf falls from the tree. One idea gives birth to another and one moment gives way for the next, but nothing in this world will last forever in the same form. But even matter never dies, as the atoms and molecules reconfigure into the next form.

Seasons and Cycles

"Why are we so surprised, sometimes even shocked, when something comes to an end? *Failure* is the name we give to something that stops. Stopping does not indicate failure; it signals that the end of one cycle and adventure has come so that we may advance into the next. The outer world is continually changing like an endless dance and kaleidoscope of variation. Nothing is supposed to stay the same, but people work very hard at making worldly things permanent.

"In time, even the pyramids will be no more. The stones from which the pyramids are made will turn into sand, and someone will come along and make cement out of the sand and build another so-called indestructible structure. Knowing the principle of cycles and change allows us to understand that everything material is temporary, but we, as the constant, move through one experience to the next. Suffering comes when we attach ourselves to the temporary and changing rather than to the eternal. God is our forever source and supply, not the outer world of ever-changing molecules, textures, and patterns. Our happiness never did come from some thing but from within us, as us. We are happiness, love, and bliss personified, and since these qualities are our very nature they will manifest when we are true to our spiritual nature.

We Are Love Personified

"The love and happiness we experience stay with us, as they are qualities of the soul and not of the ever-changing material energy. Losing a loved one or a friend naturally causes us to grieve, but it isn't the body we miss; it's the person. The body without the person is actually repulsive and must be immediately burned, so as to not create distress or disease in others. Knowing God as our unchanging, eternally loving Source, we are able to allow anything and everything to change around us, including our bodies, and still remain virtually unaffected in a state of bliss under any and all circumstances.

"Here is the point: We become like that with which we identify. By identifying with spirit, as we should, for God is our home and goal, we continually move up the spiral to more elevated states of mind and consciousness. An apple falls from the tree to the earth because it came from the earth and must return. A flame burns upward in its attempt to return home to the sun, but the person is spirit whose home is with Spirit. By identifying with Spirit, instead of dense matter, naturally we'll feel enthusiastic, light, and even elated. Time can become our friend rather than enemy when we use time righteously to advance our spiritual nature and also attain the material wealth we need to carry out our worthwhile projects.

Keeping a Steady Mind

"Dejection comes to those who believe that somehow whatever happens to 'their' things has happened to them. An example is the person whose car has been in an accident and totaled. Most often when this happens, the person goes through some form of mental, emotional, and physical shock even when no harm has been done to the body. Feeling hurt, devastated, and dejected because a thing has been damaged, stolen, or taken from us, we allow our precious consciousness to sink into the depths of despair. Nothing at all has happened to us. All that happened was a rearrangement of molecules. At this point it is wise to affirm: **'What happened happened to a thing and not to me. Everything about me is in perfect order and I am safe, sound, and secure. Infinite Intelligence is working in and around and through this situation and all is well.'** Success mantras and affirmations help us to focus our minds on the truth and keep us in a positive mental state so we can find our solutions rather than getting lost in some dismal swamp of dark despair and hopelessness. What we think affects our attitude and the outcomes of what we strive for, so whatever the situation, it is best to be positive, hopeful, and encouraged.

"The stock market will go up and down, as this is the nature of material life. Why be excited when it goes up, for you will be depressed when it goes down? Learn how it works if you want to take the gamble, but keep your mind elevated, calm, and enthused under any and all circumstances. Those who can do this are actually in control of their mind, time, finances, and life. Instead of making decisions based on fear and scarcity, one would be wise to make decisions based on good judgment and righteous discrimination. Great people are ordinary people who act great under any and all circumstances because they always remember who they are and they do not allow the outer world of appearances to control them."

If you have been lamenting the loss of anyone or anything, please describe what or who that is.

I have been:

What is this costing you?

It is costing me:

What would you gain by letting this go?

I would gain:

Success mantra: **"I identify myself with Spirit, God, Divine Intelligence, and Love knowing that whatever happens around me is never happening to the real me. The real me is forever peaceful, full of love and bliss, and eternally safe and beautiful."**

The Body Will Age, but You Are Eternally Youthful

"Those who believe themselves to be this temporary body feel and act older, as the body changes. The body is changing, but the person inside the body remains the same. We are told in Vedic scripture that the soul is eternally youthful and untouched by any outer worldly condition, including an aging body. It is we who say, 'I am too old.' It is we who say, 'I am ruined because my business failed.' Those who do not allow outer conditions to control their attitude will go on to the next success. Because things are changing around us, including the body, we do not need to identify with the changes, for we can remember who we are as pure spirit, and remain detached.

Success mantra: **"I am eternally youthful, full of vitality and energy."**

Success mantra: **"I am not a body; I have a body. I am an eternal spirit soul with godlike qualities."**

You Are Perfect

"By consciously changing our understanding and behavior we are not changing the self or soul, but we are bringing our mind and actions into harmony with the true godlike, perfect person that we are already and always will be. Our true life's work is to become conscious of who we are and then endeavor to bring this self into active full expression. This self is never in want because it is part of God and is always one with God and yet also a separate living entity. If we experience fear or lack in any way, it is because we have forgotten who we are and are drifting mentally in the far country, the world of scarcity and fear. The solution is to reunite with God and reconnect mentally with the truth of our eternal godlike qualities and the endless supply of all that we need and desire.

Qualities and Traits of a Real Human Being

"The great scriptures of the world tell us over and over that we are made in the image and the likeness of God. Our work is to become more godlike, which means to become a real human being.

"Some human and godlike qualities, attitudes, and behavior include:

- compassion toward all living entities
- love
- strength
- intelligence
- fearlessness
- working to purify one's life
- cultivating spiritual and material knowledge
- charity
- controlling of mind, behavior, and senses
- nonviolence
- truthfulness and honesty
- avoiding faultfinding
- opulence
- consciousness
- power
- creativity

- enthusiasm
- being religious
- being service oriented
- responsibility
- beauty
- youth
- talent
- tolerance
- being free of anger
- peacefulness
- gentleness
- being free of envy
- humility
- determination
- forgiveness
- cleanliness
- happiness
- enthusiasm
- being desirous of fame so as to be an inspiration to others
- being desirous of accumulating wealth to use for worthwhile purposes
- possessing artistic abilities.

"The most powerful change we can initiate is a change in our consciousness and behavior to better express our true godlike nature. Change in this manner brings us the maximum possible benefit. How awful it would be if we couldn't change our thoughts, attitudes, desires, feelings, behavior, associations, and environment. Let's rejoice in the challenge of change and if life hands you a bag of lemons, make lemonade, sell it, and get rich. We are either the agents for positive change or we are the victims of change, and the choice is ours. Here are the Three Ways of Change, and you choose which one you want to work with.

Three Ways of Change

- *"Green Light Changers:* These are the people who are doing extremely well. For them, life is an adventure. Traveling the road of life, they choose to pay attention to what is going on both within them and around them. They are alert to the signs of change, danger, and opportunities to prosper. Because they are in touch with Infinite Intelligence and their intuitive guidance system, they make change work for them. Never waiting until it is too late to avoid disaster, they see far in all directions, including glancing in the rearview mirror from time to time in case there is something that needs to be noticed. I would say that these people pay close attention to their intuitive and sixth sense, as well as to the outer signs. Green light changers are positive people who desire the topmost in life, and they make sure they get what they want. They consciously and constantly endeavor to achieve their goals and improve their relationships, health, finances, attitude, and situations simply because they choose to.

- *"Yellow Light Changers:* Yellow light changers are those people who make changes after the warning light of impending danger and problems has been turned on and is flashing. Perhaps they cannot tolerate their job or they're fighting with their mates, feeling sick, their money is running out, their addictions are ruining their lives, etc. Yellow light changers only do something different when things are not going well. They are reactors rather than actors. Instead of designing their lives as they would like them to be, they live by default. Making changes only when things are on the brink of disaster, a yellow light changer lives with constant anxiety and tension. Nothing is ever in prime condition for yellow light changers, as they just get by and maintain. The problem with maintaining is that everything around us is moving toward disintegration, so doing nothing means failure. Once the yellow warning light turns on, for sure this is the time to make positive changes, but why not make them before?

- *"Red Light Changers:* Red light changers go from one disaster to the next, never having any idea that they could have prevented them. These people live with their heads buried in the sand. They only consider the remote possibility of doing something different from what they have been doing when they have no other choice. Even then, many red light changers give up rather than exerting any effort on their own behalf. The doctor gives them a couple of months to live, they are fired from their job, their mate leaves, their home goes into foreclosure, they put all their money in the stock market and it crashes, the children are in deep trouble, etc. We call these red light changers perennial victims, when all along they could have been successful agents for positive and fruitful change. Because they consider themselves to be victims and at the mercy of fate and chance, they are. They go along never seeing the warning signs. Ignoring their intuition, the actions and words of others, and the changing conditions around them they run full speed ahead directly into dangerous, alligator-infested, murky swamp water. Most often these people crash and burn, over and over again. Having no idea that they could have made beneficial decisions at the green- and even yellow-light stages and everything would have been fine, even wonderful, they continue to believe that it's always someone else's fault, even God's, but never theirs."

What is your predominate way of making changes?

I make changes when:

What are the major changes that are happening around you at this time?

1.
2.
3.

Finishing up what I thought would be one of my last Sunday morning lessons, I gave them a list of don'ts and do's when it comes to change:

The Don'ts and Do's of Making Change Work for You

A. Don't place your full dependence upon anything that is temporary and subject to change.

B. Do be certain that you are eternal and that God is your Source and Supply, not a job, money, people, organizations, governments, places, or things. If one avenue dries up or changes and flows away from you, immediately look for another avenue or avenues to flow to you. This is called taking responsibility.

C. Do look around at the various things you see and say, "I am not that. I am spirit soul." This helps to remind you that you are a person and not a temporary, changing thing.

D. Don't believe that your good is coming from just one person or one avenue.

E. Do remember that your good is coming to you directly from God and through many avenues, people, situations, etc.

F. Do remember that you are self-employed, even if you are salaried or appear to be working for others. Take responsibility for your prosperity and make as much money as you can and invest it, so that your money is making money.

G. Do work to improve and upgrade your skills, talents, and knowledge.

H. Don't believe that there is not enough and that what you desire is in scarce supply.

I. Do believe that there is an abundant supply of every good and wonderful thing you will ever need or desire.

J. Don't affirm the negative in any situation, but choose to look for the positive and beneficial and affirm that.

K. Don't listen to negative people tell you how bad it is, or complain to others who may simply agree with your fear and negativity.

L. Do remember that when one door closes, another door opens to an even better situation and opportunity. BE POSITIVE AND ENTHUSIASTIC.

M. Don't believe, think, or say that you are too old, not talented enough, or lacking in any way.

N. Do believe that you are valuable, talented, and have what it takes to reach your goals.

O. Don't consider a simple or a complicated change as the end of your world.

P. Do realize that any challenge is there because there is a gift and seek to find the gift and receive the blessing and empower yourself with it.

Q. Do use your challenges to make you stronger, richer, happier, healthier, and more empowered.

R. Don't think of yourself as a victim, complain to others, or tell them your problems.

S. Do take responsibility and understand what you did, if anything, to bring this about. Do learn and apply the lesson.

T. Do remember that you always get another chance, so keep on keeping on.

U. Don't place all your money in one place.

V. Do believe in yourself and be confident that all is well.

W. Do a Personal Worth Inventory to maximize your potential and help you to remember that you are valuable and have marketable assets and much to offer.

Personal Worth Inventory

1. List your expertise, talents, and skills

A.   D.

B.   E.

C.   F.

2. What are your negotiable personal assets (that which you can trade for money, products, and services)?

A.   D.

B.   E.

C.   F.

3. What performance skills have you demonstrated in the past?

A.   D.

B.   E.

C.   F.

4. What have you accomplished that people not only respect but also desire to learn and utilize in order to gain the same or similar benefits for themselves or their companies?

A.   D.

B.   E.

C.   F.

5. Analyze and reconstruct all the monumental things you have experienced, produced, and contributed to.

A.   D.

B.   E.

C.   F.

6. What are the gifts and talents that others tell you that you possess?

A.   E.

B.   F.

C.   G.

D.   H.

The World Is Transformed One Person at a Time

My last words that Sunday were "Now it's your turn to take what you have learned from your studies and experience and share that with as many people as possible. If this ministry was a success, it will be proven by the work that you do from here on out. They say that a master is known by how many of her or his students become masters, and I know that each one of you is a master."

> "Not he is great who can alter matter, but he who
> can alter my state of mind."—*Ralph Waldo Emerson*

In what ways do you or can you share the principles of successful living with others?

I share the principles of successful living by:

1.

2.

3.

4.

How do you feel when you inspire someone else to believe in him- or herself?

I feel:

The End of One Life and the Beginning of Another

PEARL
Always make a dramatic exit.

Two weeks later on Easter Sunday, speaking to five thousand people, I said good-bye and made my grand exit, just as my college drama teacher had instructed me to do. He said, "Make a grand entrance onto the stage and a grand exit off, for most of your audience will forget everything else in between." The press enjoyed my leaving in this abrupt manner, as they had a marvelous time speculating on the reasons behind my departure, but I refused to give any interviews. What can you say when you have already told the story? How can you explain yourself to those who do not understand? Only those who have passed through where you are and where you are going can ever understand and appreciate your real reasons. Trying to convince others that what you are doing is the right thing is next to impossible, unless they have the same mindset. You know what you need to do and this is your life, so go and do it. As far as I was concerned, I was on a mission: a mission of God.

List the names of those in your life, excluding your mate, who seem
to think that you owe them an explanation for what you choose to
do with your life.

1.

2.

3.

Success mantra: **"It is perfectly right for me to do
that which I believe is for my highest good
and not explain myself."**

Getting in Touch with Mother Nature

Turning over the details of finishing up the business of the ministry to competent people, I packed my clothes, gave away most of my things to friends and staff, sold my white Mercedes convertible, moved out of my home, and set out on the first leg of my journey to "I had no idea." Maui, Hawaii, seemed like a good place to start, so I bought a ticket. Memories of myself when I was little girl running amidst the pine trees in the Sierra Nevada Mountains had always brought me good feelings of peace, comfort, and freedom. I needed to feel these feelings again, as I had been on a fast track and it was time to slow down, go within, and commune with Mother Nature. The further out we go, the deeper we need to go within in order to stabilize and balance. Since I had been about as far out as one could go I needed my time to dive deep into the reservoir of spirit to be refreshed and nourished. Some call what I went through "burnout," or a "midlife crisis"; others may have seen it as my unwillingness to accept all the wealth, fame, and success that was coming to me. I just called it the next step in my continuing spiritual and material education.

Visiting the Holy Sites

Leaving wasn't a spur-of-the-moment, whimsical decision—not at all. A couple of events led up to this dramatic point of departure for parts unknown. A few months before I closed the doors to the ministry, I took my television crew first to Israel and then on to Nepal and India. One of my purposes behind these trips was to bring back footage to show to the American public the manner in which people in these spiritually rich countries lived and practiced their faith and devotion. The West is strong on endeavor and the East is strong on fate, and it seemed to me that the most successful path through life would be a blend of endeavor and fate, action and inaction, and faith and good deeds.

Traveling throughout Israel, I felt as if I had lived there before. As I walked the streets of the old city of Jerusalem, the thought that kept running through my mind was "Jesus and his disciples, including Mother Mary, walked these same streets." Visiting holy places of pilgrimage offers the spiritual seeker great value, as the higher spiritual vibration at these sacred sites is very strong and the vibration alone can give one access to more elevated levels of sacred knowledge, peak experiences, and inner vision. Energy is stored in rocks, metals, and crystals; besides, when enough spiritually aware and devotional people visit sacred places, this also increases the spiritual vibration and the healing power of these already potent sites. Multitudes visit these sacred shrines for the purpose of healing, and many are healed. Perhaps they are healed because they have faith and believe they will be healed?

Something was definitely happening to me, as I visited these holy sites. I didn't understand it at the time, but I was retracing my religious heritage, looking for clues. There had to be more than what I had attained so far, but where was it and what was it? I was getting a taste of spiritual life that was more intriguing to me than what I had known, and it was this taste that would cause me to leave my television ministry to continue my search for God.

Remembering a Past Life

Visiting each of the locations where Jesus performed his miracles had a powerful impact on me because of the healing energy and the visible light that emanated from each of these places. Seeing the underground jail where Jesus was imprisoned before he was sentenced to the ordeal on the cross validated a recurring past-life experience of mine. At various times throughout my life, I had had the vision of myself as a Roman prison guard who was sent to bring Jesus upstairs to Pilate to be sentenced. Every time I'd remember this, perhaps past-life experience, I would sob and feel great sorrow. Nowhere had I ever read or heard that Jesus was imprisoned in an underground prison, so when I saw it, my past-life experience was validated and I knew for certain that I had been there.

Never allow anyone to talk you out of your "special" experiences, for they are real. Those who lack spiritual understanding may not appreciate your very real spiritual or supernatural experiences. But you should never doubt what you know to be true. Just because we do not understand something does not mean it did not happen or does not exist. It's important for us to accept these kinds of supernatural experiences as gifts. They are blessings from God for the purpose of helping us to get a sense of our own immortality and an awareness of the possibility of the existence of worlds beyond the immediate world of our material senses, limited beliefs, and rational thinking.

Part of what I would come to learn and understand was the science of you-always-get-another-chance, or what most people call reincarnation. Finding out as much as I could about reincarnation and remembering a few of my past lives gave me great comfort knowing that I, as a person, would always exist and so would everyone I loved.

Do you remember any of your past lives? If so, describe them. Even if you have a vague recollection of a past life or you are not sure if your recollection is real or imagined, still write it down in as much detail as possible.

Where were you?

Who were you?

How old were you?

Who was there with you?

What was happening?

What was the lesson?

More About Reincarnation

Past-life recalls happen because the subtle body made of ego, intelligence, and mind contains the memory of our past lives. The subtle body surrounds the soul and travels with us, as we transmigrate from body to body. Actually the subtle body contains the blueprint for our next set of circumstances, including our next body. All the information having to do with our desires, consciousness, and activities is stored in the subconscious and the memory banks of the subtle body. All this information is taken into consideration. When the person leaves one body, perfect parents and circumstances are then selected that will produce the exact body and environment to match that person's desires, consciousness, and past actions. Nothing happens at random or by accident.

A location, situation, smell, person, or a healing practice of some kind can trigger the memory of some previously forgotten time. Past lives are not at all as important as our present life, but a past-life memory, if it comes, does bring a comfort and cognizance that we have lived before and we shall continue to live. Sometimes a past-life realization can shed some light on a present-time situation or give us clarity as to why we are involved with a certain person.

Have you ever wondered why you have an instant liking for or an instant aversion toward someone? This is also a past-life recollection. Both love and hate are strong enough to bind us to other souls and bring us together again and again for the purpose of learning the lesson of love. Once we resolve the hatred and emotionally detach ourselves from the other person, we are free and never do we need to meet her or him again. As for loving relationships, because love is eternal, there can virtually be no end to our time together, either in this world or another. Reincarnation is a gift from God for the purpose of fulfilling our desires. Even if a person does not achieve an important desire in this lifetime he or she will be given the faculty to attain it in the next. The greater purpose behind reincarnation is to give us the chance to recognize and bring forth our true godlike nature, graduate from this world when it is our time to pass, and be elevated to the higher spiritual realms.

One Continuous Life

Because we always get another chance, no matter who we were yesterday or what we did five minutes ago, right now in this moment we have the power to change our lives for the better. Simply drop the past, stop talking about it and thinking about it, and shift your awareness to the present moment and to where you want to be when the future becomes now. It's good to know that what we contemplate, hope for, and do today has a greater impact on us than who we were or what we did yesterday. The point is that unless we consciously change our current direction, we will wind up where we are headed, over and over again. Without the complete picture people give up at a certain age or they quit because of mistakes and failures, believing that their lives are over. *Over* and *finished* are not words that apply to us. Wherever we leave off in one moment or one life, that is the starting point of the next moment and the next life. Reincarnation also explains why we are attracted to certain places and feel drawn to them, as I was being drawn to India.

Many Paths to the Same Goal

The thought of India both intrigued and frightened me. I had no idea of what to expect. Perhaps the cause of my anxiety was that I knew on the subconscious level that after visiting India my life would change dramatically. My television crew and I started our adventure not in India but in Nepal. Getting off the plane in Nepal, a country right next to India, I felt as if I had stepped into a time capsule that had taken me back thousands of years. Having been in the land of Moses, Abraham, Jesus, and Mother Mary, now I was in the Land of Buddha, Shiva, Krishna, and the Goddess of Fortune, Laxmi. Whereas in Jerusalem it had been the smell of spices that filled the air, here it was the smell of incense.

Each morning of my stay in Jerusalem as I drank my cup of Turkish coffee right near the gate leading to the road to Damascus, I'd watch the colorful parade of religious garb and customs before me. Drinking Chai tea flavored with yak butter, as I sat in the doorway to my primitive hotel in Kathmandu, I observed with fascination a totally different parade of religious garb and customs. There were differences and similarities. All the many different types of people I saw, young and old, male and female, in both these countries appeared to be centered on the same subject: God. Looking around me, I saw hundreds of people engaged in prayer and the contemplation of God. This was my kind of life!

As I wandered through the streets of this old city of Kathmandu, everywhere I went I could hear the penetrating drone of Buddhist monks chanting *Om Mani Padme Om*, as well as the celestial sounds of bells ringing in honor of the deities being worshiped in the many Hindu temples.

Cream Rises to the Top

"Pay attention to the obvious. Oftentimes the highest truth is missed because it is so obvious" was a wise bit of information I had gleaned from one of my teachers. Our eyes and ears get accustomed to perceiving things as they are so we don't usually look for something special or profound in what appears to be normal. A good example of this is the animal whose fur has been made to blend in with the surroundings, so as not to be noticed by its predator. One must train one's senses to perceive the supernatural in the natural.

Using this wisdom, I began to take note of the obvious having to do with the religious practices and teachings that the various religions had in common. There are many differences in the way various cultures practice their religions. Yet there are many similarities, and I used the similarities to give me clues as to where I might find my secret treasure. The way I had it figured was that truth prevails and cream always rises to the top, meaning that the most important rituals and truths tend to remain through time and can be found in every religion. Catholics chant in Latin, counting each chant on a rosary; the Buddhists and Hindus chant in Sanskrit and count each chant on wooden beads, usually 108 in number. Rosaries have fewer beads.

Sound is important in all religions. In the Holy Bible the first chapter of the book of Genesis states: "And God said, Let there be light; and there was light." God used sound to create every aspect of the universe, including the human body. Science tells us that everything material can be reduced to sound. Let us look in John 1:1 in the New Testament: "In the beginning was the Word, and the Word was with God, and the Word was God." Definitely the audible word as sound is most important, and here we read that the word is God. This gives us a definite clue that God and the original creating word are the same. Right here it's worth noting that every religion I studied had this one activity, as the most important ritual and activity that anyone could possibly do to bring the greatest benefit to themselves and others, and that was to sing the Holy Names of God.

Scripture is important, and a teacher, priest, rabbi or guru is absolutely a must. Clothes were also significant, as a way to honor one's devotional path. Catholic nuns wear their habits as part of their vows and also to communicate those vows to others. You cannot help but think, "Here is a woman who is married to Jesus." At least this is what I think. Another very important clue lay in the commonality that the scriptures of many religions have not just one, but at least two meanings: the literal meaning for the common person and the hidden, esoteric, and true meaning for the initiated and advanced. Each religion has its initiation. In the West we have baptisms by water and bar mitzvahs, and in the East they have initiations through fire ceremonies and through the transference of secret mantras and sounds from the teacher to the disciple. There had been a time when I had belittled ritual simply because I did not understand it and also because over time people tend to do things by rote, forgetting the real meaning and purpose behind the ritual. Performing rituals and remembering the meaning and purposes behind them is a most powerful and sacred experience. A simple ritual like saying grace before eating a meal helps us to remember that God has provided the food and fills us with the feeling of gratitude.

Religion in the East was more a way of life and something that the people engaged in every day, rather than a once-a-week ritual on Sunday morning. People lived around the temple, which placed God at the center of their personal as well as business lives. Whatever it was, it caught hold of me and I was hooked. Something deep inside of me was resonating to the idea of a totally devotional life, but I was concerned that if I did this, how would I earn a living and take care of my physical needs? This life was quite a contrast to the glitzy, almost show-business, celebrity lifestyle I had been living. I loved what I was hearing, tasting, touching, smelling, seeing, and feeling. All around me was a sumptuous banquet for my material and spiritual senses.

The Land Where the One God Has Many Forms

During this first mystical trip, we flew from the airport at Kathmandu bound for the mysterious Mother India. Landing in New Delhi, I felt overwhelmed by the numbers of people and the seeming dichotomy between their rich spiritual heritage and the material poverty and chaos. I was fascinated by the art, the sounds, the religious rituals, and the ornate and elaborate temples of worship. It appeared that they worshiped many gods, but they actually only worshipped one god. The Hindu scriptures teach of One God, Who is a being with unlimited spiritual form. The faithful worship the form of God to which they are most attracted. Of course, why would God limit himself to any one or anything? Because we are limited, we project limitation onto our concept of the Divine. That's our finite mentality that wants to make God into our image and likeness to fit into our little box of beliefs, prejudices, and assumptions.

I longed to find out about this One God, Who was a being with limitless spiritual forms. People cannot investigate and explore religion if they are steeped in dogma and fear about God. Because my parents allowed me to choose my own spiritual path, I felt perfectly fine researching any discipline and religion that interested me. How could God be angry with anyone who just wanted to find out more about God?

Besides bringing back wonderful footage that I would show to the people of America, Canada, Guam, Puerto Rico, and Mexico via television, I came home feeling that I had made a connection with an ancient system of enlightenment and God-realization that actually worked. I vowed I would return.

> "Again, the kingdom of heaven is like unto treasure
> hid in a field; the which when a man hath found, he
> hideth, and for joy thereof goeth and selleth all that
> he hath, and buyeth that field." —*Matthew 13:44*

Shangri-la

As it happened, I returned in one year. The legendary Himalayan Mountains in Nepal, the most sacred and revered of all mountains, had been calling me since childhood. Since having seen the movie *Lost Horizon* so many years before, I had been fascinated with the possibility of finding a Shangri-la, a secluded paradise populated by spiritually advanced and highly principled people. Perhaps I would be led to the temples of saints and mystic masters like the ones I had read about in the *Life and Teaching of the Masters of the Far East*? I had heard that great beings who had been in the same body for hundreds, even thousands, of years lived high up in these mountains. Tucked away in caves and special places, they spent their time in prayer, meditation, and in working for the uplifting of humankind. I longed to find these mystic masters, observe them, and learn their secrets. Walking through walls, traveling to anywhere throughout the universe at the speed of thought, manifesting things, food, and jewels right out of the air, levitating and healing with just a word or a thought were a few of their special abilities. If only I could meet and study with these people. For certain they would know where I could find my treasure of treasures.

Seeking My Treasure in the Holy Himalayan Mountains

My long-awaited trip to the Himalayan Mountains was to be a vision quest. Trekking in the Himalayan Mountains is an invaluable experience for the serious spiritual seeker. If others had found this sacred journey valuable, then I, too, wanted to find the secrets and treasures hidden from the eyes of the masses. Before I left America and all during the trek, I prayed to God to reveal to me the lessons I needed to learn. I also prayed to be shown my life's work from this point on, but meeting saintly persons and mystic masters who would give me the secrets of life was my real goal and hidden agenda. These aren't things you tell others, as most wouldn't understand. When you ask for something with all your heart and soul, it will come to you, but how it comes will always be a surprise.

Arriving at the Base of Mount Everest

After arriving in Kathmandu some of my students, who were accompanying me on this trip, and I chartered a small plane that flew us up to the tiny Nepali village of Lukla, right at the base camp of Mount Everest. Looking up, I saw a spectacular sight. As the clouds, wind, and snow swirled together in a majestic dance of the elements, I could almost see to the top of the most famous of all mountains. Awesome beauty and danger were playing together and calling anyone who had the inclination to risk it all, just to make it to the top. I had a mountain in mind, but my mountain was a figure of speech having to do with achieving my topmost goal. Whether the mountain one is climbing is a real mountain or a figure of speech, the steps are identical. My Seven-Step Sacred Treasure Map to Spiritual and Material Riches is the exact system every real mountain climber uses, just as it's the same system, whether they know it or not, that every person uses to achieve any objective. Over the years our goals and dreams may change; but the map remains a constant. The laws of the universe do not change; it is our creations that change.

Camping out in an open field with our spectacular view being the slopes of Mount Everest, we spent our first night in awe of where we were. Before I closed my eyes, I prayed with all my might that I meet the right teacher and holy person who would share with me the highest secret of life. I had heard stories about spiritual pilgrims who, after giving up everything in search of the absolute truth, finally found the wise old sage, and all the sage had to say was "You are God; there is nothing more, and this is all there is. Ha! Ha! Ha!" But I knew this was not the truth—someone's belief, perhaps, but not the real story. Anyway, I had tried that path and it was dismal, leading only to a miserable impersonal dead end. I was certain there was an Ultimate Truth, and my goal was to find it.

The Journey of a Lifetime

Early the next morning our Sherpas, the mountain men of the Himalayas, put our things and supplies on their backs and we started out on our three-day trek to Nam Bazaar, a Tibetan village and mountain marketplace at an elevation of 13,000 feet. Our ultimate goal was a Buddhist temple at 18,000 feet. Legend had it that there was a holy man who lived near this temple and various trekkers had been able to receive his blessing and teachings. Perhaps he was my teacher.

Not feeling well, I found that it took all the strength and willpower I had to keep on climbing, but into the third day I was dragging and barely able to walk. I was never going to make it. Altitude sickness, hypothermia, dehydration, and some unknown virus caused me to make the painful decision to turn back from my goal of reaching 18,000 feet, the Tibetan Buddhist temple, and the possibility of finding my teacher. My intuition told me that I had to get off this mountain immediately or I would leave my body. Having come all this way and now teetering on the edge of death, my body forced me to give up my search. You can imagine my dejection at having failed to reach my most important goal. I had given up a successful international television ministry and my life's work, and now nothing.

The only way down, since there were no helicopters, horses, telephones, or emergency facilities, was on the back of one of the Sherpa men, who weighed thirty pounds less than I and walked barefoot, even across the snow. Three arduous days later we reached the base camp of Mount Everest. No words could express my gratitude, and all he charged me was two dollars a day to carry me all that way. Perhaps he was the saint I was hoping to meet disguised as a mountain man? They say that saints and mystics take on the appearance of simple people, sometimes even very ugly people, just to test our compassion, love, generosity, and gentleness of heart. The Sherpa man never complained, was always positive, sometimes sang, and was respectful of me at all times. Yes, he was a saint, but maybe not the saint I was seeking, or was he? I didn't even know his name, but he saved my life.

I gave him my ski jacket, shoes, woolen socks, and everything I had that he could use. I can still see his shining face smiling at me, as the tiny plane raced down the steep runway. At the last moment before we would have fallen thousands of feet into the deep valley below, the plane lifted up and we flew out and over the tallest mountains in the world. Landing in Kathmandu, I felt relieved that I was a little closer to civilization in case I needed a doctor, but I was certain I wasn't going to visit one in this primitive town.

> "And Jesus answering saith unto them,
> 'Have faith in God.'" —*Mark 11:22*

Healing by an Angelic Choir

Not being able to walk, I was carried to the hotel and promptly fell into bed, almost unconscious. For three days, on the edge of death, all I could hear were choirs of angels singing to me continuously. Their singing was the most beautiful music I had ever heard. Now I know they were looking after me as I passed through my near-death experience. Their celestial singing was healing me through the power of God's Holy Name. Someone kept appearing and disappearing, and I couldn't tell if I was hallucinating or having a true, bona fide mystic vision. When he'd appear, he'd talk to me, as if he were my teacher, and I'd listen and take it all in. Even if he was my hallucination, he made good sense. Off and on for three days he taught me sacred knowledge, with the constant singing of the angelic choir as background music. Knowledge poured forth from his lips and into my ears, as I drank in each precious and sacred word. I was being fed and nourished at the level of my soul. Never before had I heard any knowledge that compared to what I was hearing now. Oh yes, he had white hair and a beard, golden Indian skin, a sweet personality, and yet he was serious and stern.

Right away, he told me not to worry because it wasn't my time to leave my body, as I still had a lot of work to do both on myself and in service to God and others. Teaching spiritual principles would continue to be my life's work, but it would be awhile before I would know all that I was to teach. He said that this was a time of purification for me because I was burning off some negative energy of past misdeeds. He said, "At this time, you aren't ready to be initiated, but if you continue to be sincere, within a few years you will receive the treasure of treasures you are seeking. You must desire with all your heart and also earn the right to receive, what some call, the pearl of great price." Before he went away for the last time, he told me that he was my teacher and that we would meet again.

Clearly, as I lay there barely hanging on to life, I could see my faults and mistakes and I vowed to work to make amends, put in the corrections, and give my all to becoming a better person. Finally the angels stopped singing, and I knew I was well enough to go back to America.

Flying up and out of the Kathmandu Valley and looking down at the majestic Himalayas I thought, "The mountains have done it again. One more person had a mystical experience that completely transformed her life." No, I didn't find the treasure, as yet, but I did have a most awesome experience beyond my greatest expectations. I actually got everything I wanted and the promise that I would eventually achieve my topmost goal. But my story wasn't the only story that unfolded during that trek. As I was finishing this chapter, I said to God, "Please tell me if I need to add anything to the Himalayan Mountains story." When I checked my e-mail that evening, this letter was waiting for me. Mind you, I hadn't heard from these two in years.

Dear Terry,
We are fine. I (Jim) retired in 1994 and trade stocks for a living now. The analyses of stock prices and radar signals have a lot in common. I'm right in my element and doing just fine, thank you.

Lois always wanted to teach, so she proposed a syllabus to the local community college and is now a professor of drama and speech. I am so proud of her!

All this can be traced to a certain teacher of prosperity and possibility whom we both shared. We went on a spiritual journey (to Nepal even!) seeking we knew not what and found each other. Haven't really had a chance lately to say thanks for helping us to create all this. We will be grateful eternally.
Love,
Lois & Jim

The Wonders Never Cease

Twenty-four of my students had made that trek with me, and each had a profound experience. Lois had been the one to come down the mountain with me. Her quest had been to find the right husband, which she did. Everyone got what he or she went for but no one, including me, had a clue as to how it would happen. Lois and Jim had to go to the Himalayan Mountains to find each other when they lived only forty miles apart in Southern California.

As the World Turns

As the years passed I used my time to travel to various holy sites around the world, write books, conduct retreats, give speeches and seminars, study the scriptures of some of the great religions, as well as the teachings and rituals of what many call unorthodox spiritual philosophies, and tend my organic garden. After seven years of living in semiseclusion in the woods of the Pacific Northwest, I felt the call to return to Los Angeles and civilization in order to pursue my spiritual studies. Three things were missing from my life: the topmost unknown treasure, a mission, and a husband. How was I to know that God was saving all three of these riches to come to me at the same time?

It all started as a simple prayer: "God, if you have a husband for me, I ask that you bring us together. If there is someone who can help me attain my ultimate spiritual goals, and if he has the same spiritual goals and I can also help him, then I pray for us to be together, as life mates and partners. But, God, if there is no one for me who fits this description, then I will be alone and that will also be all right. Thank you, God." Prayer must be sincere and from the heart. Prayer is a one-way conversation from your heart to God's ears. Doing God's will was most important to me and if it was His will that I be married, then I wanted this marriage to happen; but if not, then I would continue on my spiritual path alone.

Sometime before this prayer for my right and perfect husband, I had made it all right for me to be a religious zealot. I wasn't interested in being well adjusted according to the secular world but was completely absorbed in spiritual life. Call me an extremist, if you will, but this was my life to live as I chose, and I had chosen the path of religiosity. There are five goals of human life, according to Vedic scripture: 1., religiosity; 2., economic development; 3., sense gratification; 4., liberation; and 5., love of God. By choosing the path of religion I would also come to attain the other five, for the purpose of religion is to give us the knowledge and tools whereby we can reach our material and spiritual goals. Religion is a not a destination but a path one can follow to reach his or her topmost destination. Religion for the sake of religion goes nowhere and leads to fanaticism, wars, and conflicts. If only the followers of each religion practiced the systems and teachings of their particular religion, there would be love, prosperity, and peace on earth. To me scriptures contain the secrets of life, and anyone who chooses can apply the teachings and attain the ultimate that is possible for any person to attain.

Take the Best and Dump the Rest

Religion had given me a life with purpose, direction, and meaning. Religious scriptures and my teachers had blessed me with instruction about God and how to live. As I traveled the mountain of life in pursuit of spiritual and material riches, I used the system of taking the best and dumping the rest. As a child I'd eat candy in that same way. I'd poke a hole in the bottom of the chocolate and if I liked what was inside, I'd eat it; but if I didn't, I'd discard it or give it to one of my sisters if they wanted it. There are so many man-made rules that really have no bearing on one's spiritual life, so if something didn't feel right, taste right, or sound right to me, I'd let it go and continue to quest for the best. Here are the criteria I used to determine if a philosophy or religion had merit and was worth exploring or keeping: What is the goal of this religion and teaching? Who are the living examples of it? Do these teachers have it? Would I want to become like the teacher? Does this information deliver on the promise? Does this teach about how to attain supreme love and bliss? Can I apply this knowledge and live a successful life on all levels? Does this teach of the Ultimate Truth? With these criteria I didn't keep much, but still each step led me to the next. I dumped much more than I kept. To date, no religion or philosophy had passed the test.

God Did Have a Perfect Husband for Me

At this stage of my journey I had become enthralled with the scriptures of the Vedas, the sacred knowledge that comes to us from India. I had found a Hindu temple and was taking classes and doing devotional service, or what most call volunteering. While giving of my time in service to God, through this temple, I met another religious zealot, just like me. Neither of us thinking of the possibility of our being mates, we spent hours sharing our spiritual realizations and the scriptures we were reading. This seeker was very advanced in spiritual life and a Sanskrit scholar, so he also became my teacher. He too was searching for the Ultimate Truth, and a perfect teacher. Most people give up searching for the Ultimate Truth and just settle for another good fantasy, but both of us didn't want a fantasy life; we wanted the real thing. It was wonderful becoming friends with someone who had found the same clues and had come to the same conclusion and the same point in life as I.

One day I said something about what I had read and he said, "No! What you read is wrong." At first I was surprised, but what he then explained to me intrigued me. I thought about the ramifications of what he had told me, and what he had said made perfect sense and actually cleared up some of my questions on this particular subject. Having an open and inquisitive mind is a blessing. A closed-minded person can never taste the higher sweetness of life because he or she knows it all. How can anyone know it all? The next time I saw him, I asked him to tell me more; as he did, I cried tears of joy, for I knew that there was hope for me to reach my ultimate goal of God realization. The missing piece of the puzzle had been given to me. He gave me a cassette tape of a lecture from a certain teacher who lived in India, and as I listened I knew that this teacher possessed the topmost treasure. One of the truths of life is that you can only get something from someone who has it. A miserable person cannot give you bliss, but someone who is blissful can tell you what you can do to also be supremely blissful. Only someone who has love of God can give you love of God and teach you how to get it for yourself.

Both of us were ecstatic. A couple of books were available and a few more tapes. Together we listened and discussed what we were hearing, and together we read the books and savored every precious word. As our friendship grew, so did our love, and then we knew we just had to get married and live out our days together following our spiritual path. Right after our marriage, we booked our tickets to India. Our mission was to meet this teacher and to find out if what we felt, understood, and hoped would be there was really there.

India Once Again

Arriving in New Delhi, we hired a cab to take us on the three-hour ride to our destination. The little village where our teacher lived was crowded, as there was a religious festival going on, which just added to the pleasure of the adventure. First we found a place to stay, and then we walked to the temple and school of our soon-to-be teacher. As we knocked on the door, we were excited, for we were certain that this was the moment of Truth. Our teacher's main disciple welcomed us and invited us to come in to wait until the teacher he called Maharaja came to meet us. This teacher was virtually unheard-of outside of this village, so to have received his writings and lessons on audiotape was itself a miracle. Since God is in the heart of every person and obviously knows what is in our hearts, it really isn't strange at all that we meet up with the right people at the perfect right time; it's natural and how things work.

When the student is ready, the teacher appears; and we must have been ready, for in a few minutes Maharaja walked in and sat down. I was stunned! Maharaja was the same person who had come to me in the vision or hallucination I had had in my hotel room in Kathmandu, some fifteen years before. He had told me then that he was my teacher and that we would meet again, and it had happened. My husband asked if we could be initiated, and our teacher replied that he would initiate us in fourteen days. The time had to be most opportune for such an auspicious event to take place.

The Top of the Mountain

We counted the days, read his books, and attended classes. Maharaja gave us instruction as to what we needed to do to prepare for our initiation. The day of our initiation came, and we walked the mile to the temple as we seriously contemplated the blessing of this day. Maharaja first beckoned to me to enter the temple. Sitting down next to him, I felt myself in the presence of God. His consciousness was so pure that there was not the slightest trace of fear, anxiety, anger, greed, envy, doubt, pride, or arrogance. He emanated pure sweetness, gentleness, strength, love, compassion, and brilliance. Leaning over to me, he began my initiation. I stayed perfectly conscious and aware, for I wasn't going to miss a thing. This was it, and I wanted to make sure that whatever was to come I would be fully present, alert, and receptive.

Quietly he spoke secret mantras into my ears and as the sound penetrated deeply to the core of my soul, I was awakened from the dream of material life and given a glimpse of the glories of God and the awesome beauty of the spiritual world. My heart expanded in love to where I could not experience even one drop more. The missing something had been found, but there were no words to explain this to anyone who had not also had the same experience. Maharaja continued to speak each of the secret mantras, and one by one the inner doors to the treasure house of God's kingdom of ecstatic bliss, supreme love, sacred knowledge, and celestial opulence were opened and I was able to immerse myself to my heart's content. This was it! This inner experience was what I had been seeking. I sat there for a while relishing the fullness and nectar of the moment. Maharaja gave me my neck beads and handed me beads upon which to chant these secret mantras. Finishing up, he instructed me about what I was to do on a daily basis, as the initiation wasn't the end; it was the beginning of my devotional life. The initiation gave me the title of one who was twice born, meaning that I had just been born into my spiritual life. During the initiation Maharaja had transferred to me his experience, but now I had to learn how to get this for myself, which would take some time and dedicated endeavor. In time I, too, would be able to pass this, the treasure of treasures, on to others. For now, however, I had much to learn and apply.

A Return to My Mission

My husband and I had planned to live in India for the rest of our lives, but Maharaja instructed us to return to America and resume my ministry work in the world. Besides, we were building a school in India so that those who were interested in higher knowledge could come and learn from our teacher. We were told not to share the secret mantras and certain parts of the knowledge that we had been given. Maharaja said, "In time, one by one the serious students will come forth, make themselves known, and ask. After a period of purification and training the committed students will be ready, and they too will receive the treasure of treasures to be found at the top of the mountain. The fruit at the top of the tree is the sweetest, and sacred knowledge and initiation into the spiritual realms does not come cheaply for it is the most precious gift that anyone can ever receive."

Flying back to America, I was enthused and fired up about my mission and thrilled to be able to give a powerful and life-transforming message once again. I had come full circle, but I was going back richer and fuller than when I had left. Now, however, I had something I had never had before: a direct experience of God and access into the celestial realms of absolute bliss, supreme love, and opulent beauty. I wasn't seeking anything anymore, for God-consciousness naturally gives us everything we have ever desired and more, but I had much work to do to serve God by serving others. No way could I ever explain my initiation experience to others, but I could teach the method by which they could enter the kingdom. I couldn't help but marvel at the wonder, perfection, and adventure of it all.

When I gave up the ministry in San Diego, I thought I was finished. I had no thought of returning at that time, but now I was going home to start a whole new ministry and a whole new work. How would I do it? I'd do the same thing I had done before to attain every one of my heart's desires, including finding my teacher, my husband, my mission, and my treasure of treasures. You guessed it! I would follow my Seven-Step Sacred Treasure Map to the Spiritual and Material Riches of Life.

Seven-Step Sacred Treasure Map to the Spiritual and Material Riches of Life

1. Desire the topmost.
2. Pray and ask for what you desire.
3. Seek knowledge of how to attain the ultimate.
4. Do what works, and don't do what doesn't.
5. Control your mind and be positive.
6. Upgrade on a regular basis.
7. Keep on keeping on.

I looked over at my precious husband and spiritual partner and contemplated all that had happened and was continuing to happen. "Just imagine," I thought, "the best is yet to come. Thank you, God, for everything."

P.S.: You can be anything, do anything, and have anything you desire, if you follow this Seven-Step Sacred Treasure Map to the Spiritual and Material Riches of Life. Looking back, would I have done anything different from what I did? Of course. Wouldn't you? That's the point. We are supposed to learn as we go, correct our errors, and then do the right thing. No use lamenting the past or sacrificing your life because of a mistake or error; get back up and try again and again until reach your topmost goal. You can do it. I know you can, if you remember that "with God and you all things are possible."

> "You don't have to give up anything you need, but
> you will be asked to give up what you don't need.
> If it's gone, you don't need it."
> —*Terry Cole-Whittaker*

About the Author

Super speaker, motivator, bestselling author, television producer, television personality, minister, and business executive, Dr. Terry Cole-Whittaker is a catalyst for greatness!

"Bubbly, bouncy and relentlessly upbeat, Terry Cole-Whittaker preaches a gospel of happiness, success, and prosperity now." —*The Wall Street Journal*

A former Mrs. America runner-up and Mrs. California, Terry Cole-Whittaker is the American Woman's success story. After being ordained in The United Church of Religious Science—and without any formal business training, just a strong desire and passion to achieve her mission and attain her goals—Cole-Whittaker took a tiny group of twenty-five people and grew them into a thriving television audience of millions worldwide in a few short years. In 1983, Terry's *How to Have More in a Have-Not World* became a #1 *New York Times* bestseller.

Women of Power, a bestselling book by Laurel King, lists Terry Cole-Whittaker as one of the ten most powerful and motivating women in the world. Throughout her career, Dr. Cole-Whittaker has reshaped the concept of what it is possible to achieve. She offers her diverse audience of business, civic, educational, philosophical, and entrepreneurial groups the principles and formulas that will consistently turn their ideas, goals, visions, and dreams into tangible reality.

Dr. Terry Cole-Whittaker has also served as a mentor for many of today's expert speakers, leaders, and authors, including Anthony Robbins, Mark Victor Hansen, and Neale Donald Walsh. The people who have been touched and inspired by Dr. Cole-Whittaker's work reads like a Who's Who of global leaders, movie and television stars, bestselling authors, motivational speakers, spiritual leaders, politicians, educators, and business leaders. Diana Ross, Gavin MacLeod, Lily Tomlin, Linda Grey, George Burns, Melanie Griffith, Jesse Jackson, plus countless other celebrities are among the members of her celebrated audience and friends.

Recently Dr. Cole-Whittaker founded Innerfaith Ministries in Palm Springs, California. She can be contacted at her Website www.terrycolewhittaker.com.